IFIP Advances in Information and Communication Technology 576

Editor-in-Chief

Kai Rannenberg, Goethe University Frankfurt, Germany

Editorial Board Members

IFIP – The International Federation for Information Processing

IFIP was founded in 1960 under the auspices of UNESCO, following the first World Computer Congress held in Paris the previous year. A federation for societies working in information processing, IFIP's aim is two-fold: to support information processing in the countries of its members and to encourage technology transfer to developing nations. As its mission statement clearly states:

IFIP is the global non-profit federation of societies of ICT professionals that aims at achieving a worldwide professional and socially responsible development and application of information and communication technologies.

IFIP is a non-profit-making organization, run almost solely by 2500 volunteers. It operates through a number of technical committees and working groups, which organize events and publications. IFIP's events range from large international open conferences to working conferences and local seminars.

The flagship event is the IFIP World Computer Congress, at which both invited and contributed papers are presented. Contributed papers are rigorously refereed and the rejection rate is high.

As with the Congress, participation in the open conferences is open to all and papers may be invited or submitted. Again, submitted papers are stringently refereed.

The working conferences are structured differently. They are usually run by a working group and attendance is generally smaller and occasionally by invitation only. Their purpose is to create an atmosphere conducive to innovation and development. Refereeing is also rigorous and papers are subjected to extensive group discussion.

Publications arising from IFIP events vary. The papers presented at the IFIP World Computer Congress and at open conferences are published as conference proceedings, while the results of the working conferences are often published as collections of selected and edited papers.

IFIP distinguishes three types of institutional membership: Country Representative Members, Members at Large, and Associate Members. The type of organization that can apply for membership is a wide variety and includes national or international societies of individual computer scientists/ICT professionals, associations or federations of such societies, government institutions/government related organizations, national or international research institutes or consortia, universities, academies of sciences, companies, national or international associations or federations of companies.

More information about this series at https://link.springer.com/bookseries/6102

Marco A. Wehrmeister ·
Márcio Kreutz · Marcelo Götz ·
Stefan Henkler · Andy D. Pimentel ·
Achim Rettberg
Editors

Analysis, Estimations, and Applications of Embedded Systems

6th IFIP TC 10 International
Embedded Systems Symposium, IESS 2019
Friedrichshafen, Germany, September 9–11, 2019
Revised Selected Papers

 Springer

Editors
Marco A. Wehrmeister (iD)
Federal University of Technology – Parana –
UTFPR
Curitiba, Brazil

Marcelo Götz (iD)
Federal University of Rio Grande do Sul –
UFRGS
Porto Alegre, Brazil

Andy D. Pimentel
University of Amsterdam
Amsterdam, The Netherlands

Márcio Kreutz (iD)
Federal University of Rio Grande do Norte –
UFRN
Natal, Brazil

Stefan Henkler
University of Applied Sciences
Hamm-Lippstadt
Hamm, Germany

Achim Rettberg
University of Applied Sciences
Hamm-Lippstadt
Hamm, Germany

ISSN 1868-4238   ISSN 1868-422X (electronic)
IFIP Advances in Information and Communication Technology
ISBN 978-3-031-26502-0   ISBN 978-3-031-26500-6 (eBook)
https://doi.org/10.1007/978-3-031-26500-6

This Springer imprint is published by the registered company Springer Nature Switzerland AG
The registered company address is: Gewerbestrasse 11, 6330 Cham, Switzerland

Preface

This book publishes the research and technical works presented at the International Embedded Systems Symposium (IESS) 2019. Deep and fruitful discussions occurred during the event covering several aspects of modern embedded and cyber-physical systems. This book presents tendencies and solutions for problems tightly coupled to industry, ranging from new methodologies to novel hardware designs, analysis approaches, and real-world application examples.

A broad discussion on the design, analysis, and verification of embedded and cyber-physical systems is presented in a complementary view throughout the chapters of this book. The presented research and technical works cover system-level design methods, algorithms, verification and validation techniques, estimation of system properties and characteristics, performance analysis, and real-time systems design. Also, the book presents industrial and real-world application case studies that discuss the challenges and realizations of embedded systems.

Technological advances over recent years have provided a resourceful infrastructure to embedded systems through enormous processing and storage capacity. Formerly external components can now be integrated into a single System-on-Chip. This tendency results in a dramatic reduction in the size and cost of embedded systems. Such hardware infrastructures enable increasing numbers of services, allowing embedded systems to support many application areas (including cyber-physical applications). As a unique technology, the design of embedded systems is an essential element of many innovations.

Embedded systems meet their performance goals, including real-time constraints, employing a combination of special-purpose hardware and software components tailored to the system requirements. Both the development of new features and the reuse of existing intellectual property components are essential to keep up with ever-demanding customer requirements. Furthermore, design complexities are steadily growing with an increasing number of components that must cooperate properly. Embedded system designers must cope with multiple goals and constraints simultaneously, including timing, power, reliability, dependability, maintenance, packaging, and, last but not least, price.

The significance and importance of these constraints vary depending on the target application area. Typical embedded applications include consumer electronics, automotive, avionics, medical, industrial automation, robotics, communication devices, and others.

The International Embedded Systems Symposium (IESS) is a unique forum to present novel ideas, exchange timely research results, and discuss the state of the art and future trends in the field of embedded systems. Contributors and participants from both industry and academia take an active part in this symposium. The IESS conference is organized by the Computer Systems Technology committee (TC10) of the

International Federation for Information Processing (IFIP), especially the Working Group 10.2 "Embedded Systems".

IESS is a truly interdisciplinary conference on the design of embedded systems. Computer Science and Electrical Engineering are the predominant academic disciplines concerned with the topics covered in IESS, but many applications also involve civil, mechanical, aerospace, and automotive engineering, as well as various medical disciplines.

In 2005, IESS was held for the first time in Manaus, Brazil. IESS 2005 was very successful, with 30 accepted papers ranging from specification to embedded systems applications. IESS 2007 was the second edition of the symposium held in Irvine in the US, with 35 accepted papers and 2 tutorials ranging from analysis and design methodologies to case studies from automotive and medical applications. IESS 2009 took place in the wonderful Schloß Montfort in Langenargen, Germany with 28 accepted papers and 2 tutorials ranging from efficient modeling towards challenges for designers of fault-tolerant embedded systems. IESS 2013 was held in Paderborn, Germany, at the Heinz Nixdorf MuseumsForum (HNF) with 22 full papers, and 8 short papers. IESS 2015 was held in Foz do Iguaçu, Brazil, close to the beautiful Iguaçu Falls, with 12 full papers and 6 short papers.

The sixth edition, IESS 2019, was held in Friedrichshafen, Germany, on the northern shoreline of the delightful Lake Constance (Bodensee). The articles presented in this book are the result of a rigorous review process implemented by the technical program committee. Out of 32 valid submissions, 16 full papers were accepted, yielding an acceptance rate of 50%. Also, 4 short papers are included yielding an overall acceptance rate of 62.5%. From this total, 4 full papers were published as an extended version in the International Journal of Parallel Programming, Springer. Since that journal issue was published before this proceedings volume, these were not included in this publication.

The technical program of IESS 2019 included sessions with complementary and interdisciplinary themes, e.g., embedded real-time systems, system architecture design, algorithms, embedded hardware, estimation and analysis, and applications. Remarkably interesting keynotes on diverse topics, such as computational self-awareness, a paradigm for adaptive, resilient embedded computing, were included in the technical program, along with some invited talks on evaluating soft errors in multi-core systems, digitalization in the automotive world, modern human-machine interfaces for the automotive industry, and scientific and technical presentations.

All editors of this volume cited below, besides their formal roles, were involved in the discussions and decisions made during the review phase, and during the development of this volume. We are a small group involved in the organization of this conference and previous editions, and we were pleased to organize a highly successful conference in 2019 with fruitful and lively discussions.

We thank our sponsors, ZF Friedrichshafen AG, BHTC GmbH, the IFIP WG 10.2 on Embedded Systems, the Gesellschaft für Informatik e.V. (GI), and the Hamm-Lippstadt University of Applied Sciences, for their generous financial support of this conference. Without these contributions, IESS 2019 would not have been possible in its current form. We would also like to thank IFIP as the organizational body for the promotion and support of the IESS conference. And, last but not least, we thank the authors for their interesting research contributions and the members of the technical program committee for their valuable time and effort in reviewing the articles.

December 2022

Marco A. Wehrmeister
Márcio Kreutz
Marcelo Götz
Stefan Henkler
Andy D. Pimentel
Achim Rettberg

Organization

General Chairs

Marco A. Wehrmeister   Federal University of Technology, Parana, Brazil
Andy D. Pimentel   University of Amsterdam, Netherlands

Program Chairs

Stefan Henkler   University of Applied Sciences Hamm-Lippstadt, Germany
Marcio Kreutz   Federal University of Rio Grande do Norte, Brazil

Steering Committee

Achim Rettberg   University of Applied Sciences Hamm-Lippstadt, Germany
Marcelo Götz   Federal University of Rio Grande do Sul, Brazil
Mauro C. Zanella   ZF Friedrichshafen AG, Germany
Franz J. Rammig   University of Paderborn, Germany

Technical Program Committee

Samar Abdi   Concordia University, Montreal, Canada
Christian Allmann   Audi Electronics Venture, Germany
Michael Amann   ZF Friedrichshafen, Germany
Richard Anthony   University of Greenwich, UK
Jürgen Becker   Karlsruher Institut für Technologie, Germany
Alecio Binotto   IBM Research, Brazil
Christophe Bobda   University of Arkansas, USA
Luigi Carro   Federal University of Rio Grande do Sul, Brazil
Florian Dittmann   Kromberg & Schubert, Germany
Rainer Doemer   University of California at Irvine, USA
Cecilia Ekelin   Volvo Technology Corporation, Sweden
Rolf Ernst   Technical University Braunschweig, Germany
Danubia B. Espindola   Federal University of Rio Grande, Brazil
Mohammad Al Faruque   University of California at Irvine, USA
Masahiro Fujita   University of Tokyo, Japan
Marcelo Götz   Federal University of Rio Grande do Sul, Brazil
Andreas Gerstlauer   University of Texas Austin, USA
Tayfun Gezgin   Lufthansa Cargo, Germany
Kim Grüttner   OFFIS, Germany
Andreas Hein   Carl von Ossietzky University Oldenburg, Germany

Joerg Henkel	Karlsruher Institut für Technologie, Germany
Stefan Henkler	University of Applied Sciences Hamm-Lippstadt, Germany
Carsten Homburg	dSPACE, Germany
Uwe Honekamp	Vector Informatik, Germany
Michael Huebner	Ruhr-University Bochum, Germany
Marcel Jackowski	University of Sao Paulo, Brazil
Ricardo Jacobi	University of Brasilia, Brazil
Michael Keckeisen	ZF Friedrichshafen, Germany
Timo Kerstan	Vector Informatik, Germany
Amin Khajeh	Intel, USA
Doo-Hyun Kim	Konkuk University, Korea
Hermann Kopetz	Technical University Vienna, Austria
Marcio Kreutz	Federal University of Rio Grande do Norte, Brazil
Horst Krimmel	ZF Friedrichshafen, Germany
Thomas Lehmann	HAW Hamburg, Germany
Armin Lichtblau	Mentor Graphics, Germany
Patrick Lysaght	Xilinx Research Labs, USA
Roger May	Altera, UK
Adam Morawiec	ECSI, France
Wolfgang Nebel	Carl von Ossietzky University Oldenburg, Germany
Markus Oertel	Vector Informatik, Germany
Mike Olivarez	Freescale Semiconductor, USA
Carlos Eduardo Pereira	Federal University of Rio Grande do Sul, Brazil
Franz Rammig	University of Paderborn, Germany
Achim Rettberg	University of Applied Sciences Hamm-Lippstadt, Germany
Stefan Schimpf	ETAS, Germany
Juergen Schirmer	Robert Bosch, Stuttgart, Germany
Aviral Shrivastava	Arizona State University, USA
Charles Steinmetz	University of Applied Sciences Hamm-Lippstadt, Germany
Joachim Stroop	dSPACE, Germany
Hamed Tabkhi	Northeastern University Boston, USA
Hiroyuki Tomiyama	Ritsumeikan University, Japan
Flavio Rech Wagner	Federal University of Rio Grande do Sul, Brazil
Marco Wehrmeister	Federal University of Technology Parana, Brazil
Marilyn Wolf	Georgia Institute of Technology, USA
Mauro Zanella	ZF Friedrichshafen, Germany
Jianwen Zhu	University of Toronto, Canada

Co-organizing Institution

IFIP TC 10, WG 10.2 and WG 10.5

Contents

Algorithm and System C

Analysis

Embedded Real-Time Systems

A Real-Time Operating System for Cyber-Physical Systems Based on Physical Time and Logical Time

Keiko Amadera[1], Ayumu Ichimura[1,2], Takanori Yokoyama[1]([✉])(iD),
and Myungryun Yoo[1]

[1] Tokyo City University, 1-28-1, Tamazutsumi, Setagaya-ku, Tokyo 158-8557, Japan
{tyoko,myoo}@tcu.ac.jp
[2] Presently with RISO KAGAKU CORPORATION, Tokyo, Japan

Abstract. The paper presents a real-time operating system (RTOS) of a time-triggered distributed computing environment based on physical time and logical time for cyber-physical systems. In the environment, input and output tasks are activated synchronized with physical time and computation tasks are activated by the reception of timestamped messages and managed based on logical time. The control performance is affected by the jitters of input and output tasks but not affected by the jitters of computation tasks, so the jitter of the computation task activation is tolerated. However, the response time of low priority computation tasks may be increased in fixed-priority scheduling, which is used by most RTOSs. The paper presents a RTOS with mixed scheduling, in which fixed scheduling is used for input and output tasks to minimize the jitters and earliest deadline first (EDF) scheduling based on logical deadlines is used for computation tasks to minimize the response time. The logical deadline is not affected by the task activation time and higher priority is assigned to a computation task with an earlier logical deadline even if its activation is delayed, so the response time is improved. We have evaluated the performance of the RTOS and have confirmed that the performance is acceptable for practical embedded control systems.

Keywords: Real-time operating system · Cyber-physical systems · Embedded systems · Time-triggered architecture

1 Introduction

Cyber-physical systems (CPS) are real-time systems that affect physical processes [1]. Embedded control systems are hard real-time CPS, in which the delay and jitter may lead to performance degradation [2]. The time-triggered architecture (TTA) is suitable for building a hard real-time distributed system with minimal jitter [3]. TTA utilizes a time-triggered network such as TTP (Time-Triggered Protocol) [4] and FlexRay [5], which supports clock synchronization. Tasks on

© IFIP International Federation for Information Processing 2023
Published by Springer Nature Switzerland AG 2023
M. A. Wehrmeister et al. (Eds.): IESS 2019, IFIP AICT 576, pp. 3–14, 2023.
https://doi.org/10.1007/978-3-031-26500-6_1

each node are managed according to the synchronized system time. However, the static scheduling of network communication compromises the flexibility.

Researches on distributed control systems utilizing the synchronized system time but not requiring static scheduling of network communication have been done. Henzinger et al. have presented an abstract programmer's model based on TTA called Giotto [6]. Giotto provides platform-independent development environment. Benveniste et al. have presented Loosely Time-Triggered Architecture (LTTA), which does not require clock synchronization [7,8]. Lee et al. have presented event-triggered distributed systems with time synchronization [9] and a programming model called PTIDES to provide a coherent temporal semantics based on the synchronized time [10].

Recently, distributed control systems with wireless communication such as vehicle-to-vehicle (V2V) and vehicle-to-infrastructure (V2I) communications are increasing. The communication time of such systems varies and the message transfer order may be disturbed when the routing is dynamically changed. However, the disturbance of the message transfer order is not considered in Giotto and LTTA. PTIDES permits out of order processing events by utilizing timestamped events. PTIDES, however, requires that the clocks of all nodes must be synchronized. A distributed computing environment that tolerates the variation of communication time and the disturbance of the message transfer order is required.

A distributed embedded control system generally consists of tasks that perform sensor input operations, actuator output operations and computations. The jitter of input and output operations must be minimized in CPS. However, the jitter of computation is tolerated unless it affects the input and output operations. So, we have presented a time-triggered distributed computing environment in which input and output tasks are activated synchronized with physical time and computation tasks are activated by events of receiving timestamped messages and managed based on logical time [11]. The jitter of computation task activation caused by the variation of communication time is tolerated in the environment. The previous version of the environment uses OSEK OS [12] or AUTOSAR OS [13], the fixed priority of which may increase the response time of computation tasks with low priorities.

We present a real-time operating system (RTOS) to minimize the response time of computation tasks in this paper. The RTOS utilizes mixed scheduling, in which fixed scheduling is used for input/output tasks to minimize task activation jitter and earliest deadline first (EDF) scheduling [14] based on logical deadlines is used for computation tasks to minimize the response time. The logical deadline of a computation task is not affected by the activation time and a higher priority is assigned to a computation task with an earlier logical deadline even if its activation is delayed, so the response time is improved.

The rest of the paper is organized as follows. Section 2 describes the time-triggered distributed computing environment based on physical time and logical time. Section 3 describes the RTOS with the mixed scheduling. We evaluate the RTOS in Sect. 4. Section 5 concludes the paper.

2   Distributed Computing Environment

2.1   Logical Time-Triggered Processing

Figure 1 shows the structures of an example distributed embedded control system, which consists of four nodes and four periodic tasks; *Input Task*, *Computation Task A*, *Computation Task B* and *Output Task* are distributed to each node.

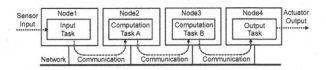

Fig. 1. Example distributed embedded control system

Figure 2 shows an example time chart of a time-triggered distributed system with a time-triggered network, the structure of which is the same as shown by Fig. 1. Each task is periodically activated in the period *10*. Each numbered rectangle shows a job of a task, which receives a message from its predecessor task and/or sends a message to its successor task. For example, a job of *Computation Task A* receives the message from *Input Task* and sends a message to *Computation Task B*. We call the difference between the time to activate a task and the time to activate its successor task *the inter-task delay time*. In this example, all the inter-task delay times are *10*.

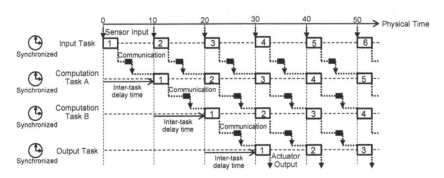

Fig. 2. Time chart of time-triggered architecture

Figure 3 shows an example time chart of a distributed system built with the time-triggered distributed computing environment based on physical time and logical time, the structure of which is same as shown by Fig. 1. This system utilizes a network with varying communication time delays. *Input Task* and *Output Task* are synchronously activated according to *physical time*. On the other hand, *Computation Task A* and *Computation Task B* are asynchronously activated by message reception events. The jitters of computation task activation are caused by varying communication time delays.

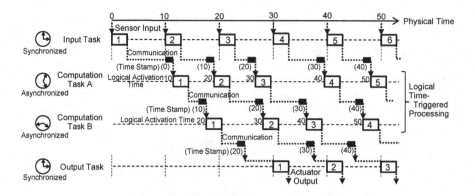

Fig. 3. Time chart of logical time-triggered processing

We introduce *logical time*, which is used to manage computation tasks. We call the activation time represented by logical time *the logical activation time*, which is given as same as the physical activation time in the corresponding TTA shown by Fig. 2. We also call the processing in which tasks are activated based on logical time *logical time-triggered processing*.

2.2 Timestamped Message

Timestamped messages are used to be tolerant with varying communication time delays. When a job of a task sends a message, the logical activation time of the job is attached to the message as a timestamp. The timestamps of messages are shown in parentheses at the receiver tasks in Fig. 3.

We call the inter-task delay time represented by logical time *the logical delay time*. The logical delay time is a constant and is defined to be equal to the corresponding inter-task delay time in TTA shown by Fig. 2. The logical delay time is statically designed considering the task execution time and the message communication time. The relation between the logical activation time, the timestamp of the received message and the logical delay time is indicated by the following formula (1).

$$Logical\,Activation\,Time = Timestamp + Logical\,Delay\,Time \qquad (1)$$

When a message to a computation task is received, the sum of its timestamp and the logical delay time is checked to be equal to the logical activation time of the next job of the computation task. If so, the next job is activated. Otherwise, the activation is postponed because it means that the order of message transfer is disturbed. When a message with the timestamp equal to the next logical activation time is received, the postponed jobs are activated. Thus, the environment can utilize a network in which the order of message transfer may be disturbed.

2.3   Task Scheduling

The priorities of input/output tasks should be higher than the priorities of computation tasks. Fixed priority scheduling such as Rate Monotonic (RM) scheduling [14] is suitable for input/output tasks because the jitter of the activation of a task with a high priority is small. However, fixed priority scheduling is not suitable for computation tasks. If the activation of a computation task with a low priority is delayed by the communication delay, the response time of the computation task may be increased.

Figure 4 shows the structures of an example distributed embedded control system, which consists of three nodes. *Computation Task A* and *Computation Task B* reside on *Node2*. *Computation Task A* is activated when receiving a message from *Input Task A* on *Node1* and *Computation Task B* is activated when receiving a message from *Input Task B* on *Node3*.

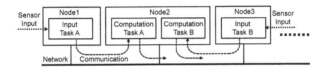

Fig. 4. Another example distributed embedded control system

Figure 5 shows an example time chart of the system when the computation tasks on *Node2* are scheduled by fixed priority scheduling. The priority of *Computation Task A* is higher than the priority of *Computation Task B*. We call the absolute deadline represented in logical time *the logical deadline*. The logical deadline of each job is calculated by adding the relative deadline of the task to the logical activation time. In this example, the relative deadline is *10*, which is same as the period of the task. The response time of *Computation Task B* is much larger than the response time of *Computation Task A* because the jobs of *Computation Task B* are preempted by the jobs of *Computation Task A*. For example, the first job of *Computation Task B* is activated at physical time *11* and completed at physical time *24* because it is preempted by the second job of *Computation Task A*.

We adopt EDF scheduling based on logical deadlines for computation tasks. Earlier the logical deadline of a job is, higher the priority of the job is. Thus, a higher priority is assigned to a task with an earlier logical deadline even if its activation is delayed.

Figure 6 shows the time chart of a system, in which the computation tasks on *Node2* are scheduled by EDF scheduling. The response time of *Computation Task B* is improved. For example, the first job of *Computation Task B* is not preempted by the second job of *Computation Task A* and completed at physical time *19* because the priority of the first job of *Computation Task B* with logical deadline *20* is higher than the second job of *Computation Task A* with logical deadline *30*.

8 K. Amadera et al.

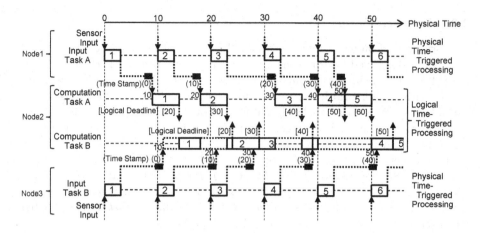

Fig. 5. Time chart of fixed priority scheduling

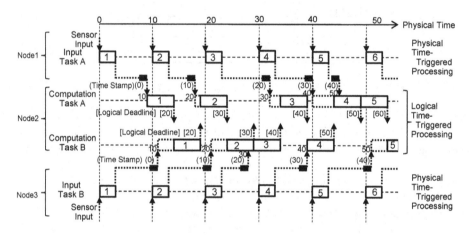

Fig. 6. Time chart of EDF scheduling

The response time of computation tasks is minimized because the logical deadline of the job of a computation task is not affected by the activation time and higher priority is assigned to a job with an earlier logical deadline even if its activation is delayed.

We call this scheduling the mixed scheduling, the mechanism of which is described in Sect. 3.1.

2.4 Software Structure of Distributed Computing Environment

Figure 7 shows the software structure of the distributed computing environment. The distributed computing middleware [11] runs on the RTOS presented in this paper.

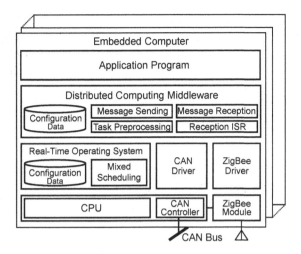

Fig. 7. Software structure

We develop the RTOS by extending an OSEK-compliant RTOS called TOP-PERS/ATK1, which has been developed by TOPPERS Project [15]. We use a time synchronization mechanism based on GNSS (Global Navigation Satellite Systems) [16] for nodes in which input or output tasks reside. The system time synchronization is not needed if input tasks and output tasks reside on the same node.

The middleware supports timestamped message communication and consists of modules that performs *message sending*, *message reception*, *task preprocessing* and *reception ISR* (Interrupt Service Routine). The middleware also supports message communication through CAN network [17] and ZigBee wireless network [18].

3   Real-Time Operating System

3.1   Mixed Scheduling

We extend the scheduler of TOPPERS/ATK1 to support mixed scheduling. The scheduler deal with three kinds of tasks: input/output tasks, computation tasks and non real-time tasks. Input/output tasks and non real-time tasks are scheduled by fixed scheduling and computation tasks are scheduled by EDF scheduling based on their logical deadlines. The priorities of input/output tasks are higher than the priorities of computation tasks. The priorities of non real-time tasks are lower than the priorities of computation tasks.

Figure 8 shows the mixed scheduling mechanism of the RTOS. There are ready queues with priority levels, in which tasks with state *ready* are queued according to their priority levels. One of the ready queues is used for computation tasks scheduled by EDF scheduling. The ready queues with higher priority levels are used for input/output tasks and the ready queues with lower priority levels are used for non real-time tasks. The number of ready queues and the priority level of the computation task ready queue can be statically defined by a developer. In the case of Fig. 8, there are sixteen priority levels: the priority levels from *8* to *15* for input/output tasks, the priority level *7* for computation tasks, and the priority levels from *0* to *6* for non real-time tasks.

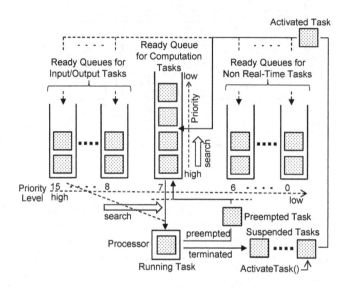

Fig. 8. Mixed scheduling mechanism

When a task is activated, the scheduler shifts the state of the task to *ready* and enqueues the task into a ready queue according to its priority level. If the priority level of the activated task is higher than the priority level of the running task, a preemption occurs and the preempted task is enqueued into a ready queue. When a running task is terminated, the scheduler selects the first task in the highest-priority no-empty ready queue to be executed by the processor.

Computation tasks with state *ready* are queued in a single ready queue according to their logical deadlines, which mean priorities. When a computation task is activated, the scheduler calculates the logical deadline by adding the relative deadline to the logical activation time and inserts the computation task into the computation task ready queue comparing its logical deadline and other queued tasks' deadlines. The task with the earliest logical deadline other than the running computation task is to be at the head of the ready queue. If the logical deadline of the activated computation task is earlier than the logical deadline of the running computation task, a preemption occurs and the preempted computation task is enqueued into the computation task ready queue. When a running computation task is terminated, the scheduler selects the computation task at the head of the ready queue to be executed by the processor.

3.2   Task Activation Mechanism

In an OSEK OS or AUTOSAR OS, periodic tasks are activated by an alarm associated with the system counter, which counts the system time. Thus, the system counter represents physical time. The upper part of Fig. 9 shows the system counter and alarms for input/output tasks. The system counter is updated by the tick interrupt, which is periodically issued by a hardware timer. If a non real-time task is a periodic task, it is also activated by an alarm associated with the system counter.

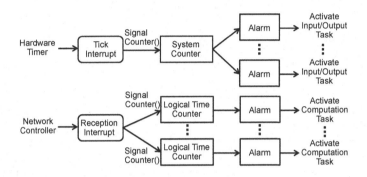

Fig. 9. Counters and alarms

A counter other than the system counter can be defined in an OSEK OS or AUTOSAR OS. A user-defined counter is used to represent a logical time and an alarm to activate a computation task is associated with the counter. The lower part of Fig. 9 shows logical time counters (user-defined counters for logical times) and alarms to activate computation tasks.

3.3   Logical Time Updating

TOPPERS/ATK1 provides the API *SignalCounter()* to update a counter. When a message for a computation task is received, the reception ISR (Interrupt Service Routine) of the middleware is issued. The reception ISR calls *SignalCounter()* if the timestamp of the received message meets the following formula (2).

$$Timestamp = Next\,Logical\,Activation\,Time - Logical\,Delay\,Time \qquad (2)$$

If the order of message transfer is disturbed and the timestamp does not meet the formula (2), the ISR does not call *SignalCounter()* and the task activation is postponed. When a message with the timestamp corresponding to the next logical activation time of the task is received, the ISR repeatedly calls *SignalCounter()* and the postponed jobs are sequentially executed together.

Figure 10 shows a time chart that illustrates the behavior of computation task activation. The period of the message communication is *10* and the logical

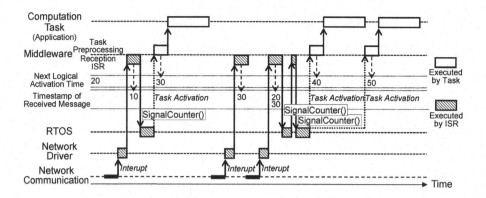

Fig. 10. Time chart of computation task activation

delay time is *10* in this example. The initial value of the next logical activation time is *20*.

When the first message with timestamp *10* is received, the reception ISR of the middleware is issued. The reception ISR stores the timestamp and the data of the received message into the buffer and calls *SignalCounter()* to update the logical time counter because the timestamp of the received message meets the formula (2). Then, the computation task is activated by the alarm of the RTOS. When the computation task is activated, the task preprocessing is executed before executing the application. The task preprocessing updates the next logical activation time.

In this example, the timestamp of the second message is *30* and the timestamp of the third message is *20* because the message transfer order is disturbed. The reception ISR does not call *SignalCounter()* when the second message is received and calls *SignalCounter()* twice when the third message is received. Thus, the distributed computing environment is tolerated with the disturbance of the message transfer order.

The logical time counter is updated by the period of the message communication at a time. If the period of the task is n times of the message communication period, the task is activated once in n times of message reception.

4   Implementation and Evaluation

We use an evaluation board in which a microprocessor called H8S/2638F is installed. The H8S/2638F has on-chip memories: the 256 kBytes ROM and the 16 kBytes RAM. The clock rate of the microprocessor is 20 MHz. The H8S/2638F also has two on-chip CAN controllers. An XBEE wireless module that supports ZigBee protocol is connected to the H8S/2638F through UART serial communication.

We have measured the CPU execution time of the task management system calls of the developed RTOS to evaluate the overhead of the mixed scheduling.

We have measured the CPU execution time of *ActivateTask()*, *TerminateTask()*, *ChainTask()* and *Schedule()* in the case of fixed scheduling and in the case of EDF scheduling. We have separately measured the execution time of *Schedule()* in the case without dispatching and in the case with dispatching.

Table 1 shows the CPU execution time of the system calls. The execution time of task activation in EDF scheduling is 27% larger than in fixed priority scheduling because of ready queue search. The table also shows the CPU execution time of original TOPPERS/ATK1 that supports just fixed scheduling for comparison. We think that the overhead is practically acceptable because the overhead is less than 9% in fixed scheduling.

Table 1. Execution time of task management system calls

System call		Execution time [μsec]		
		Developed RTOS		TOPPERS/ATK1
		Fixed scheduling	EDF scheduling	
ActivateTask		21.9	27.9	20.1
TerminateTask		8.3	8.3	7.8
ChainTask		18.3	21.6	17.5
Schedule	without dispatch	21.2	22.0	20.3
	with dispatch	27.3	28.1	26.4

5 Conclusion

We have presented a RTOS for time-triggered distributed computing environment based on physical time and logical time, which is suitable for cyber-physical systems utilizing networks with varying communication time. The RTOS schedules input/output tasks by fixed scheduling and schedules computation tasks by EDF scheduling based on their logical deadlines. The response time of computation tasks is minimized because a higher priority is assigned to a computation task with an earlier logical deadline even if its activation is delayed. We have evaluated the CPU execution time of the task management system calls of the RTOS and have confirmed the overhead is practically acceptable.

The distributed computing environment just supports periodic tasks. The future work is to extend the RTOS and the middleware to support not only periodic tasks but also aperiodic tasks. We are considering to adopt another scheduling algorithms such as a fixed priority server or a dynamic priority server to support aperiodic tasks. We are also extending the middleware to support other wireless communications such as IEEE802.11p.

Acknowledgment. The authors would like to thank the developers of TOPPERS/ATK1. This work was supported by JSPS KAKENHI Grant Number JP18K11225.

References

1. Lee, E.A.: Cyber physical systems: design challenges. In: Proceedings of 11th IEEE International Symposium on Object Oriented Real-Time Distributed Computing, pp. 363–369 (2008)
2. Cervin, A., Henriksson, D., Lincoln, B., Eker, J., Arzen, K.: How does control timing affect performance? Analysis and simulation of timing using jitterbug and TrueTime. IEEE Control. Syst. **23**(3), 16–30 (2003)
3. Kopetz, H.: Should responsive systems be event-triggered or time-triggered? IEICE Trans. Inf. Syst. **E76–D**(11), 1325–1332 (1993)
4. Kopetz, H., Grunsteidl, G.: TTP-A protocol for fault-tolerant real-time systems. IEEE Comput. **27**(1), 14–23 (1994)
5. Makowitz, R., Temple, C.: FlexRay - a communication network for automotive control systems. In: Proceedings of 2006 IEEE International Workshop on Factory Communication Systems, pp. 207–212 (2006)
6. Henzinger, T.A., Horowitz, B., Kirsch, C.M.: Giotto: a time-triggered language for embedded programming. In: Henzinger, T.A., Kirsch, C.M. (eds.) EMSOFT 2001. LNCS, vol. 2211, pp. 166–184. Springer, Heidelberg (2001). https://doi.org/10.1007/3-540-45449-7_12
7. Benveniste, A., Caspi, P., Guernic, P.L., Marchand, H., Talpin, J.-P., Tripakis, S.: A protocol for loosely time-triggered architectures. In: Sangiovanni-Vincentelli, A., Sifakis, J. (eds.) EMSOFT 2002. LNCS, vol. 2491, pp. 252–265. Springer, Heidelberg (2002). https://doi.org/10.1007/3-540-45828-X_19
8. Baudart, G., Benveniste, A., Bourke, T.: Loosely time-triggered architectures: improvements and comparisons. In: Proceedings of the 12th International Conference on Embedded Software (EMSOFT'15), pp. 85–94 (2015)
9. Lee, E.A., Matic, S.: On determinism in event-triggered distributed systems with time synchronization. In: Proceedings of 2007 IEEE International Symposium on Precision Clock Synchronization for Measurement, Control and Communication, pp. 56–63 (2007)
10. Eidson, J.C., Lee, E.A., Matic, S., Seshia, S.A., Zou, J.: Distributed real-time software for cyber-physical systems. In: Proceedings of the IEEE, vol. 100, no. 1, pp. 45–59 (2012)
11. Ichimura, A., Yokoyama, T., Yoo, M.: A time-triggered distributed computing environment for cyber-physical systems based on physical time and logical time. In: Proceedings of 2018 IEEE Region 10 Conference (TENCON'18), pp. 1516–15210 (2018)
12. OSEK/VDX: Operating System, Version 2.2.3 (2005)
13. AUTOSAR: Specification of Operating System, Release 4.3.0 (2016)
14. Liu, C.L., Layland, J.W.: Scheduling algorithms for multiprogramming in a hard-real-time environment. J. ACM **20**(1), 46–61 (1973)
15. TOPPERS Project. http://www.toppers.jp/. Accessed 9 May 2019
16. Yokoyama, T., Matsubara, A., Yoo, M.: A real-time operating system with GNSS-based tick synchronization. In: Proceedings of IEEE 3rd International Conference on Cyber-Physical Systems, Networks, and Applications, pp. 19–24 (2015)
17. Kiencke, U.: Controller area network - from concept to reality. In: Proceedings of 1st International CAN Conference, pp. 11–20 (1994)
18. Aliance, Z.: http://www.zigbee.org/. Accessed 9 May 2019

A Proposal to Trace and Maintain Requirements Constraints of Real-time Embedded Systems

Fabíola Gonçalves C. Ribeiro[1](✉) , Achim Rettberg[2] , Carlos E. Pereira[3] ,
Charles Steinmetz[4] , and Michel S. Soares[5]

[1] Federal Institute Goiano, Goiânia, Brazil
`fgcr.ufg@gmail.com`
[2] University of Applied Science Hamm/Lippstadt and CvO University Oldenburg,
Hamm, Germany
`achim.rettberg@iess.org`
[3] Federal University of Rio Grande do Sul, Porto Alegre, Brazil
`cpereira@ece.ufrgs.br`
[4] University of Applied Science Hamm/Lippstadt, Hamm, Germany
[5] Federal University of Sergipe, São Cristóvão, Brazil

Abstract. The development of Real-Time Embedded Systems (RTES) considering critical and volatile system and software requirements is a difficult and error-prone activity. The capability to describe system components while highlighting and maintaining their correlations at different abstraction levels and refinements has a significant impact on RTES development. Most techniques for designing RTES present many problems and limitations regarding tracing RTES constraints along of architectural design. Moreover, there is a gap in integrated strategies to evaluate the correctness of these constraints from model specification to the system models realization. This article aims to perform a study on Model-Driven Systems Engineering approaches applied in the design and traceability of specific RTES constraints. The main objective of this study is to automatically perform an evaluation of traced non-functional concerns and provide feedback to the developers regarding the validity of the simulated constraints. In order to achieve this objective, this study, initially, develops a formalized manner to specify RTES constraints in architectural viewpoints and a tool to evaluate the real simulated values of these specifications.

Keywords: SysML · MARTE · Real-time systems · Non-functional constraints

1 Introduction

RTES have been increasingly present in human activities and many of them present high level of complexity, smartness and automation. For instance,

© IFIP International Federation for Information Processing 2023
Published by Springer Nature Switzerland AG 2023
M. A. Wehrmeister et al. (Eds.): IESS 2019, IFIP AICT 576, pp. 15–26, 2023.
https://doi.org/10.1007/978-3-031-26500-6_2

controlling the diversity of infrastructures - water, energy, transportation and so on - improving citizens access to services, which leads to smart, heterogeneous and complex software controllers [15, 16].

Traceability is an important knowledge for improving the artifacts of software and systems and processes related to them. Even in a single system, various kind of artifacts exist, and each of them relates to different kinds of artifacts. Traceability over them has thus large diversity. In addition, developers in each process have different types of purposes to improve their artifacts and processesResearch regarding traceability can be categorized and analyzed so that such a developer can choose one of them to achieve his/her purposes.

The most common approach to write requirements specifications for software is through natural language [10]. Natural languages have no mathematical structure, thus they present difficulties to be properly analyzed [3]. As a result, problems such as imprecision, difficulty of understanding, ambiguity and inconsistency are common when natural language is used [20]. However, as the main mean of communication between stakeholders, natural language can not be simply avoided. Structured languages [20] allow the designer to write requirements using a pre-formatted pattern. Their main characteristic is to contain most part of the ease of expression and understanding of natural languages, ensuring that some degree of uniformity is imposed in the specifications. However, structured natural languages are neither formal nor graphical and, in some cases, are inadequate for modern programming languages and paradigms [18].

Managing traces between large, complex real-time systems artefacts has been a concern of many studies in past years [4,5,17,19,23]. In a study performed by Gills [23], an issue discussed about traceability of requirements is that most companies create their own trace metamodel almost from scratch, which normally leads to huge effort and frustration. In addition, traces are poorly recorded and almost never consulted as a support for other software development activities. According to Gills, using a well-known modeling language, such as the one proposed in this article, can diminish these problems. The SysML language has been successfully applied to model and to trace requirements. The work presented in [17] refers to the application of the SysML Requirements diagram for the specification of system requirements.

In [2], a method to facilitate the development of systems with safety-critical requirements, linking the functional design phase using SysML is proposed. In [22], SysML is used together with *Alloy*, a modelling and design tool, to formally specify the semantics and syntax of SysML Requirements diagrams. In [6], SysML is used for the analysis of requirements of military aircraft. The choice in this article is not to start from scratch, as criticized by Gills, but to start elements provided by the SysML language to deal with the traceability problem in software systems. The choice is based on two facts. First, SysML is derived from UML, a well-known modeling language both in academia and industry. Second, and most important, the SysML metamodel brings a new diagram which is specific to model and to trace requirements. However, the current state of the language is not complete enough to satisfy many of the needs of representation, description, trace, and manipulation of requirements for RTS.

This paper focuses on three important contributions to the RTES development while highlighted traceability strategies to architectural models. (1) Automatic Code Generation from Papyrus to C++ Code, highlighting non-functional constraints, in order to favorize the implementation of the designed RTES. (2) Automatic Code Generation, from Papyrus to XML format, in order to extract, from graphical models, information of constrained model elements. It focuses on the values of the periodic and deadlines constraints. (3) A tool to evaluate the designer's assumptions versus the runtime system behavior.

2   A Proposal to Trace MARTE Constraints

Traceability of RTES constraints is performed, in this study, by the adoption of enumerated and standard labels. A strategy is developed to trace the constraints along the system viewpoints. A specific constraint has different nomenclature in its ID at distinctive abstraction levels. However, the integer number which is part of the ID does not change in each viewpoint.

In the architectural models each constraint of the MARTE profile is labeled as an specific "ID". Figure 1 shows the trace of non-functional constraints in different viewpoints. For example, a periodic constraint, of the Logical viewpoint, has the following L_Nfp_T"x" identification where:

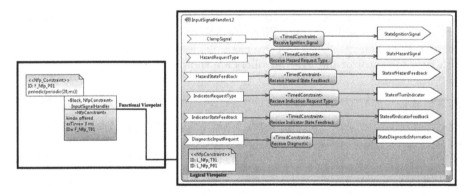

Fig. 1. Trace of $\ll NfpConstraint \gg$ from functional viewpoint to logical viewpoint.

- The first parameter identifies the viewpoint. For example, **L** corresponds to the Logical viewpoint.
- The second parameter relates to the type of the constraint. In the example, **Nfp** recognizes a non-functional constraint.
- The third parameter defines an immutable number to identify the constraint. The variable "**x**" is an integer variable. This number represents a value which traces and distinguishes a constraint in different views and viewpoints.

- In the case that the constraint is labelled by $\ll NpfConstraint \gg$ stereo-type, the label **P** or **F** is also applied in the third part of the ID. These characters describe if $\ll NpfConstraint \gg$ relates to a periodic time (**P**) or timing duration (**T**). For example, **T** sets this constraint as computation time value (for example, deadline);

Figure 1 shows slices of the architectural viewpoint models labeled by suggested labels. As detailed in [12], automatic code generations are performed in order to provide an executable version of the system. Once the authors consider the proposed standard of the MARTeSys^{ReqD} methodology, as introduced in this paper, in different abstraction levels the generated code also receives the translated non-functional annotations. Thus, the automatic translation, performed here, is able to generate graphical constraints, of viewpoint models, as textual information in the source code. After complete development of the system, partially manually made, the developed tool can combine, evaluate and compare the constraints values.

3   Case Study in the RTES Domain

The proposed case study and the architectural models were already detailed in [11,13]. This study relates to the Turn Indicator Controller System (TICS). The TICS is manipulated by drivers when they want to use the lights system to signalize the intention to change the directions of the car.

Requirements specification of TICS are defined in [13]. Figure 2 shows a usage scenario of the Turn Indicator. In this example, features which are related either with turn indicator or hazard controllers are shown.

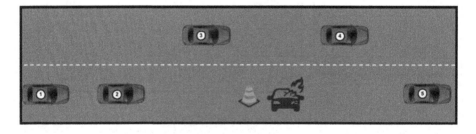

Fig. 2. An example scenario of turn indicator system.

In Fig. 2 the labels 1 to 5 represent distinctive positions of the car based on the driver's actions as follows:

1. Driver identifies an accident and turns the hazard lights;
2. Driver needs to change lane and turns the flashing lights in hard manner to the left side;

3. Driver turns off the flashing lights;
4. Driver needs to change lane and turns the flashing lights in soft manner to the right side;
5. Driver overpasses the anomaly situation and turns off the hazard lights.

RTES constraints have been annotated in architectural models following the MARTeSys^{ReqD} methodology. From these annotations, as depicted in Fig. 3, an early dynamics analysis of timing and precedence constraints to the developed system is performed. In order to perform the trace and analysis of the annotated constraints this study suggest the **NFP Constraints Simulation** and the **Comparison of Constraints** phases in order to suggest/allow the improvement and examination of the designers assumptions and runtime behavior of the tasks.

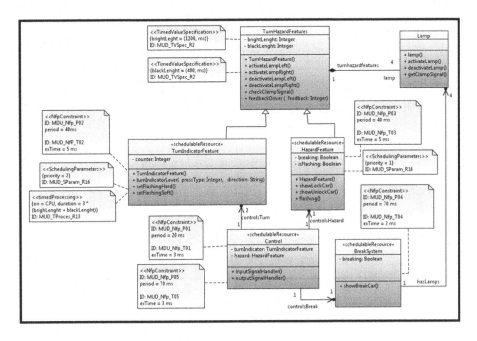

Fig. 3. Classes diagram, from the model and unit model, with RTES constraints.

NFP Constraints Simulation adopts empirical/experimental techniques to evaluate the system services realization and the constraints which are imposed on these services. The main objective of this Phase is to describe a common manner to simulate timing, schedulability and precedence constraints of RTES. **Comparison of Constraints** provides strategies to check if the constraints, under the system services, are reached in the final development stage. This phase provides automatic comparisons of constraints from different abstraction levels regarding the implemented system. If any inconsistency between architectural constrained models and the final implementation models is identified, an error message appears as a recommendation to the designers.

3.1   Manual Analysis and Comparison of Constraints

The designer assumptions, already annotated in architectural models, can be compared with the executable values, from system' tasks. Figures 4 and 5 depicts, in average, the period of 1500 executed samples to the constrained and periodic *TurnIndicatorFeature* and *HazardFeature* classes (see Fig. 3). In the implemented system, the system constraints are respectively imposed in tasks *taskTurnFlashing* and *taskHazardFlashing*.

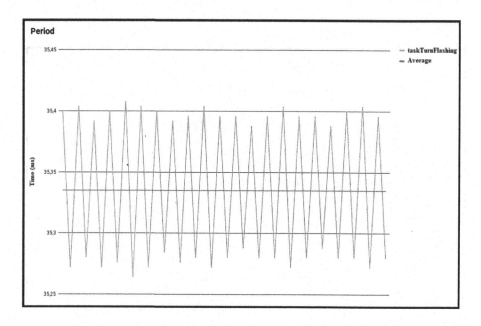

Fig. 4. Period of turn flashing task.

The empirical validation considers the runtime behavior of tasks. It allows timing measurements of design and development models. Moreover, it enables, by simulation techniques, to validate the constrained runtime behavior.

The tasks *taskTurnFlashing* and *taskHazardFlashing* have the same constrained period of 40 ms. Figures 4 and 5 present the results of the simulation activity of the mentioned tasks and it shows that the real period occurs within 35, 33 ms. In this case, as detailed in following, τ_1 and τ_2 were executed respecting their predefined deadlines. The measurements of processor utilization of τ_1 and τ_2 are, respectively, $U_3^m = 1, 1/35, 3 = 0, 031$ and $U_4^m = 1, 1/35, 3 = 0, 031$. In this study, it is considered processor utilization [8], described in Eq. 1, to analyse the feasibility of a given task set.

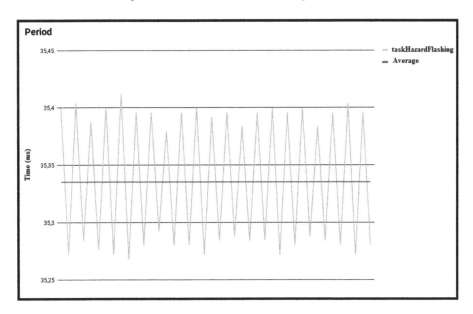

Fig. 5. Period of hazard task.

Function 1 shows that the utilization factor should be less or equal the U_{lub}. The attendance to this inequality ($U \leq U_{ulb}$) is sufficient, but not necessary to guarantee the feasibility of a given task set.

$$\sum_{i=1}^{n}(C_i/T_i) \leq n * (2^{1/n} - 1) \tag{1}$$

From the proposed analysis, a tool to analyze the models assumptions and the runtime behavior of the tasks is proposed. It is possible to connect information from validating results (**NFP Constraints Simulation** phase) with early design artefacts and improve them (**Comparison of Constraints**). This analysis can denote that the RTES constraints can be represented in early design viewpoints, fulfilled at different abstraction levels and reached and simulated in the final development phase. Moreover, it proves that there is consistency between the architectural constrained models and the final model implementation regarding constraints estimation. Finally, it also indicates that constrained parameters, which are related with real-time schedule/precedence, can be satisfied and evaluated.

4 Proposed Tool to Automatic Analysis of Timing Constraints

The tool *constraintChecker* performs the interface between the architectural models, more specifically the .xml files, automatically generated from the Class diagram modeled on Papyrus tool [9], and the system developed. This tool allows automatic discovering of errors in the model's assumptions to the non-functional constraints. Figure 6 depicts the tool interface.

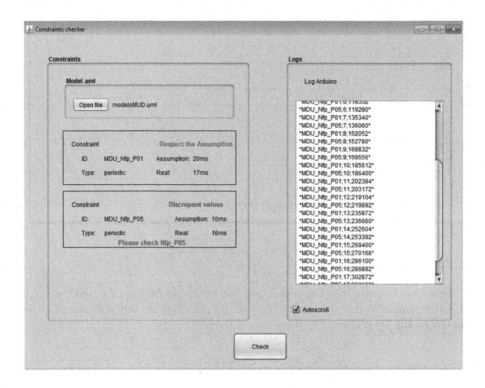

Fig. 6. RTES Constraints Checker.

The proposed tool reads the models in order to get pre-defined constraint values (Assumption field) and compare them with runtime behavior (Real field) of the related task. As can be observed in Fig. 6, on the right side, these values are calculated based on Arduino execution logs that contain period/deadline values of the occurrence of each task. Finally, the phrase "Respect the Assumption" or "Discrepant values" is presented in the tool interface in order to inform whether the constraint is respected by designer assumptions. These messages collaborate with guidelines of necessary adaptations, refinements of requirements and improvements of architectural models since early stages of RTES development.

It is not a simple activity to categorize the period and deadline constraints. The authors consider, in the evaluation of periodic constraints, if a task is executed respecting its initial assumption. It means the task deadline is $\leq |period|$. Otherwise, if the task has a deadline $\geq$ period an error message and the constraint identification is presented to the user.

The developed tool provides a strategy to trace and verify the constraints at different perspectives. Thus, it is possible to check the constraints from the architectural design models, as for example, the Class diagram constraints, against the implemented/executed constraints. In this case, it is possible to evaluate the real values of timing constraints which were previously annotated by MARTE stereotypes.

5   Discussion

Modeling, simulation and verification activities describe some of the most powerful techniques in modern RTES development [24]. Thus, in RTES development, it is very important the adoption of well-defined, reliable and automated techniques to timing prediction since the initial design stages [25].

The study proposed in [24] depicts a real-time simulation proposal for automotive systems. The simulator works analyzing the XML format file of a UPPAAL model and transforming it into a model into the C++ code. The timed automata in UPPAAL [21] can be simulated based on the C++ code analyzing clock and event constraints.

An approach to automated timing prediction of real-time systems is presented in [14]. The authors develop a pivot model and transformation rules which favoring the design process and allowing the verification of the system timing behavior at the early design stages. It considers a timing pivot model that must be followed in order to adapt all design models in the verification tool semantic. Thus the verification models can be created and analyzed. In our case, instead of creating an interface between two different tools - modeling tool (CAPELLA [1]) and model-checking tol (ROMEO [7])-, we develop a tool which performs data analysis of timing constraints based on designers assumptions and runtime system behavior.

The proposed modelChecker allows annotating real-time embedded constraints and provides a standard manner to describe important system properties. Moreover, it allows tracing these constraints/properties in different abstraction levels. The developed tool can be applied at different scenarios of RTES development without needing transformation rules or extra-knowledge to perform the proposed timing analysis.

In this study, simulation and measurements of constraints values are performed in order to check correctness, consistency and feasibility of initial timing annotations. These measurements are performed regarding execution time and scheduling policy of each task. Here, the empirical evaluation of RTES constraints aims to answer **two questions**:

1. Do the system tasks hold their deadline?
2. Does the periodic task set fulfil the requirements of the scheduling policy?

Simulation of RTES constraints can support correctness of design decisions, favour quantitative analysis of non-functional concerns and contribute to refinements of these constraints even after system implementation. Furthermore, it contributes to investigation of empirical evaluation questions.

The system implementation respects and follows the traced constraints from the Class diagram model of Fig. 3. From these annotations, timing analysis of annotated constraints are dynamically performed. The empirical analysis and the generated feedback also contributes to maintenance of timing constraints at different viewpoints. Therefore, it is possible to figure out possible discrepancies between the predefined values of constraints and the ones which come from the automated verification activities. Refinements can be proposed when there are inconsistencies between the initial values, which were modeled by designers, and the simulated values, after dynamic execution, of constrained values. Besides, if it is necessary to improve the models or to evaluate the design decisions regarding the software or hardware platform.

6   Conclusion

This paper presents an strategy to trace and evaluate consistency between models assumptions, performed by designers, and runtime behavior considering the developed system. Moreover, a technique to define and annotate constraints in architectural models, at different abstraction levels, is developed in order to provide a common manner to label related constraints along of architectural models.

Contributions of this research can be summarized the following: (1°) it traces RTES constraints along of architectural design to the system realization, (2°) it automatically compares annotated timing constraints against system implementation results and (3°) it shows an strategy to design and trace RTES constraints along architectural design.

The developed tool can visualize if the model constraints the timing constraints are fulfilled, and that they can be reached in the final development phase. Moreover, it proves that there is a consistency between the architectural timed constrained models and the final model implementation regarding constraints estimation. Finally, it also indicates that real-time schedule constrained parameters are satisfied.

As future work, it is necessary to improve the toolset to automatically provide guidelines for improvement of affected viewpoints and their models. In this case, more than the identification of the constraints (by its ID), for refinement, the proposed tool can link directly these changes to the support tool. Moreover, the authors aim to apply the proposed approach in other case studies.

References

1. CAPELLA: https://polarsys.org/capella/ (2018). Accessed 15 May 2019
2. David, P., Idasiak, V., Kratz, F.: Reliability study of complex physical systems using SysML. Reliab. Eng. Syst. Saf. **95**, 431–450 (2010). 2011.5979460
3. Gervasi, V., Nuseibeh, B.: Lightweight validation of natural language requirements. Softw. Pract. Exper. **32**, 113–133 (2002)
4. de Jesus, T.O., Soares, M.S.: An event-based technique to trace requirements modeled with SysML. In: Gervasi, O., et al. (eds.) ICCSA 2017. LNCS, vol. 10409, pp. 145–159. Springer, Cham (2017). https://doi.org/10.1007/978-3-319-62407-5_10

5. Kaiya, H., et al.: Preliminary systematic literature review of software and systems traceability. In: KES, Procedia Computer Science, vol. 112, pp. 1141–1150. Elsevier (2017)
6. Li, L., Ma, L., Wang, N., Yang, Q.: Modeling method of military aircraft support process based SysML. In: International Conference in Reliability, Maintainability and Safety (ICRMS), pp. 1247–1251. IEEE (2011). 2011.5979460
7. Lime, D., Roux, O.H., Seidner, C., Traonouez, L.-M.: Romeo: a parametric model-checker for petri nets with stopwatches. In: Kowalewski, S., Philippou, A. (eds.) TACAS 2009. LNCS, vol. 5505, pp. 54–57. Springer, Heidelberg (2009). https://doi.org/10.1007/978-3-642-00768-2_6
8. Liu, C.L., Layland, J.W.: Scheduling algorithms for multiprogramming in a hard-real-time environment. J. ACM **20**(1), 46–61 (1973). https://doi.org/10.1145/321738.321743
9. Papyrus, T.: Papyrus: www.eclipse.org/papyrus/ (2018). Accessed 03 April 2019
10. Pohl, K., Hnninger, H., Achatz, R., Broy, M.: Model-based Engineering of Embedded Systems: The SPES 2020 Methodology, 1st (edn). Springer Publishing Company, Heidelberg (2016)
11. Ribeiro, F.G.C., Pereira, C.E., Rettberg, A., Soares, M.S.I.P.: An approach for architectural design of automotive systems using MARTE and SysML. In: CASE, pp. 1574–1580. IEEE (2018)
12. Ribeiro, F.G.C., Rettberg, A., Pereira, C.E., Botelho, S.C., Soares, M.S.: Guidelines for using MARTE profile packages considering concerns of real-time embedded systems. In: 15th IEEE International Conference on Industrial Informatics, INDIN, pp. 917–922 (2017). 2017.8104894
13. Ribeiro, F.G.C., Rettberg, A., Pereira, C.E., Steinmetz, C., Soares, M.S.: SPES methodology and MARTE constraints in architectural design. In: ISCC, pp. 377–383. IEEE (2018)
14. Rioux, L., Henia, H., Sordon, N.: Using model-checking for timing verification in industrial system design. In: ICST Workshops, pp. 377–378. IEEE Computer Society (2017)
15. Santana, E.F.Z., Chaves, A.P., Gerosa, M.A., Kon, F., Milojicic, D.S.: Software platforms for smart cities: concepts, requirements, challenges, and a unified reference architecture. ACM Comput. Surv. **50**(6), 1–37 (2017)
16. Silva, B.N., Khan, M., Han, K.: Towards sustainable smart cities: a review of trends, architectures, components, and open challenges in smart cities. Sustain. Urban Areas **38**, 697–713 (2018)
17. Soares, M.S.: Architecture-driven integration of modeling languages for the design of software-intensive systems. Ph.D. thesis, Deltf University of Technology, Delft, Holanda (2010)
18. Soares, M.S., Vrancken, J., Verbraeck, A.: User requirements modeling and analysis of software-intensive systems. J. Syst. Softw. **84**(2), 328–339 (2011). https://doi.org/10.1016/j.jss.2010.10.020
19. Torkar, R., Gorschek, T., Feldt, R., Svahnberg, M., Akbar, R.U., Kamran, K.: Requirements traceability: a systematic review and industry case study. Int. J. Softw. Eng. Knowl. Eng. **22**, 385–433 (2012). https://doi.org/10.1142/S021819401250009X
20. Umber, A., Bajwa, I.S.: Minimizing ambiguity in natural language software requirements specification. In: 2011 6th International Conference on Digital Information Management, pp. 102–107 (2011). https://doi.org/10.1109/ICDIM.2011.6093363
21. Uppaal, T.: http://www.uppaal.org/ (2018). Accessed 11 Jan 2019

22. Valles, B.F.: A formal model for the requirements diagrams of SysML. Lat. Am. Trans. IEEE **8**, 259–268 (2010). https://doi.org/10.1109/TLA.2010.5538400
23. Winkler, S., Pilgrim, J.: A survey of traceability in requirements engineering and model-driven development. Softw. Syst. Model. **9**(4), 529–565 (2010). https://doi.org/10.1007/s10270-009-0145-0
24. Yan, X., Li, Y., Li, X.: Real-time simulation of automotive systems based on UPPAAL. In: 8th IEEE International Conference on Software Engineering and Service Science (ICSESS), pp. 173–176 (2017). 2017.8342890
25. Yang, C.H., Vyatkin, V., Pang, C.: Model-driven development of control software for distributed automation: a survey and an approach. IEEE Trans. Syst. Man Cybern. Syst. **44**(3), 292–305 (2014)

A Comparative Analysis Between SysML and AADL When Modeling a Real-Time System

Quelita A. D. S. Ribeiro[1], Achim Rettberg[2]([✉]),
Fabíola Gonçalves C. Ribeiro[3], and Michel S. Soares[1]

[1] Federal University of Sergipe Sao Cristovão, Sao Cristovão, Sergipe, Brazil
[2] University of Applied Science Hamm/Lippstadt and CvO University Oldenburg,
Hamm, Germany
achim.rettberg@iess.org
[3] Federal Institute Goiano, Goiânia, Brazil

Abstract. System Architecture has a primary role in communication between stakeholders, in addition to planning and structuring the whole architectural process. Architecture Description Languages (ADLs) should be helping within architectural activities. However, most ADLs have not yet been widely used in industry. Another limiting factor for the effective use of ADLs is the difficulty of these languages in concretely expressing complex systems architecture. Considering this situation for the effective use of ADLs, UML has been often used in past years for architecture modeling. However, UML itself presents difficulties in representing characteristics which are pertinent to real-time systems, such as security or real-time restrictions. One of the advantages of UML is its extensibility, ability which allows creation of profiles. Thus, this work presents the Systems Modeling Language (SysML), a UML profile used for system architecture modeling. SysML and Architecture Analysis & Design Language (AADL) languages were both applied to a case and compared. As a conclusion, it was noticed that SysML is better than AADL when modeling abstract characteristics, such as decision making and loops functionality, which are not well-described in AADL.

Keywords: SysML · AADL · Real-time system · System architecture

1 Introduction

As complexity of real-time systems and embedded applications increase, there is the continuous need of more abstract representation of such systems. Modeling systems architecture is a challenging task, since these systems are not only of great magnitude, but are also significantly different [5]. Moreover, challenges and difficulties happen when developing these systems, due to specific characteristics, including mobility and security or real-time restrictions [6,7]. One of the main challenges to be faced in the development of solutions is to connect domain

© IFIP International Federation for Information Processing 2023
Published by Springer Nature Switzerland AG 2023
M. A. Wehrmeister et al. (Eds.): IESS 2019, IFIP AICT 576, pp. 27–38, 2023.
https://doi.org/10.1007/978-3-031-26500-6_3

specific requirements, expressed by business analysts, with specific technological solutions designed by software architects [1,3].

Since UML is a popular language in the software industry, and UML-based modeling tools are fully available [12], the UML community has been working with the purpose of presenting a way of modeling real-time system's properties. One of these efforts related to embedded systems is the SysML (Systems Modeling Language) profile. SysML offers additional resources to UML, including requirements modeling [7,9,11], and specification of several structural, behavioral and temporal aspects of real-time systems [5,10].

Characteristics of SysML have been recognized for requirements engineering [2,7] and for real-time systems requirements modeling [5]. These advantages were evidenced and have been analyzed for modeling systems' architecture [4, 12]. In this paper we present a case on an automatic headlight modeling in an automotive system in two languages, SysML and ADDL. The objectives of developing architectural representation with two different languages are: (1) to analyze the weak and strong points of each language, (2) to offer a comparative example and (3) to propose SysML as an architectural description language.

Authors of paper [12] describe a survey among 60 possible ADLs for development of automotive systems. After analysis, 3 languages for architectural description were chosen: AADL, MARTE and SysML. MARTE (UML profile) was used in a complementary way to SysML in order to model the systems execution time. However, the author considers AADL as a better alternative for architectural representation, based in criteria of code generation, formal verification, error modeling and variability modeling.

A survey of modeling languages of real-time software systems is presented in [4]. For the authors, each language has its advantages and disadvantages and, in order to properly describe the architecture of the real-time software system, is almost certain the need of complementary use of two or more languages. In the referred work, AADL, UML, SysML and MARTE are explored in the context of comprehending the contribution that each language brings to software engineering and to determine if it is viable to combine aspects of the four modeling languages in order to obtain a wider coverage in architectural descriptions.

2   Headlight Control System Details

The software requirements presented in this Section were primarily collected through reading and research in automobile manuals, web-site and the book [13]. After this stage the requirements were identified and organized for the automatic headlight control system.

In the headlight control system, the headlights are activated through a photoelectric sensor. The sensor is activated or deactivated by lightning conditions, and may be dark or light. Thus, the automatic control of headlights switches on the lights whenever the sensor feels the dark environment. For instance, the system will activate the headlights when a car enters in a tunnel or when an environment presents heavy clouds.

In this example, according to the characteristics previously listed, and to the results of the detailed domain analysis, the functional and non-functional system requirements are described in Table 1:

Table 1. Description of the system requirements

ID	Description
FR1	The light control system shall turn off the front lights in exactly 3 min after engine is shut down
FR2	The light control system shall schedule simultaneous requests in memory every 50 ms
FR3	The light control system shall evaluate the functioning of all components every 50 ms
FR4	The light control system shall recognize sensor status of the front lights every 50 ms
FR5	The light control system shall recognize when the sensor detects a dark environment in a maximum of 50 ms
FR6	If the FR5 is satisfied, the light control system shall turn on the front lights in a maximum of 50 ms
FR7	The light control system shall recognize when the sensor detects light environment in a maximum of 50 ms
FR8	If the FR7 is satisfied, the light control system shall turn off the front lights in a maximum of 50 ms
FR9	The light control system shall get signal of the lights sensor every 50 ms
FR10	The light control system shall recognize the status from light actuator every 50 ms
FR11	The light control system shall notify to user the malfunction of any light component, with a light on the dashboard, in a maximum of 50 ms
FR12	The light control system shall modify light intensity[1] in a maximum of 50 ms, when there is variation of external lighting
FR13	The light control system shall allow the driver to turn off the automatic lights
FR14	The light control system shall allow the driver to turn on the automatic lights
FR15	The light control system shall allow the driver to turn on the lights manually
FR16	The light control system shall allow the driver to modify manually the lights intensity
FR17	The light control system shall allow the driver to turn off the lights manually
FR18	When driver uses the lights manually, the light control system shall notify to user if the driver leaves the lights on after engine is switched off (by audio)
FR19	The light control system shall run requests of requirement FR2 every 50 ms
NFR01	The car shall have reliability lights system, tests shall guarantee lowest rate (0.10%) to software failures
NFR02	When the car is in operation, the light control system shall be available 99% of the time while the car is on

3 Headlight System Modeled with SysML

SysML Requirements diagram allows each requirement to have an identification (ID) and a textual information using natural language in order to describe the requirement.

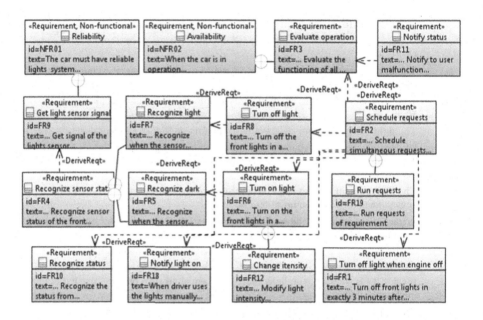

Fig. 1. SysML requirements diagram of the headlight system.

The Headlight control Requirements diagram is depicted in Fig. 1. The diagram includes an incomplete description because, due to space limitation, the description was omitted. In Sect. 2 there is a complete textual description of the requirements. Functional requirements 13, 14, 15, 16, and 17 were not shown in Fig. 1 because these are manual requirements, and the concern in this paper is automatic requirements.

Relationship *"DeriveRqt"* relates a derivative requirement with its origin requirement. *"Containment"* relationship, (represented by the symbol ⊕—— in diagram in Fig. 1) specifies the hierarchy between requirements, its use prevent the reuse of requirements in different contexts, once a specific element of the model can only exist in a *"Containment"*. *"Trace"* relationship is of general purpose between a requirement and any other element of the model and its use occurs only for traceability reasons [8].

SysML also allows the representation of requirements, their properties and relationships in a tabular format which can be seen in Table 2.

Table 2. Requirements table (SysML) of the headlight system.

Id	Name	Type	Derived Req	DerivedFrom Req	Containment Req
FR8	Turn off light	Functional	FR2	FR7	
FR10	Recognize status	Functional	FR2		
FR11	Notify status	Functional		FR3	
NFR01	Reliability	Non-functional			FR9
NFR02	Availability	Non-functional			FR3
FR1	Turn off light when engine off	Functional	FR2		
FR2	Schedule requests	Functional		FR1, FR3, FR6, FR8, FR10, FR18	FR19
FR6	Turn on light	Functional	FR2	FR5	FR12
FR4	Recognize sensor status	Functional		FR9	FR5, FR7
FR5	Recognize dark	Functional	FR6		
FR3	Evaluate operation	Functional	FR2, FR11		
FR18	Notify light on	Functional	FR2		
FR7	Recognize light	Functional	FR8		
FR9	Get light sensor signal	Functional	FR4		
FR12	Change intensify	Functional			
FR19	Run requests	Functional			

3.1   Block Definition Model

SysML provides two diagrams which are useful for system architecture modeling: Block Definition Diagram (BDD) and Internal Block Diagram (IBD).

In the case study, BDD was developed for modeling components which are involved in the headlight system. The specified functions are implemented for secure communication with other components and with local sensors/actuators. SysML BDD is represented in Fig. 2.

A SysML BDD can describe general structural elements, varying from small to very large. SysML Blocks can be used to represent the hardware architecture, the data and procedures of a system [8]. In the example of the headlight system, 10 related blocks are defined. The relationship between blocks was represented by composition associations. The composition instance is synchronous, that is, if an instance is destroyed, finishing the execution, the other executions are also going to be finished. *"Clock"* Block controls time synchronicity. *"Light system"* block communicates with other blocks which are not directly part of the headlight system through the *"Communication control"* block, this communication is essential for the necessary information to the execution of the headlight system to be conducted.

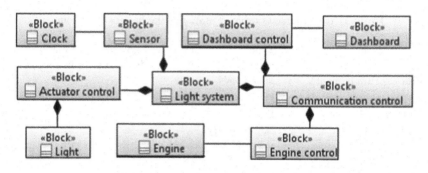

Fig. 2. BDD headlight system.

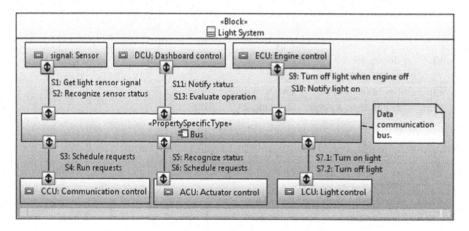

Fig. 3. IBD headlight system.

3.2 Internal Block Model

SysML IBD (Fig. 3) models the internal operations of the *"Light System"* block. The doors connect to external entities and interact with a block through connectors. A flow door specifies the entrance and exit items which can flow between a block and its environment. The doors specify the flow path, data communication, operations, receptions and hardware resources (BUS). For modeling a flow path, *"FlowPort"* was used, specifying entrance and exit items which can flow between a block and its environment. Flow doors relay entrance and exit items for a connector which connects blocks to the internal parts. The connectors are labeled by messages which represent operations between two parts.

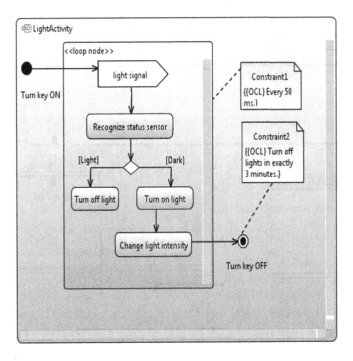

Fig. 4. Activity diagram of the headlight system.

3.3 Activity Model

The main headlight activity is depicted in Fig. 4. Initial and final activities were modeled, decision node which represents the action of switching the headlights on and off, interactive loop with ⟨⟨loop node⟩⟩ and restrictions with OCL for repetition of the loop and to switch the headlights off in exact 3 min after the car is switched off.

4 Headlight System Modeled with AADL - External Specification

AADL descriptions consist in basic elements named components. The modeling of the interface (External specification) of components is given by the AADL type definition. A component type declaration defines the interface elements of a component and externally observable attributes, such as devices which are part of the interaction with other components and connections (see Fig. 5).

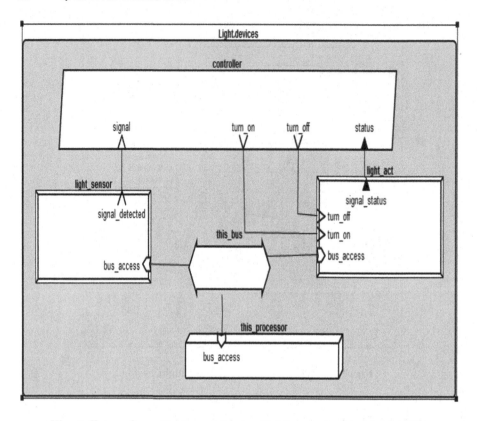

Fig. 5. External specification of the headlight control system in AADL.

The headlight control system, as shown in Fig. 5, is described in the AADL language. The system consists in a system unity, which contains a processor, a process and two devices. The system unity receives entrance signals coming from a sensor device named as *"light_sensor"*. When the absence or presence of light is detected, the *"light_sensor"* sends a signal through a door to the process named *"controller"*. The process receives a signal and the system starts to be executed with the information which was transmitted by the sensor. With the goal of executing a software, it was used a memory processor. The memory is a subcomponent of the processor, in memory the code is stored while the processor is in execution. The *"this_bus"* is required for loading data, controlling signals and establishing data and events interchange between hardware and software components, such as in the communication between the process and the sensor.

```
--process
⊖   process comm controller
        features
            signal: in event port;
            status: in data port;
            turn_off: out event port;
            turn_on: out event port;
    end comm_controller;


⊖   process implementation comm controller.threads
        subcomponents
            thread_readSignal: thread readSignalSensor.impl;
            thread_sendSignal: thread sendSignalAct.impl;
            thread_controlLight: thread controlLight.impl;
        connections
            Readsignal_thread_conn: port signal -> thread_readSignal.signal_in;
            Sendsignal_thread_conn: port status -> thread_sendSignal.status_in  ;
            controlLight_thread_conn: port thread_controlLight.turn_off_out-> turn_off;
            controlLightOn_thread_conn: port thread_controlLight.turn_on_out -> turn_on;
    end comm_controller.threads;
```

Fig. 6. Process code in AADL.

4.1   Internal Specification of AADL Headlight System

Internal specification is specialized by an external implementation. A components implementation declaration defines an internal structure of a component in terms of subcomponents, subcomponents connections, subprogram calls sequencies, modes, flow implementations and properties. Usually, external and internal specifications are performed by alternately repeating two stages. Source code of Fig. 6 presents an internal definition and the implementation of an AADL process. The process, named *"comm_controler"*, and the implementation of the process contains and controls the threads.

In the headlight control system, *threads* are subcomponents of the process, that is, they are an internal specification of the process and are presented in Fig. 7. These *threads* must be able to receive as entrance the light intensity value coming from the (*"thread_readSignal"*) sensor, to process the signal and transmit to the actuator the response regarding the automatic ignition of the headlights (*"thread_controlLight"*). These threads are connected with event doors, because this kind of door allows the rowing of the event associated data. The last thread must receive, as response from actuators, the current state of the headlights (*"thread_sendSignal"*).

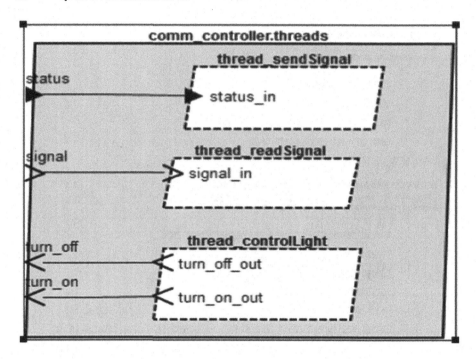

Fig. 7. Internal specification of the headlight control system in AADL.

A highlight of the AADL language is that, besides allowing both textual and graphical description of the system, it relates both.

5   A Comparative Analysis: SysML x AADL

In practical terms, it was observed that abstract features such as decision making, repetition of a functionality (loop), start and end representation of an activity, characteristics that are related to reality, and consequently, to the system, are not described in AADL. The lack of these characteristics was observed while the headlights were being modeled in AADL.

Currently, AADL does not provide a specific diagram/representation to show requirements or behavior by means of actions, such as the SysML Activity diagram. In addition, it is not possible to show the relationship of requirements with the systems design in AADL, and also relationships between system design and software design.

Connectors in AADL are not differentiated, when two types of systems are related, one can only relate them as "extension", in other words, one system only extends another. There is no other classification for connections like there is in SysML, for example, "Trace, Derive, ou Containment".

In AADL, component is identified only by name, there is no Identifier (ID). ID is essential to identify and track easily a requirement, as shown in the SysML example in Table 2.

Developing models in the AADL graphical language is a complex activity, it is necessary to manipulate the internal diagram so that the connections are changed in the external diagram, sometimes this manipulation of the internal diagram to the external or from the external to the internal becomes confused because of the ports and connections, connections are difficult to implement in the graphical model.

SysML provides diagrams for behavior modeling, such as the Sequence diagram, Activity diagram (Figure 4) and State Machine diagram. SysML obviously has strong ability to model system behavior. On the other hand, AADL provides a limited vocabulary for behavior modeling [12].

6 Conclusion

In this paper, the main focus is to show that the SysML language can be used to systems architecture modeling. The comparison between the SysML and AADL languages is performed to understand the limitations that SysML presents and to propose improvements in the architectural aspect.

It was observed that SysML can be used extensively for modeling abstract features. SysML accurately captures the requirements, management of system complexity is developed from the initial stages of production of a system with the expressiveness of the Requirements diagram.

Block diagram and Internal Block diagram capture the systems and subsystems, provide communication between them and the necessary resources. The Activity diagram can represent the steps required for a given activity to be completed successfully, or may display a predicted deviation. This diagram also captures the main strategic decisions of a system, and serves for communication between stakeholders.

We can conclude that the Requirements, Activities, Blocks and Internal Blocks diagrams are suitable for software architecture modeling. However, SysML needs to be expanded for classification of components, implementation of the model through textual syntax and description of time properties to have features necessary for modeling the architecture of real-time systems.

References

1. Van der Auweraer, H., Anthonis, J., De Bruyne, S., Leuridan, J.: Virtual engineering at work: the challenges for designing mechatronic products. Eng. Comput. **29**(3), 389–408 (2013). https://doi.org/10.1007/s00366-012-0286-6
2. Behjati, R., Yue, T., Nejati, S., Briand, L., Selic, B.: Extending SysML with AADL concepts for comprehensive system architecture modeling. In: France, R.B., Kuester, J.M., Bordbar, B., Paige, R.F. (eds.) ECMFA 2011. LNCS, vol. 6698, pp. 236–252. Springer, Heidelberg (2011). https://doi.org/10.1007/978-3-642-21470-7_17
3. Brown, A.W.: Model driven architecture: principles and practice. Softw. Syst. Model **3**(4), 314–327 (2004). https://doi.org/10.1007/s10270-004-0061-2

4. Evensen, K., Weiss, K.: A comparison and evaluation of real-time software systems modeling languages. In: AIAA Infotech@ Aerospace 2010, p. 3504. American Institute of Aeronautics and Astronautics, California, USA (2010)

5. Khan, A.M., Mallet, F., Rashid, M.: Modeling systemverilog assertions using SysML and CCSL. In: Electronic System Level Synthesis Conference, ESLsyn Conference, Proceedings (2015)

6. Koopman, P.: Better Embedded System Software. Drumnadrochit Education, Pittsburgh (2010)

7. Marques, M.R.S., Siegert, E., Brisolara, L.: Integrating UML, MARTE and SysML to improve requirements specification and traceability in the embedded domain. In: Proceedings of the 12th IEEE International Conference on Industrial Informatics (INDIN), pp. 176–181. IEEE (2014)

8. OMG: OMG systems modeling language (OMG SysML). OMG Document: 03 June 2015, p. 346 (2015)

9. Ribeiro, F.G.C., Pereira, C.E., Rettberg, A., Soares, M.S.: Model-based requirements specification of real-time systems with UML, SysML and MARTE. Softw. Syst. Model. 17(1), 343–361 (2016). https://doi.org/10.1007/s10270-016-0525-1

10. Ribeiro, Q.A.D.S., Ribeiro, F.G.C., Soares, M.S.: A technique to architect real-time embedded systems with SysML and UML through multiple views. In: 19th International Conference on Enterprise Information Systems (ICEIS), 2(1), pp. 287–294 (2017)

11. dos Santos Soares, M., Vrancken, J.L.: Model-driven user requirements specification using SysML. JSW 3(6), 57–68 (2008)

12. Shiraishi, S.: Qualitative comparison of ADL-based approaches to real-world automotive system development. Inf. Media Technol. 8(1), 196–207 (2013)

13. Zurawski, R.: Embedded Systems Handbook, 2-Volume Set. CRC Press Inc, Taylor and Francis Group (2009)

Design, Implementation, and Evaluation of a Real Time Localization System for the Optimization of Agitation Processes

Andreas Heller$^{(\boxtimes)}$, Ludwig Horsthemke$^{(\boxtimes)}$, and Peter Glösekötter$^{(\boxtimes)}$

Münster University of Applied Sciences, Steinfurt, Germany
{andreas.heller,l.horsthemke,peter.gloesekoetter}@fh-muenster.de

Abstract. This work describes the setup of an ultrawideband (UWB) realtime localization system (RTLS) for tracking of particles. We describe how the RTLS obtains distances and positions through radio waves and the setup and evaluation of a real world system is stated in detail. In the proposed system the particles track a subtrates surface flow inside a biogas plant for verification of agitation processes.

Keywords: UWB · RTLS · Biogas plant optimization

1 Introduction

The mixing process in biogas plants plays an important role in its effectiveness [2]. Simulations for different biogas mixing concepts are carried out, with the aim of maximizing the gas yield. The here described system provides a means to assessing the surface flow of substrates in biogas plants to validate such simulations [3]. Lemmer et al. [7] pointed out that a combination of intrusive and non-invasive research methods tends to be applied for the research on mixing quality in biogas digesters as done in this work.

The UWB RTLS consists of fixed nodes mounted above the biogas plant and small floating units which positions are tracked over time. By reconstructing the path from the captured positions and calculating the time derivative, flow velocities can be deducted. With a high number of tags and long runtimes a dependable data base for evaluation of simulations can be constructed. UWB has been chosen in contrast to other ranging techniques like received signal strength indication, (assisted) global navigation satellite system (GNSS) or ultrasound due to its high accuracy (≤ 15 cm) relatively low cost and low power [10].

2 Main

This section offers a detailed look into the systems logic. First the distance determination via ultra wide band communication (UWB) with subsequent position determination is explained. In following, the system structure is described and key parameters are examined. Finally, results of a real world test are provided.

© IFIP International Federation for Information Processing 2023
Published by Springer Nature Switzerland AG 2023
M. A. Wehrmeister et al. (Eds.): IESS 2019, IFIP AICT 576, pp. 39–50, 2023.
https://doi.org/10.1007/978-3-031-26500-6_4

2.1 Distance Determination

The proposed system is based on UWB localization, which relies on time measurement to extract distances between two communication partners. To calculate these distances, we simply measure the time a signal needs to travel from one communication partner to another. To extract the distance based on the measured time, we take the signals velocity into account. That however is, like it is for all electromagnetic waves, the speed of light c. Lastly a simple multiplication of c and time t provides the distance ρ, we are looking for ($\rho = c \cdot t$).

Measuring the distance like proposed above would simply not be possible, since the two communicating sides do not know send or receive times of the opposing side. Thus a scheme called Alternative Double Sided Two Way Ranging (AltDS-TWR) is deployed. In comparison to other TWR-schemes, such as Single Sided-TWR (SS-TWR), Symmetric Double Sided-TWR (SDS-TWR), or Asymmetric Double Sided-TWR (ADS-TWR), AltDS-TWR offers good robustness and accuracy [9]. Another widely presented method for UWB based distance measurement is called Time Difference of Arrival (TDoA). It offers great performance and usually good accuracy, however all the components in a TDoA based system have to be properly synchronized to achieve reasonable accuracies. The two communication partners are called *tag* and *anchor*, where *tag* usually refers to the mobile node which position is tracked and the anchors positions are known. Figure 1 shows the DS-TWR scheme in which three messages are exchanged. The respective nodes note the times at which messages are received or transmitted. The results of this scheme are six time stamps, from which intervals can be calculated. These are marked in Fig. 1 as t_{XS} and t_{XR}. When subtracting the tags first send- and the receive-time stamp, the result is a *round trip time*, marked as T_{Ra}, same goes for the round trip time for the anchor, marked as T_{Rb}. The time interval noted as T_{Dx} is the processing time each component needs to compute a received message, prepare and send the answer message. If

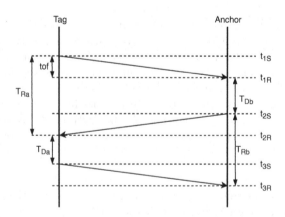

Fig. 1. Alternative double sided two way ranging.

we subtract a processing time from a round trip and take the result by half, we calculate the *time of flight tof* for SS-TWR. To take maximum advantage of *DS-TWR* however we have to take into account, that the clock speeds of the two communication partners will vary. Errors from diverging clocks are called *clock-* and *frequency drifts* which play a huge role in the optimization of UWB based localization systems. Since the signal travels with the speed of light, small deviations in measured time can cause great errors in calculated distances. Lastly the following formula will take all this into account and calculate the time of flight as

$$tof = \frac{T_{Ra} \cdot T_{Rb} - T_{Ra} \cdot T_{Rb}}{T_{Ra} + T_{Rb} + T_{Da} + T_{Db}}. \tag{1}$$

If the anchor calculates the distance, the sent-time stamp for the final message can be pre calculated and embedded into the final message, thus the anchor knows all time slots and is able to calculate without needing to wait for another message.

2.2 Lateration

In previous section we covered the measurement of distances between two components. Here we will take distances from components with static positions, called anchors, to one tracked component, called tag. In this section an example with three anchors and one tag is presented, where the tag can be tracked in two dimensions. We will also cover how to track the tags position in the third dimension and what restrictions the system has in each case. Figure 2 schematically shows this system. The measured ranges from each anchor A_i to the tag T_0, is marked as ρ_X. As marked in the figure, the ranges can be interpreted as circles around the anchors positions. Thus the intersection of all the circles mark the tags position. Mathematically a circle is described as

$$\rho_i^2 = (x - x_{A_i})^2 + (y - y_{A_i})^2 \tag{2}$$

where x_{A_i} and y_{A_i} are the coordinates of the i-th anchors location. When solving Eq. 2, there will be squared terms left for the x- and y- coordinates, which we are looking for. The difference to another circle will solve this problem. In this example we subtract the circle in the origin, this way the terms for the anchors position are set to zero

$$x_{A_0} = y_{A_0} = 0 \tag{3}$$

thus resulting to a solvable linear equation system with two equations and two variables

$$\rho_1^2 - \rho_0^2 = -2x(x_{A_1} - x_{A_0}) - 2y(y_{A_1} - y_{A_0}) + x_{A_1}^2 + y_{A_1}^2 - x_{A_0}^2 - y_{A_0}^2, \tag{4}$$

$$\rho_2^2 - \rho_0^2 = -2x(x_{A_2} - x_{A_0}) - 2y(y_{A_2} - y_{A_0}) + x_{A_2}^2 + y_{A_2}^2 - x_{A_0}^2 - y_{A_0}^2. \tag{5}$$

Additional to the resulting equation system, also the context to the amount of anchors and the trackable dimensions becomes clear. If we want to track a tag in N dimensions, we have to provide $N + 1$ anchors.

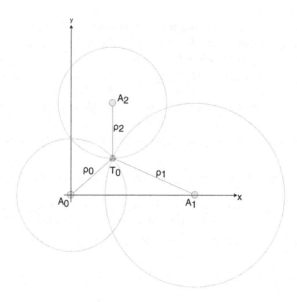

Fig. 2. Trilateration visualization.

A more straightforward view is achieved by displaying the system using a matrix equation

$$b = A \cdot \begin{pmatrix} x \\ y \end{pmatrix} \tag{6}$$

where

$$b = \begin{pmatrix} \rho_1^2 - \rho_0^2 - x_{A_1}^2 - y_{A_1}^2 + x_{A_0}^2 + y_{A_0}^2 \\ \rho_2^2 - \rho_0^2 - x_{A_2}^2 - y_{A_2}^2 + x_{A_0}^2 + y_{A_0}^2 \\ \vdots \\ \rho_n^2 - \rho_0^2 - x_{A_n}^2 - y_{A_n}^2 + x_{A_0}^2 + y_{A_0}^2 \end{pmatrix} \tag{7}$$

and

$$A = -2 \cdot \begin{bmatrix} x_{A_1} - x_{A_0} & y_{A_1} - y_{A_0} \\ x_{A_2} - x_{A_0} & y_{A_2} - y_{A_0} \\ \vdots & \vdots \\ x_{A_1} - x_{A_0} & y_{A_1} - y_{A_0} \end{bmatrix} \cdot \tag{8}$$

The system displayed in Fig. 2 can now be described as

$$b = A \cdot \begin{pmatrix} x \\ y \end{pmatrix} \tag{9}$$

$$\begin{pmatrix} \rho_1^2 - \rho_0^2 - x_{A_1}^2 - y_{A_1}^2 + x_{A_0}^2 + y_{A_0}^2 \\ \rho_2^2 - \rho_0^2 - x_{A_2}^2 - y_{A_2}^2 + x_{A_0}^2 + y_{A_0}^2 \end{pmatrix} = \begin{bmatrix} x_{A_1} - x_{A_0} & y_{A_1} - y_{A_0} \\ x_{A_2} - x_{A_0} & y_{A_2} - y_{A_0} \end{bmatrix} \cdot \begin{pmatrix} x \\ y \end{pmatrix} \tag{10}$$

This equation is now solved by multiplying it with A^{-1}. This however is not as trivial. One requirement for inverting matrices requires it to be symmetric. With more anchors the matrix $\boldsymbol{A}$, only grows in one direction. Moores pseudoinverse $\boldsymbol{A}^+$ however does not require symmetry. It is calculated as

$$\boldsymbol{A}^+ = (\boldsymbol{A}^T \cdot \boldsymbol{A})^{-1} \cdot \boldsymbol{A}^T. \tag{11}$$

Now tag positions are obtainable no matter the dimensions of matrix $\boldsymbol{A}$.

In conclusion the system can track positions in two dimensions with any amount of anchors (more than three). In the case of this paper however it is substantial to track the tags in three dimensions leading to a single adjustment to the mathematical foundation. So instead of the circles, denoted by the ranges from anchors to the tag, the third dimension will create a sphere around each anchor. Thus the adjusted system builds up on

$$\rho_i^2 = (x - x_{A_i})^2 + (y - y_{A_i})^2 + (z - z_{A_i})^2. \tag{12}$$

Finally the matrix equation changes to

$$b = A \cdot \begin{pmatrix} x \\ y \\ z \end{pmatrix} \tag{13}$$

with adjustments to $\boldsymbol{b}$ and $\boldsymbol{A}$ as

$$b = \begin{pmatrix} \rho_1^2 - \rho_0^2 - x_{A_1}^2 - y_{A_1}^2 - z_{A_1}^2 + x_{A_0}^2 + y_{A_0}^2 + z_{A_0}^2 \\ \rho_2^2 - \rho_0^2 - x_{A_2}^2 - y_{A_2}^2 - z_{A_2}^2 + x_{A_0}^2 + y_{A_0}^2 + z_{A_0}^2 \\ \vdots \\ \rho_n^2 - \rho_0^2 - x_{A_n}^2 - y_{A_n}^2 - z_{A_n}^2 + x_{A_0}^2 + y_{A_0}^2 + z_{A_0}^2 \end{pmatrix}, \tag{14}$$

$$A = -2 \cdot \begin{bmatrix} x_{A_1} - x_{A_0} & y_{A_1} - y_{A_0} & z_{A_1} - z_{A_0} \\ x_{A_2} - x_{A_0} & y_{A_2} - y_{A_0} & z_{A_1} - z_{A_0} \\ \vdots & \vdots & \vdots \\ x_{A_1} - x_{A_0} & y_{A_1} - y_{A_0} & z_{A_1} - z_{A_0} \end{bmatrix}. \tag{15}$$

2.3   System Structure

Anchors and tags are based on simple printed circuit boards which include a DecaWave DWM1000 UWB transceiver module, a STM32F103 ARM Cortex-M3 processor and a low quiescent current, low drop out voltage regulator as shown in Fig. 3. Anchors are additionally equipped with circuitry for RS485 communication and buck converters for power supply from the backbone.

Figure 4 shows the basic structure concept. It can be divided into a backbone and the mobile tags. The backbone is comprised of a Single Board Computer (SBC) as a central unit which delivers power to the anchor nodes and connects to them via RS485. The anchors are distributed around the perimeter of the biogas reactor, usually on the outside with direct line of sight (LOS) to the

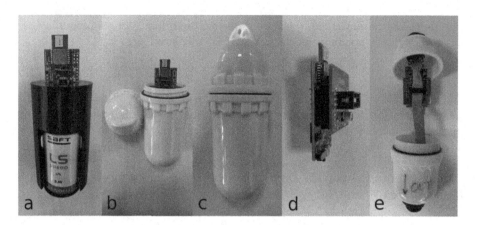

Fig. 3. a) Tag PCB and battery in supporting frame. b) Tag assembly in enclosure. c) Closed enclosure of tag. d) Anchor PCB with additional circuitry. e) Opened anchor assembly.

substrates surface, except for the film hood on the reactor and the nodes plastic enclosures. The anchors positions have to be determined manually when setting up the system. Distance records are stored in the anchors memory until the SBC retrieves and stores them at a period of 10 s. Additionally the stored records and information about the systems state are uploaded to a server via cellular connection. This way the system can be constantly monitored and the gathered data are available for offline processing while the measurements are still running. Also a backup battery ensures the uninterrupted operation of the system for several days, should a power outage occur.

The mobile tags are powered by 61.2 Wh Li-SOCl$_2$ primary cells which enable runtimes of several months. The weight distribution in the case was chosen in a way that the top part tends to always protrude from the substrate to ensure the best possible reception of the radio. The cases are made of ABS and feature a smooth surface which prevents the substrate in the biogas reactor from adhering to it and attenuating the RF propagation.

In the ranging process a tag carries out AltDS-TWR successively with each of the four anchors. This process takes approximately 20 ms with the radio settings listed in Table 1 which means that a capacity of 50 tags can not be exceeded. These settings are chosen as a compromise to give high ranges and high accuracies while keeping the transmission time low to give the aforementioned capacity of tags and the best ranging performance. As Mikhaylov et al. [12] already mentioned on channel 5 the standard deviations of the results do not seem to change much with the distance between tag and anchor and show an overall lower deviation of the measurements. This behaviour was also observed in this work after less extensive tests which is why channel 5 was chosen for this system.

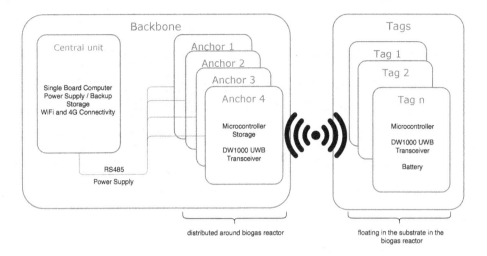

Fig. 4. Basic structure of the system.

Table 1. Communication configuration of radio.

Parameter	Value
Channel number	5
Center frequency	6,489 GHz
Bandwith	499.2 MHz
Pulse repetition frequency	16 MHz
Preamble length	1024
Preamble acquisition chunk size	32
Preamble code in RX and TX	3
Data rate	110 kbps

2.4 Distance and Accuracy

For a maximum distance estimation the link margin which is the difference of received signal level P_R and the receiver sensitivity can be examined. P_R can be calculated from the path loss formula

$$R_P[dBm] = T_P[dBm] + G[dB] - L[dB] - 20\log_{10}\frac{4\pi f_C d}{c} \qquad (16)$$

with transmit power T_P, gain of receive and transmit antennas G, losses from PCB, cables and connectors L, the center frequency of the used channel f_C, distance d and speed of light c [1]. At channel 5 the center frequency equals 6.489 GHz and the transmit power was set to the legal limit of -41 dBm/MHz. From the DWM1000 datasheets antenna diagram combined loss and antenna gain of 0 dB to -5 dB per transceiver is assumed. The receiver sensitivity at

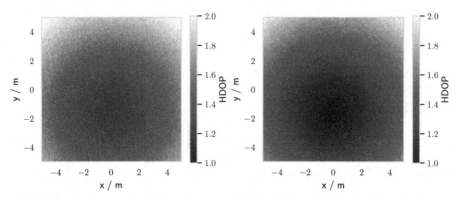

(a) **HDOP distribution for fill level of** 0.8 m (b) **HDOP distribution for fill level of** 3.4 m
(3 m between anchor and tag planes).   (0.4 m between anchor and tag planes).

Fig. 5. Simulation of HDOP for two different fill levels of constellation from Fig. 8a. Anchor positions are set to $(0, -5), (5, 0), (0, 5), (-5, 0)$ with the origin in the center of the tank.

the used configuration is determined from the datasheet as -100 dBm [4] with a crystal trimmed to ± 2 ppm. The resulting link margin leads to communication ranges of 79 m to 23 m. State of the art biogas plants include fermenter tanks of up to 40 m diameter though most of todays plants are smaller. The attenuation by the enclosures and the film hood cover of the biogas plant is expected to be low as they are made of ABS and PVC respectively which offer low dissipation factors $\tan \delta$ and dielectric constants near to 1. With the anchor placement right at the tanks perimeter and high expected fill levels the maximum needed ranges are of the same dimensions. This could imply a necessary change of the radio configuration in favor of range with the disadvantage of lower accuracy or system capacity.

The quality of measurements also depends on the constellation of anchor and tag positions which can be quantified by the dilution of precision (DOP). It is an indicator for the error gain of a certain constellation and has been introduced for time of arrival (TOA) based systems like GNSS [6]. As in this work the height of the tags will be at the constant or slowly changing fill level of biogas tanks and the planes of anchor placement and tags will be parallel to each other, only the horizontal part (HDOP) is of interest. The HDOP is defined as the ratio of error in the horizontal plane to the error of pseudoranges [8]

$$\text{HDOP} = \frac{\sqrt{\sigma_X^2 + \sigma_Y^2}}{\sigma_\rho} \tag{17}$$

with the errors in x- and y-direction σ_X, σ_Y. The best HDOP can be achieved when the two mentioned planes are coplanar. A stochastic simulation for the constellation depicted in Fig. 8a has been carried out for two different fill levels. The results in Fig. 5 show the best values can be expected in the center of the

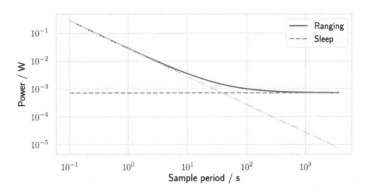

Fig. 6. Power consumption of tag as a function of sample period from $10\,\mathrm{Hz}^{-1}$ to $1\,\mathrm{h}$.

slurry tank while amplifications of error rise up to HDOP = 2 at the edge of the tank. With decreasing fill levels the distances between the planes and so the HDOPs increase.

Another source of error is message loss, which can occur due to submerged tags. This systems backbone however, can detect message loss and only takes sets of messages into account, that provide feasible position calculations.

2.5 Power Management and TDMA

To minimize power consumption and thus ensure long runtimes the tags initiate the ranging process at a regular interval and enter a low power state in between. For wait times between the ranging processes the microprocessor was put into the lowest power state from which it can only be woken up by an external interrupt which is generated by the DW1000 built in sleep timer. After calibration as explained in [5, P.39] the timers actual frequency is determined. As the frequency can be approximately $7\,\mathrm{kHz}$ to $13\,\mathrm{kHz}$ and the upper 16 bits of the 28 bit counter can be set, the minimum wait duration can be $585\,\mathrm{ms}$ to $315\,\mathrm{ms}$. Using this timer the rest of the DW1000 can be put to sleep in addition to the host microcontroller.

An update rate of $1\,\mathrm{Hz}$ was chosen for this system because it gives good temporal resolution at the expected flow velocities at the surface of biogas plants. From the variation of the timers frequency follows that the exact wait times for $1\,\mathrm{Hz}$ operation can not be met. Also the collision of two tags ranging initiations has to be prevented. This makes it necessary to introduce a time division multiple access (TDMA) scheme. It is coordinated by one of the anchors which acts as a master and sends synchronization information during the ranging procedure. This master has to know of all active tags and based on the number of tags and the systems update rate assign each a unique time slot. Should a tags ranging initiation drift over time leaving its assigned slot the master anchor will calculate a wait time which is used once by the tag for resynchronization.

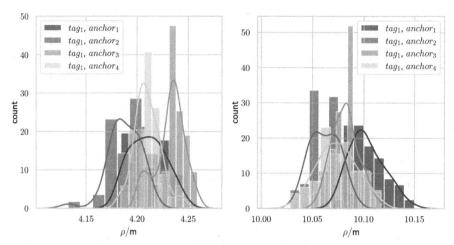

(a) Real distance $r = 4.2\,\text{m}$, Mean measured distances $\bar{\rho}_1 = 4.21\,\text{m}$, $\bar{\rho}_2 = 4.19\,\text{m}$, $\bar{\rho}_3 = 4.23\,\text{m}$, $\bar{\rho}_4 = 4.21\,\text{m}$, Standard deviations $\sigma_{\rho,1} = 17\,\text{mm}$, $\sigma_{\rho,2} = 15\,\text{mm}$, $\sigma_{\rho,3} = 14\,\text{mm}$, $\sigma_{\rho,4} = 13\,\text{mm}$.

(b) Real distance $r = 10.1\,\text{m}$, Mean measured distances $\bar{\rho}_1 = 10.1\,\text{m}$, $\bar{\rho}_2 = 10.06\,\text{m}$, $\bar{\rho}_3 = 10.08\,\text{m}$, $\bar{\rho}_4 = 10.07\,\text{m}$, Standard deviations $\sigma_{\rho,1} = 17\,\text{mm}$, $\sigma_{\rho,2} = 14\,\text{mm}$, $\sigma_{\rho,3} = 13\,\text{mm}$, $\sigma_{\rho,4} = 19\,\text{mm}$.

Fig. 7. Histograms and fitted probability density functions of $n = 120$ rangings between one tag floating in water and four anchors at two fixed distances.

The power consumption of a tag is dominated by the active ranging which was measured to be $27{,}7\,\text{mW}$ at the given update rate. This leads to an operational time of 92 days with the chosen battery. During sleep times the power could be reduced to $724\,\mu\text{W}$. Figure 6 shows the power consumption of tag as a function of sample period. The mean dynamic power used by the ranging drops below the static power at a sample period above $40\,\text{s}$. Self discharge of the battery has not been accounted for.

2.6 Evaluation

To assess the expected quality of distance measurements a tag was placed inside an open tank of $10\,\text{m}$ by $5\,\text{m}$ filled with water at two different fixed locations. Four anchors were placed $2\,\text{m}$ above the ground next to each other and to the perimeter of the tank. Figure 7 shows the resulting histograms of 120 measurements at each location. The results show standard deviations of less than $20\,\text{mm}$ and maximum differences of mean and real value under $50\,\text{mm}$. These results show a comparable performance to open space measurements deducted by Michler et al. [11]. This leads to the conclusion that the placement of the UWB transceiver right above a plane of water has no detrimental effect on the ranging performance.

In a next step a test with two tags in a slurry tank was performed. This tank has similar properties to those of biogas plants and the advantage of an open

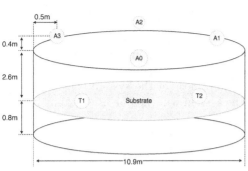 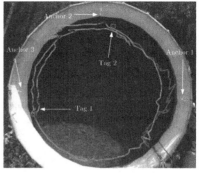

(a) Schematic of tank with dimensions, fill level indication and anchor placements.
(b) Top view of tank with reconstructed traces of two tags overlayed after 2 minutes of operation.

Fig. 8. Test setup and reconstructed position records in slurry tank.

top. So it was possible to have an unmanned aerial vehicle capture a video for later comparison to the reconstructed positions. Figure 8 shows a schematic of the tank with dimensions, fill level indication and anchor placements as well as reconstructed traces of two tags overlayed after 2 min of operation. The anchors were placed 0.5 m to the inside and 0.4 m above the walls of the tank which would also be the positions right on top of the hood cover if the tank was a biogas plant. The low fill level resulted in a difference of 3 m between the plane of anchors and the substrate surface. This can be considered a worst case scenario in terms of the HDOP as biogas plants are expected to operate at medium to high fill levels. No systematic loss of messages due to too high distances could be detected in this test.

A reconstruction of the traces was projected onto the horizontal plane and overlayed to the stabilized video capture of the UAV. Traces and video were synchronized in time and scaled accordingly using two timestamps with known positions. Because errors from perspective distortion have not been accounted for, the reconstructed path gives only an indication of the dynamic deviation to the actual position.

3   Conclusion and Future Work

This paper describes the concepts and system structure of a UWB based real-time localization system for the tracking of substrate flow on the surface of biogas plant digesters. The system can operate continuously over a period of three months with up to 50 concurrent tags and offers a sufficient accuracy for the evaluation of flow simulations. The field of use however does not end with substrate flow tracking as it can be used for all kind of tracking tasks where other systems e.g. global navigation satellite systems fail.

Future work includes the implementation of a novel ranging scheme (TOF-CR) described by Rebel et al. [13] to benefit of the accurate ranging of DS-TWR while keeping transmit times and power consumption low. Furthermore the amount of anchors will be increased and the number of anchors a tag communicates to will be made flexible and chosen at runtime based on the anchors in reach and the resulting DOP. Therefore most of the system control will be moved to the SBC in the backbone. The system will then be used extensively to build a database for simulation verification.

Acknowledgement. This project has been funded by the Federal Ministry of Education and Research in Germany, the grant ID reads 03FH002IX4.

References

1. APS017: Maximising range in DW1000 based systems (2015)
2. Annas, S., Czajka, H., Jantzen, H.A., Janoske, U.: Influence of the viscosity and speed on the fluid flow of a paddle agitator (2017). https://doi.org/10.13140/RG.2.2.26620.03205
3. Annas, S., Elfering, M., Volbert, N., Jantzen, H.A., Scholz, J., Janoske, U.: Einfluss der rührwerksposition auf den mischprozess in biogasanlagen anhand eines paddelrührwerks. Chem. Ing. Tec. **91**(7), 969–979 (2019). https://doi.org/10.1002/cite.201800116
4. DecaWave Ltd.: DW1000 IEEE802.15.4-2011 UWB-Transceiver Datasheet (2015)
5. Decawave Ltd.: DW1000 Device Driver Application Programming Interface (API) Guide, Version 2.4. Decawave Ltd. (2017)
6. Langley, R.B.: Dilution of Precision. GPS World (1999)
7. Lemmer, A., Naegele, H.J., Sondermann, J.: How efficient are agitators in biogas digesters? Determination of the efficiency of submersible motor mixers and incline agitators by measuring nutrient distribution in full-scale agricultural biogas digesters. Energies **6**(12), 6255–6273 (2013). https://doi.org/10.3390/en6126255
8. Li, B., Dempster, A., Wang, J.: 3D DOPs for positioning applications using range measurements. Wirel. Sens. Netw. **3**, 343–349 (2011). https://doi.org/10.4236/wsn.2011.310037
9. Lian Sang, C., Adams, M., Hörmann, T., Hesse, M., Porrmann, M., Rückert, U.: Numerical and experimental evaluation of error estimation for two-way ranging methods. Sensors **19**(3), 616 (2019). https://doi.org/10.3390/s19030616
10. Liu, H., Darabi, H., Banerjee, P., Liu, J.: Survey of wireless indoor positioning techniques and systems. IEEE Trans. Syst. Man Cybern. Part C: Appl. Rev. **37**, 1067–1080 (2007). https://doi.org/10.1109/TSMCC.2007.905750
11. Michler, F., Deniz, H., Lurz, F., Weigel, R., Koelpin, A.: Performance analysis of an ultra wideband transceiver for real- time localization. In: Proceedings of the 48th European Microwave Conference (EuMC), pp. 1141–1144 (2018). https://doi.org/10.23919/EuMC.2018.8541672
12. Mikhaylov, K., Petäjäjärvi, J., Hämäläinen, M., Tikanmäki, A., Kohno, R.: Impact of IEEE 802.15.4 communication settings on performance in asynchronous two way UWB ranging. Int. J. Wirel. Inf. Netw. **24**(2), 124–139 (2017). https://doi.org/10.1007/s10776-017-0340-9
13. Rebel, G., González, J., Glösekötter, P., Estevez, F., Romero, A.: A novel indoor localization scheme for autonomous nodes in IEEE 802.15.4a networks (2016)

Estimations

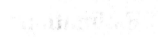

Improving Estimations for Latencies of Cause-Effect Chains

Max J. Friese[1,2(✉)], Thorsten Ehlers[1], and Dirk Nowotka[1]

[1] Department of Computer Science, Kiel University, Kiel, Germany
{mjf,the,dn}@informatik.uni-kiel.de
[2] Mercedes-Benz Car Development, Sindelfingen, Germany
max_jonas.friese@daimler.com

Abstract. The reaction of a cyber-physical system to a stimulus typically requires the processing of several tasks. A task in this context is an aggregation of different working steps, where each step comprises a dedicated piece of software called runnable. The delay between stimulus and reaction depends of the interaction of the software pieces and is subject to timing constraints. Therefore, tight bounds on the delays are needed at any stage of the engineering processes. We present an extension for an approach to estimate such bounds more precisely than previously possible.

Keywords: Cyber-physical systems · Cause-effect chains · Analytical models · Formal estimations · end-to-end latencies

1 Introduction

For many systems, like cars, safety and comfort features rely on the seamless processing of physical values by electronic control units (ECUs). Those values are captured by sensors and the collected data is used to control actuators to the user's needs. Systems where physical data is processed and physical processes are monitored and controlled by networks of ECUs are called cyber-physical systems (CPS) [15]. In many cases the time for such a system to react to an input is subject to constraints. Thus, a performance analysis with respect to different latencies is an important part of system engineering. The complexity of performance analysis increases with the ongoing digitalization of technical systems.

Constraints on the temporal behavior of CPS usually exists between a physical stimulus and a physical reaction. To estimate an end-to-end latency, the processing between stimulus and reaction is divided in different segments. One of these segments is the software running on the ECUs. The temporal behavior of the software can be determined in several ways. It can be measured in the end-product or with testbed hardware, determined with simulation or estimated by analytical approaches as described in [19]. For measurements and simulations no formal abstraction of the system is needed. The temporal behavior is analyzed

© IFIP International Federation for Information Processing 2023
Published by Springer Nature Switzerland AG 2023
M. A. Wehrmeister et al. (Eds.): IESS 2019, IFIP AICT 576, pp. 53–64, 2023.
https://doi.org/10.1007/978-3-031-26500-6_5

using existing parts of the system. However, choosing the right measurement scenarios or simulation stimuli to definitely observe the worst-case behavior is known to be a hard problem [8]. Therefore, a disadvantage of measurement-based analyses is the lack of guarantees for the measured values to be safe bounds.

On the contrary, approaches based on formal analysis give guarantees for the calculated bounds. These guarantees come with the price of an overestimation due to assumptions and abstractions in the modeling process. However, overestimations can be reduced by making use of more detailed system models. More details inevitably lead to more complexity, resulting in greater computational effort. This results in a trade-off between precision and computing time. The presented approach provides a new level of detail while breaking the time-precision trade-off.

1.1 Problem Statement

In this paper we focus on systems in which data propagation through the software can be described in terms of so-called cause-effect chains. Such a chain is a sequence of tasks where he successor of a task reads at least signal value produced by its successor. A task can occur multiple times within such a chain and a system function might have multiple associated chains.

The temporal constraints on cause-effect chains can be divided in two categories. One is the delay between the arrival of an input and the reaction of the last task, which is called *response time* (or *reaction time*). Another constraint is *data age* which describes the fact that an output may depend on old input values, e.g. when the task writing a signal is activated less frequent than the task reading the signal. The different semantics for latencies are depicted in Fig. 1 and are described with more detail in [5]. The first path, starting at the second instance of *Task A* shows the worst case response time for the chain *Task A* → *Task B* → *Task C* → *Task A*. The second path, starting at the 6th instance of *Task A* shows its data age. Both, the data age and response time of a chain, mainly depend on the possible relative offsets between task instances on the chain and their read and write intervals. The latter depends on the communication model of the task and its core execution time. Furthermore, task instances may influence other task instances when competing for computation time, imposing a delay on the response of the single task.

Safe and tight bounds for both types of constraints and various types of chains are needed at any stage of the development process, e.g. to evaluate the impact of changes in the system or verify the final system against timing requirements. The presented approach is the first formal estimation approach yielding safe upper bounds while allowing an analysis on intra-task level and supporting the range of activation models, communication models, and further system parameters as described below.

1.2 Our Contribution

In this paper we demonstrate improvements and extensions of the approach presented in [6].

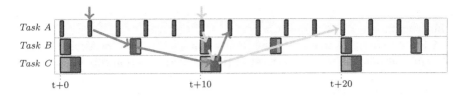

Fig. 1. Response Time (blue) and Data Age (orange) of the Chain *Task A* (Color figure online) → *Task B* → *Task C* → *Task A*

In particular,

- The authors claim that best- and worst-case execution times can easily be integrated in their model. This is true, however, it significantly increases the runtime of the analysis. We show that this increase can be minimized by adding additional constraints. Furthermore, we demonstrate that the model can also be adapted for computing data ages.
- Additionally to incorporating execution times, a further step towards precision can be made by also looking inside the tasks. We integrate software runnables, i.e. chunks of software which are processed when a task is activated, in the analysis. In order to keep runtimes low, we show how to compress the modeling of runnables such that a high precision is preserved exactly where required.
- To show the benefits of the more detailed approach we compare our outcomes with results of other approaches. A comparison between our adaption and a state-of-the-art implementation of a compositional approaches for example shows significantly tighter bounds.

1.3 Structure

This paper is organized as follows: related work is presented in the next section. Subsequently, the systems in scope are described and a set of constraints which models their temporal behavior with respect to cause-effect chains is defined. Finally, in Sect. 5 the performance of our approach when compared with a state-of-the-art implementation of a compositional approach is evaluated. The benchmarks for the experiments are industrial-scale task sets from an automotive supplier and a manufacturer of automobiles.

2 Related Work

Calculating a formal bound on a latency of a cause-effect chain in a given system consists of two main steps. Firstly, a formal representation which fits the purpose is defined or chosen. Secondly, a suitable method to analyze the temporal properties of the model is employed to obtain an estimation. Therefore, due to the descriptive nature of the presented approach, related work is found in two disciplines: modeling systems and describing timing behavior, and the estimation of end-to-end latencies.

A formal language to specify the functionality as well as the timing of real-time applications has been presented in [11]. One abstraction introduced is the logical execution time (LET). In LET the behavior of the system in terms of time is abstracted to when input is read and output is written rather than the actual execution time [12]. The LET paradigm is especially used in the automotive domain to determine end-to-end latencies [9,16]. LET massively simplifies the problem of estimating end-to-end latencies for cause-effect chains because data propagation only occurs within well-defined and fixed instances of chains. However, in the mechatronic part of the system, data rates might vary because they depend on physical factors, e.g. the engine speed of a car.

In contrast to analytical approaches, like e.g. [9], formal approaches strive after upper bounds for latencies, i.e. all response times possibly observed in the real system are lower or equal that bound. Formal approaches to tackle this complexity can be divided in two categories. On the one hand, there are holistic approaches, where chains are analyzed in one piece. The holistic approach of Becker et al. is implemented by analyzing possible data propagation paths of a chain [1]. Kloda et al. proposed an analysis algorithm with linear time complexity which makes use of the execution time of tasks [13]. However, these analyses are restricted to periodic task sets and make use of worst-case response times of tasks, rather than worst-case execution times. This can lead to load being considered which can not possibly be observed simultaneously in the real system. Another holistic approach to estimating response times was presented in [3,14]. It is based on mixed integer linear programming (MILP). For the analysis, the system's timing properties are modeled with the help of linear constraints. However, the scheduling model differs from the one considered in this work and again the possible inferences of tasks are assumed to be covered in an earlier analysis step. Another category of formal approaches if formed by the compositional analysis (CPA) approaches. In CPA, local analyses are combined to model the global system behavior to cope with the challenges in scalability. Latest work on CPA broadens the range of systems for which the approach is applicable [7] and shows how it can be used for the optimization of data ages [20]. CPA approaches also suffer from the problem that contexts of local worst-cases might not be considered in the end-to-end result.

3 Properties and Encoding of Task Sets

To model the systems temporal behavior, we use a declarative description of all possible data propagation paths for a chain within a finite interval of time. The properties of tasks and chains are encoded in a set of constraints. Searching for the worst case end-to-end latency in all satisfying assignments for these constraints yields bounds on the latencies of the encoded task sequence. These bounds are safe if the encoded system behavior models a superset of all possible behaviors of the real system. Here, safe means, that no worse data age or response time can be observed in the real system, assuming that no overload occurs.

3.1   System Model

We consider multiprocessor systems, where each processing unit has a fixed set of tasks assigned. Tasks communicate via variables which are located in shared memory. We focus on fixed priority preemptive scheduling (FPPS) in this work. Tasks have a deadline relative to their activation. We assume that each tasks instance is guaranteed to be processed before it relative deadline occurs. In the next section we give a more detailed description of our task model.

3.2   Task Properties

The three most important properties of tasks with regards to end-to-end timing analysis are activation, response time of its runnables, and the communication mode for signal values. The response time of the runnables depend on their core execution time and the interference with other runnables competing for computing time on the same processing unit. In the following, $\mathcal{T}$ denotes the set of tasks.

Task Activation. Activation patterns describe the temporal nature of how instances of tasks occur. In general, tasks exist which occurrence cannot be modeled by a periodic-with-offset activation pattern without adding too much pessimism. A typical example from the automotive domain are computations which need to be performed synchronously to the engine speed [2]. The nature of these activation patterns is rather a minimum and maximum occurrence per time interval, e.g. because the rounds per minute of a combustion engine is specified within a given range. This can be converted to a minimum and maximum temporal distance of two consecutive activation events as shown in [21]. For task where a maximum occurrence per time interval cannot possibly be estimated, our approach additionally supports a sporadic activation pattern.

Runnables. Let $\mathcal{R}$ be the set of runnables. Let $\mathcal{L} = \{(R)_{i=0}^{n} | n \in \mathbb{N}$ and $R_i \in \mathcal{R}\}$, i.e. the set of ordered lists of runnables. For a list of runnables of length n, $(R)_{i=0}^{n}$ we say $R_i \prec R_j$ if and only if $i < j$ f.a. $i, j \in \{0, \ldots, n\}$. The runnables of a task are preemptable if the task is behaving cooperative, i.e.

$$\forall i \in \mathcal{T} : \text{cooperative}(i) = \mathtt{t} \rightarrow (\forall r \in \text{rnbls}(i) : \text{preemptable}(r) = \mathtt{f}) \quad (1)$$

where $\text{rnbls}(i)$ denotes the ordered list of runnables assigned to task i. Constraint 1 is an assertion that must hold for the input data.

Communication Modes. Runnables communicate with the help of *signals*. Different *communication modes* for signal accesses are common. Direct read and write on signals as the data is being processed is called *explicit communication*. On the contrary, tasks obtaining a local copy of the data they process are said to implement *implicit communication*. In this case, results are transferred to shared memory collectively after the last runnable was completely processed. A special case of implicit communication is called *deterministic communication*. Here, all data manipulated is held in a buffer and written back only at well-defined points of time relative to the activation of the task instance, e.g. the start of the next execution period.

3.3   Encoding

In [6] the authors gave a list of constraints which need to be satisfied if a task-level data flow with no core execution times (CETs) is considered. We incorporate CETs on runnable level to add an additional level of detail. Consequently, the constraints which must hold to model the systems behavior need to be extended. The following, previously not considered, constraints must additionally be satisfied:

1. If a task is scheduled for processing, an instance of the first runnable of the task is started. Cf. Constraint 3.
2. If the processing of an runnable instance finished and the corresponding task has another runnable, an instance of this runnable is started. Cf. Constraint 3.
3. When a task instance gets activated, it may interrupt a currently processed runnable instance if the latter is preemptable and the former is preferred for execution by the scheduling policy and both are assigned to the same processing unit. The processing time of all runnable instance of the preempting task is added to the paused time of the preempted runnable. Cf. Constraint 6.
4. The time to process a runnable is at least its BCET and at most its WCET. The results of a runnable are produced between its start and end. Cf. Constraint 7.
5. An instance of a task terminates at the moment the instance of the last runnable of the task was processed. The response time is before a given deadline. Cf. Constraint 8 and Constraint 9.

Given a set of tasks and a chain, it can be derived how many task instances need to be considered for a safe estimation. Let m_i hold this number for each task $i \in \mathcal{T}$. The determination of m_i is discussed in [6] and does not change for the extended approach. To encode task instances with their runnables, each task instance and runnable instance gets three variables assigned. A task instance has an activation time α^T, an actual starting time σ^T and a termination time ε^T. The delay of a task instance is described in the difference between α^T and σ^T. Each runnable of every task instance has a starting time σ^R, a termination time ε^R and a total time it was paused from processing ι^R. In Fig. 2 the variables in the context of a task instance are depicted.

The constraints on the activation time α^T only depend on the activation model of the task. Thus, the constraints presented in [6] can be reused. After a task instance is activated, it is enqueued for processing. A possible delay of the actual start depends on other tasks running on the same core. At this point, for the new detail-level, runnables need to be consid-

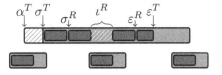

Fig. 2. Variables of task instances and runnable instances

ered. In order to list the constraints on the σ^Ts, we define two auxiliary sets. Firstly, let $D_{i,j}^{\mathrm{HP}}$ contain the termination times of all task instances that might delay instance j of task i due to higher priority. Secondly, let $D_{i,j}^{\mathrm{NP}}$ contain the termination time of all runnables which might cause a delay on instance j of task i because they are still running but might not be preempted.

The actual starting time can then be determined by taking the maximum from the aforementioned sets and the activation time of the task, i.e. for all $i \in \mathcal{T}$ and $1 \leq j \leq m_i$ holds

$$\sigma_{i,j}^T = \max\left(D_{i,j}^{\mathrm{HP}} \cup D_{i,j}^{\mathrm{NP}} \cup \{\alpha_{i,j}^T\}\right). \tag{2}$$

After a task is scheduled for processing, the first runnable of the task is processed. Each following runnable, is processed after the processing of its predecessors finished. Therefore,

$$\sigma_{i,j,r}^R = \max(\{\sigma_{i,j}^T\} \cup \{\varepsilon_{i,j,o}^R | o \in \mathrm{rnbls}(i) \wedge o < r\}) \tag{3}$$

must hold f.a. $i \in \mathcal{T}$ and $1 \leq j \leq m_i$ and $r \in \mathrm{rnbls}(i)$.

A task might be paused due to other task instance being preferred for processing. To calculate the total paused time, ι^R, we introduce two auxiliary variables for each pair of task instance and runnable. The first one, i^{HP}, is defined as

$$
i_{i,j,r,\ell,k,o}^{\mathrm{HP}} =
\begin{cases}
1 & \text{if } \sigma_{\ell,k,r}^T \geq \sigma_{i,j}^T \wedge \epsilon_{\ell,k}^T \leq \epsilon_{i,j}^T \wedge \sigma_{\ell,k,o}^R > \sigma_{i,j,r}^R \wedge \\
& \quad \mathrm{core}(i) = \mathrm{core}(\ell) \wedge \mathrm{prio}(i) < \mathrm{prio}(\ell) \wedge \\
& \quad \mathrm{preemptable}(r) = \mathbf{t} \\
0 & \text{otherwise}
\end{cases}
\tag{4}
$$

f.a. $i, \ell \in \mathcal{T}$, $j \in \{1, \ldots, m_i\}$, $k \in \{1, \ldots, m_\ell\}$, $r \in \mathrm{rnbls}(i)$, and $o \in \mathrm{rnbls}(\ell)$. This is, $i_{i,j,r,\ell,k,o}^{\mathrm{HP}}$ is 1 if the runnable o of the kth instance of task ℓ causes a pause of the runnable r of the jth instance of task i. The second one, $\gamma_{i,j,r}^R$ is the CET of r, this is

$$\gamma_{i,j,r}^R = \varepsilon_{i,j,r}^R - \sigma_{i,j,r}^R - \iota_{i,jr}^R \qquad \forall i, \ell \in \mathcal{T}, j \in \{1, \ldots, m_i\}, r \in \mathrm{rnbls}(i). \tag{5}$$

The pause time ι^R then is f.a. $i, \ell \in \mathcal{T}$, $j \in \{1, \ldots, m_i\}$, $k \in \{1, \ldots, m_\ell\}$, and $r \in \mathrm{rnbls}(i)$ given by

$$\iota_{i,j,r}^R = \sum_{\ell \in \mathcal{T} \setminus \{i\}} \sum_{k=1}^{m_\ell} \sum_{o \in \mathrm{rnbls}(\ell)} i_{i,j,r,\ell,k,o}^{\mathrm{HP}} \cdot \gamma_{\ell,k,o}^R. \tag{6}$$

To model the possible interference by other tasks for tasks scheduled cooperatively, we add an additional preemptable runnable between any two runnables where the task might return control to the scheduler.

Given the CET and the paused time, the possible termination times for the runnables can be determined. This is, f.a. $i, \ell \in \mathcal{T}$, $j \in \{1, \ldots, m_i\}$, $k \in \{1, \ldots, m_\ell\}$, and $r \in \mathrm{rnbls}(i)$

$$\varepsilon_{i,j,r}^R \geq \sigma_{i,j,r}^R + \iota_{i,j,r}^R + \mathrm{bcet}(r) \wedge \varepsilon_{i,j,r}^R \leq \sigma_{i,j,r}^R + \iota_{i,j,r}^R + \mathrm{wcet}(r) \ . \tag{7}$$

The end of processing of the last runnable of a task instance finally determines the time of termination for the task instance ε^T.

$$\varepsilon_{i,j}^T = \max\left(\{\varepsilon_{i,j,r}^R | r \in \mathrm{rnbls}(i)\}\right) \tag{8}$$

According to our assumptions, the response time of task instances is bound by its deadline, i.e.

$$\varepsilon_{i,j}^T \leq \alpha_{i,j}^T + \mathrm{deadline}(i) \qquad\qquad \forall i \in \mathcal{T}, 1 \leq j \leq m_i \ . \tag{9}$$

3.4   Model Optimization

The newly gained precision, comes with the price of larger constraint models. Especially, Constraint 4 and Constraint 6 contribute to an increase because they depend on the amount of runnables per task. However, the impact can be reduced by aggregating individual runnables to a single runnable where it has little to none effect on the estimation. More precisely, multiple runnables of a task which is not part of the analyzed chain can be aggregated to one runnable modeling the same load. For task which participate in the chain, only the first possible read access and the last possible write access are relevant to determine the temporal behavior with respect to the chain. Therefore, the runnables of such a task can be divided in three categories: the ones processed prior to the first read, the ones processed in between, and the ones processed after the last write. Each group of runnables can be aggregated as described above, resulting in three synthetic runnables for a task on the chain.

Aggregating runnables to abstract their temporal behavior collectively gives the flexibility to adjust the time-precision tradeoff by the user's needs. If fast estimations are needed, e.g. because the system model is still vague in early development stages, nearly all runnables can be aggregated. If the system design is fixed in the final product, final analyses can be performed with a greater level of detail.

4   Properties and Encoding of Cause-Effect Chains

As described above, the analysis of task sequences suffices for the analysis of end-to-end latencies in the considered systems. Let $(p^T)_{k=1}^\ell$ with $p_k^T \in \mathcal{T}$ f.a. $k \in \{1, \ldots, \ell\}$ be such a sequence of tasks and let $(p^R)_{k=1}^\ell$, with p_k^R subsequence of rnbls(p_k^T), be the corresponding sequence on runnable level f.a. $k \in \{1, \ldots, \ell\}$. The timing properties of the sequence can be characterized by an ordered sequence of points of time with two points of time for each task or runnable involved. The first point of time describes when data is read, the second point of time describes when data is written. As proposed in [6] two additional sets of variables are used. One variable holds the point of time at which values were written at index k f.a. $k \in \{1, \ldots, \ell\}$. The other holds the index of the task instance participating in the chain at index k. In the constraints on x and n the newly gained precision is reflected. Most evidently in the the constraints in the case of explicitly communicating tasks, e.g. the constraints for response time which are

$$n_k = \min \left(\{j | \min \left(\{\sigma_{i,j,r}^R | r \in p_k^R\} \right) \geq x_{k-1}\} \right) \tag{10}$$

and

$$\min \left(\{\sigma_{i,n_k,r}^R | r \in p_k^R\} \right) \leq x_k \leq \max \left(\{\epsilon_{i,n_k,r}^R | r \in p_k^R\} \right) \tag{11}$$

f.a. $k \in \{1, \ldots, \ell\}$.

Finally, the objective under the constraints on n and k and the constraints listed in Sect. 3.3 is to maximize the difference in the response time of the last task and the activation of the first task on the chain.

5 Evaluation

We evaluated the performance of the improved model in terms of quality of the results, and scalability and performance. For this, we encoded the constraints using the high-level constraint language *MiniZinc* [18]. For solving, the *MiniZinc* models are linked with a data file to create a *FlatZinc* formula [17]. We chose the parallel version of the lazy clause generation solver *Chuffed* as presented in [4] to solve the *FlatZinc*-formula. As an environment to run our tests we used *OpenMpi*[1] under *CygWin*[2]. The performance in terms of time consumption and memory usage was measured with the *time* command[3]. The experiments were carried out on a desktop computer with an Intel(R) Core(TM) i9-7940X CPU @ 3.10GHz and 128 GB DDR4 running Windows 10 Enterprise.

Besides more precise results, the evaluations show the need of sporadic activation patterns for safe and precise estimations. To evaluate precision on runnable-level, we compare our results to the results of [20] for different variants of the task-set published in [10]. Afterwards, we compare the results of the task-level approach with the results of the compositional timing analysis tool *pyCPA*. For this comparison we used a benchmark based on the task set of a power-train controller from Daimler. The data is available online[4]. The tasks $CXIY$

---

[1] https://www.open-mpi.org/.

[2] http://cygwin.org/.

[3] http://man7.org/linux/man-pages/man1/time.1.html.

[4] https://www.informatik.uni-kiel.de/~mjf/CPCPS/.

$X, Y \in \{0, \ldots, 3\}$ of the benchmark task set have an alternative sporadic activated pattern. These are used to show that approximating the behavior of a sporadically activated tasks with the help of a periodic task does not yield safe bounds.

The results of the comparison with $pyCPA$[5] are listed in Table 1. They show tighter bounds for data age and response time for all chains. The differences originate from an overestimation on relative offset between the tasks on the chain. Summing them up takes situations into consideration which can not possibly occur in the real system.

Table 1. Results for chain 0 – chain 7

Chain	Response time (μs)			Data age (μs)		
	pyCPA	task-level[1]	task-level[2]	pyCPA	task-level[1]	task-level[2]
Chain 0	22160	10650	10650	20910	10650	10650
Chain 1	21420	10740	10800	15170	6740	6800
Chain 2	15410	4750	4750	19930	8660	8720
Chain 3	34620	15250	15250	32890	15160	15220
Chain 4	36110	15240	15300	34380	15240	15300
Chain 5	27685	15780	15780	7685	5780	10549
Chain 6	16520	10015	11748	31520	25015	25734
Chain 7	5265	5015	6355	5265	5015	6355

task-level[1]: Benchmark task-set without sporadic tasks
task-level[2]: Benchmark task-set with sporadic tasks

Furthermore, we compared the results using the periodic activation patterns with the ones using their sporadic alternative. The results are also shown in Table 1. For chains containing task C0I0, the estimation increases, e.g. the response time of Chain 6. An effect on the estimations is also observed for chains only containing periodic tasks, e.g. the data age of Chain 1. The additional delay is caused by a newly possible delays of periodic tasks. This can lead to additional relative offsets between tasks, e.g. because of shifted write intervals. Depending on task set and chain, the concurrence of both effects can lead to tremendously increased estimations, e.g. for the data age of Chain 5. On the one hand, C0I0 can have a greater temporal distance to C1T0 in terms of activation time. On the other hand, a shift of C2T1 to the left and C3T3 to the right results in an additional period of C2T1 being added to the latency.

Table 2. Results for the *Bosch FMTV Challenge* model

Experiment	Chain	Data age (μs)		
		results from [20]	task-level	runnable-level
Default	Chain 2	-	148283	120101
$E\pi\phi$	Chain 2	160415	148283	120101
$E\pi\phi A$	Chain 2	134207	128283	110101
Default	Chain 3	-	4927	3148
$E\pi\phi$	Chain 3	5249	4200	3148
$E\pi\phi A$	Chain 3	4683	4981	2422

Another evaluation is based on originally published in [10]. In [20] Schlatow et al. propose different priority assignments and core mappings in order to optimize data ages. We compared the results with estimations obtained using our approach. Both, a task-level data flow and a runnable-level data flow were considered. The task level-data flow was implemented by aggregating all runnnables of a task in terms of their temporal behavior. The result are listed in Table 2. They show that the improvement from variant $E\pi\phi$ to $E\pi\phi A$ for Chain 2 is confirmed by our estimations. However, in the case of Chain 3 the estimations using a task-level data flow disagree with

---
[5] https://bitbucket.org/pycpa/pycpa.

the results obtained using a runnable-level data flow regarding an improvement. This shows the importance of reliable and precise estimations in the context of optimization. An actual improvement might not be achieved if the margin of the optimization lies within the imprecision of the estimation method.

6   Conclusion

In this paper we showed how the constraint programming approach to latency estimation can be improved to obtain tighter bounds on end-to-end latencies. The extended approach supports a wide range of task-sets and can be used to estimate data ages as well as response times. The comparison with state-of-the-art estimations shows an improved precision. This comes with the cost of additional computational effort. Nevertheless, we showed that the approach can be optimized to scale for industrial-size task-sets.

References

1. Becker, M., Dasari, D., Mubeen, S., Behnam, M., Nolte, T.: Synthesizing job-level dependencies for automotive multi-rate effect chains. In: 22nd IEEE International Conference on Embedded and Real-Time Computing Systems and Applications, RTCSA 2016, Daegu, South Korea, 17–19 August 2016, pp. 159–169. IEEE Computer Soc (2016)
2. Biondi, A., Buttazzo, G.C.: Engine control: task modeling and analysis. In: Nebel, W., Atienza, D. (eds.) Proceedings of the 2015 Design, Automation & Test in Europe Conference & Exhibition, DATE 2015, Grenoble, France, March 9–13, 2015. pp. 525–530. ACM (2015), http://dl.acm.org/citation.cfm?id=2755872
3. Boniol, F., Lauer, M., Pagetti, C., Ermont, J.: Freshness and reactivity analysis in globally asynchronous locally time-triggered systems. In: Brat, G., Rungta, N., Venet, A. (eds.) NFM 2013. LNCS, vol. 7871, pp. 93–107. Springer, Heidelberg (2013). https://doi.org/10.1007/978-3-642-38088-4_7
4. Ehlers, T., Stuckey, P.J.: Parallelizing constraint programming with learning. In: Quimper, C.-G. (ed.) CPAIOR 2016. LNCS, vol. 9676, pp. 142–158. Springer, Cham (2016). https://doi.org/10.1007/978-3-319-33954-2_11
5. Feiertag, N., Richter, K., Nordlander, J., Jonsson, J.: A compositional framework for end-to-end path delay calculation of automotive systems under different path semantics. In: Proceedings of the IEEE Real-Time System Symposium - Workshop on Compositional Theory and Technology for Real-Time Embedded Systems, Barcelona, Spain, 30 November 2008 (2008)
6. Friese, M.J., Ehlers, T., Nowotka, D.: Estimating latencies of task sequences in multi-core automotive ecus. In: 13th IEEE International Symposium on Industrial Embedded Systems, SIES'18, Graz, Austria, 6–8 June 2018, pp. 1–10 (2018)
7. Gemlau, K.B., Schlatow, J., Möstl, M., Ernst, R.: Compositional analysis for the waters industrial challenge 2017. In: International Workshop on Analysis Tools and Methodologies for Embedded and Real-time Systems (WATERS), Dubrovnik, Croatia (2017)
8. Godefroid, P., Sen, K.: Combining model checking and testing. In: Handbook of Model Checking, pp. 613–649. Springer, Cham (2018). https://doi.org/10.1007/978-3-319-10575-8_19

9. Hamann, A., Dasari, D., Kramer, S., Pressler, M., Wurst, F.: Communication centric design in complex automotive embedded systems. In: Bertogna, M. (ed.) 29th Euromicro Conference on Real-Time Systems, ECRTS'17, 27–30 June 2017, Dubrovnik, Croatia. LIPIcs, vol. 76, pp. 10:1–10:20. Schloss Dagstuhl - Leibniz-Zentrum fuer Informatik (2017)

10. Hamann, A., Ziegenbein, D., Kramer, S., Lukasiewycz, M.: Demonstration of the FMTV 2016 timing verification challenge (2016). http://www.ecrts.org/forum/download/file.php?id=35&sid=619cd45cc904f6f8a66fc526919a2ebd

11. Henzinger, T.A., Horowitz, B., Kirsch, C.M.: Giotto: a time-triggered language for embedded programming. In: Henzinger, T.A., Kirsch, C.M. (eds.) EMSOFT 2001. LNCS, vol. 2211, pp. 166–184. Springer, Heidelberg (2001). https://doi.org/10.1007/3-540-45449-7_12

12. Kirsch, C.M., Sokolova, A.: The logical execution time paradigm. In: Chakraborty, S., Eberspächer, J. (eds.) Advances in Real-Time Systems, pp. 103–120. Springer, Heidelberg (2012). https://doi.org/10.1007/978-3-642-24349-3_5

13. Kloda, T., Bertout, A., Sorel, Y.: Latency analysis for data chains of real-time periodic tasks. In: 23rd IEEE International Conference on Emerging Technologies and Factory Automation, ETFA'18, Torino, Italy, 4–7 September 2018, pp. 360–367. IEEE (2018)

14. Lauer, M., Boniol, F., Pagetti, C., Ermont, J.: End-to-end latency and temporal consistency analysis in networked real-time systems. IJCCBS 5(3/4), 172–196 (2014)

15. Lee, E.A.: Cyber-physical systems - are computing foundations adequate? Proceedings Workshop CyberPhysical Systems Research Motivation Techniques and Roadmap (2006). http://ptolemy.eecs.berkeley.edu/publications/papers/06/CPSPositionPaper/

16. Martinez, J., Olmedo, I.S., Bertogna, M.: Analytical characterization of end-to-end communication delays with logical execution time. IEEE Trans. CAD Integr. Circuits Syst. 37(11), 2244–2254 (2018)

17. Nethercote, N.: Converting minizinc to flatzinc (2014). http://www.minizinc.org/downloads/doc-1.2.2/mzn2fzn.pdf

18. Nethercote, N., Stuckey, P.J., Becket, R., Brand, S., Duck, G.J., Tack, G.: MiniZinc: towards a standard CP modelling language. In: Bessière, C. (ed.) CP 2007. LNCS, vol. 4741, pp. 529–543. Springer, Heidelberg (2007). https://doi.org/10.1007/978-3-540-74970-7_38

19. Santos, M.M.D., Ambiel, V., Acras, M., Gliwa, P.: On the timing analysis at automotive real-time embedded systems. SAE Technical Paper (2017)

20. Schlatow, J., Möstl, M., Tobuschat, S., Ishigooka, T., Ernst, R.: Data-age analysis and optimisation for cause-effect chains in automotive control systems. In: 13th IEEE International Symposium on Industrial Embedded Systems, SIES'18, Graz, Austria, 6–8 June 2018, pp. 1–9 (2018)

21. Schliecker, S., Ernst, R.: A recursive approach to end-to-end path latency computation in heterogeneous multiprocessor systems. In: Rosenstiel, W., Wakabayashi, K. (eds.) Proceedings of the 7th International Conference on Hardware/Software Codesign and System Synthesis, CODES+ISSS 2009, Grenoble, France, 11–16 October 2009, pp. 433–442. ACM (2009)

Workload Characterization for Memory Management in Emerging Embedded Platforms

Biswadip Maity$^{(\boxtimes)}$ ⓘ, Bryan Donyanavard, Nalini Venkatasubramanian, and Nikil Dutt

University of California, Irvine, USA
{maityb,bdonyana,nalini,dutt}@uci.edu

Abstract. Memory has emerged as a primary performance and energy bottleneck for emerging embedded platforms that integrate heterogeneous compute units. Applications require a balance between performance and energy-efficiency and finding the optimal operating point on embedded platforms is challenging. There exist many opportunities to manage the memory subsystem efficiently at runtime to save energy without compromising quality in the face of dynamic workloads. Previous works have used memory bandwidth utilization to determine memory requirements and develop runtime policies to configure system knobs (e.g., memory controller frequency) accordingly. However, bandwidth utilization as a singular metric is not always sufficient: policies for a range of workload scenarios require insight into an application's memory access pattern and working set size. Alternatively, memory profilers provide fine-grained information such as the memory access pattern for the entire virtual address space, and the load/store density of different regions of the memory. However, parsing this detailed information frequently at runtime induces excessive overhead. In this work, we propose a profiling mechanism that considers both (1) the working set size of running workloads and (2) memory bandwidth utilization to compute WBP (Working Set Size-Bandwidth Product). WBP can be estimated with low overhead, and the combined metric provides insights that runtime policies can use to determine desirable configurations for specific workload scenarios. Our early results show that a static configuration devised with this metric yields an optimal memory controller frequency for 8 out of 10 PARSEC workloads, demonstrating the promise of this approach.

Keywords: Main memory · Memory bandwidth · Runtime memory management

1 Introduction

Contemporary embedded systems are equipped with heterogeneous compute units with shared main memory to meet the varying memory capacity and bandwidth requirements of modern applications (e.g., Nvidia Tegra, Nvidia Xavier,

© IFIP International Federation for Information Processing 2023
Published by Springer Nature Switzerland AG 2023
M. A. Wehrmeister et al. (Eds.): IESS 2019, IFIP AICT 576, pp. 65–76, 2023.
https://doi.org/10.1007/978-3-031-26500-6_6

AMD Accelerated Processing Unit). All computational resources (e.g., CPU, GPU, DSP, on-chip accelerator) share the main memory, resulting in memory contributing as a primary performance and energy bottleneck for emerging embedded system platforms. To address this bottleneck, application developers use memory profilers to understand the runtime requirements of applications, and attempt to reduce their memory footprint through code optimization.

At runtime, resource managers monitor system state and implement policies to update system configuration (i.e., knobs) to meet the system's goals (e.g., maximize performance-per-unit-power). Traditionally, policies that target memory exploit memory bandwidth under-utilization at runtime by dynamically scaling the memory controller frequency in order to reduce power without compromising quality. However, embedded systems commonly support many hardware and software knobs which: (1) schedule applications across compute units, (2) set the frequency of heterogeneous compute units, and (3) set the degree of parallelism by changing the number of threads; all of which can affect the time required to process application data and, in turn, energy consumption.

Although memory profilers report the number of memory accesses (load/stores) and generate heatmaps (i.e., memory access density) for the profiled application, it is difficult for policies to manage the overhead of parsing this information at runtime. The overhead of analyzing the information from memory profilers makes the information impractical to consider for high-frequency runtime decision making. Thus, it becomes essential to monitor a coarse-grained metric(s), which can assist the runtime resource managers in efficiently determining the ideal system configuration.

We propose a memory-driven application classification based on multiple dimensions in order to assist in developing policies for resource allocation strategies, specifically for DRAM. We combine (a) the size of memory required (in MBs) of the working set of an application, and (b) the runtime DRAM bandwidth requirement (last-level cache miss rate) to classify an application's memory requirement. Both measurements can be made with minimal overhead and can be used at runtime to evaluate the dynamic requirements of applications. In this work, this classification is used to determine static memory controller frequency to minimize the Energy-Delay Product (EDP). However, this classification can be used generally to develop policies which decide the system configuration based on the classes of the application currently running on the system.

2   Motivation

In 1965 Gordon E. Moore predicted that manufacturers would keep doubling the number of transistors on a chip almost every two years [11]. The developments of the semiconductor industry by leaps and bounds have introduced billions of transistors on tiny dies. The law has also set the pace for software running on the underlying hardware. Small computers present in most households devices (e.g., smartwatches, smart-lights, mobile devices) and personal computers are now equipped with more resources than can be powered. With the growth in embedded compute resources, applications have now become extremely demanding.

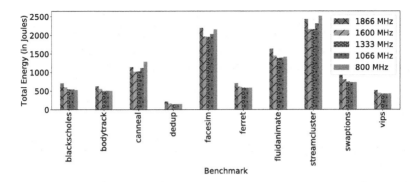

Fig. 1. Total energy consumed as memory controller frequency is varied statically from 800 MHz to 1866 MHz for PARSEC workloads on the Jetson TX2. The frequency that results in the minimum energy spent varies.

Applications generate data at a rate that tests the extremes of main memory latency and bandwidth. Thus, the performance and energy bottleneck in today's embedded system platforms is no longer the computation of data, but the transportation of that data to and from computation. One current challenge for computing systems is that the computation is performed far away from the data [7,9].

Although caching is traditionally applied to address this challenge, the working set size of applications may be significant enough to exceed the cache capacity. The growth in working set size leads to cache misses and requires main memory accesses to fetch data for the processor. The movement of data from the DRAM to the processor consumes 19% of total system power [3] and cache misses consume more than 50% of the cycles [7]. Previous works have used memory bandwidth utilization to determine memory requirements and develop runtime policies to address the issue of memory-related energy consumption. [3] proposes to set the memory controller frequency at the lowest frequency (i.e., 800 MHz) when the memory is lightly loaded (memory bandwidth is under 2000 MB/s).

Figure 1 shows the effect of memory controller frequency on total energy consumption for a variety of benchmarks executing on a contemporary embedded platform, the Nvidia Jetson TX2 [1]. A single instance of 10 workloads from the PARSEC benchmark suite [2] is executed on the Jetson TX2 with fixed memory controller frequency at various levels, and a runtime system calculates the total energy spent. The first observation we make about the workloads executed in Fig. 1 is the memory bandwidth utilization is low: it never exceeds 430 MB/s. According to the previously described policy, one would expect the lowest frequency to be the best configuration for the system for this memory bandwidth utilization.

Second, we observe that the lowest frequency leads to the minimum energy consumption for only 2 out of 10 workloads. This is due to the fact that, although the power consumption is minimal, the extended execution time results in increased energy consumption in 8 out of 10 cases. Even from this simple example, we can conclude that in order to account for additional energy consumption due to excess latency, we must consider more than just bandwidth when a policy decides on the memory controller frequency.

3 Diversity of Working Set Size in Embedded Applications

Denning defines the working set of an application as a collection of recently referenced pages of the application's virtual address space [5]. Working set is an efficient tool to measure the memory demands of an application. A similar metric, the resident set, is defined as the subset of an application's segments which are present in main memory at a given time.

3.1 PARSEC Benchmark Suite

The PARSEC benchmark suite [2] is a popular suite for evaluating multiprocessor-based embedded platforms. It consists of twelve workloads (nine applications and three kernels) from the recognition, mining, and synthesis (RMS) domain, as well as representative embedded system applications. The workloads compose a diverse representative of working set size, degree of parallelism, off-chip traffic, and data-sharing that can be representative of the workloads executed on emerging embedded platforms. Based on the working set, two broad classes of workloads are distinguished:

1. **Working set smaller than 16 MB**: These applications do not generate much memory pressure because the working set can fit in the last-level shared cache. Example applications are `bodytrack` and `swaptions`.
2. **Working set larger than 16 MB**: These applications have a very large working set generating more off-chip memory accesses to the DRAM. Example applications are `canneal`, `ferret`, `facesim`, `fluidanimate`. When the input size grows, the working set can even reach gigabytes due to algorithms that operate on large amounts of collected data.

Note that as the number of cores increases with the degree of parallelism, so does the bandwidth requirement. `bodytrack` makes off-chip memory accesses in short, but bandwidth-intensive bursts. When several instances of the same application execute concurrently, these short bursts limit the scalability.

The sampling of benchmarks from PARSEC demonstrates highly variable memory requirements that depend on multiple factors. The number of load/store operations, size of the last-level cache, and the number of parallel threads are some of the factors that affect the bandwidth requirement. These various sources of memory pressure provide opportunities for resource managers to address the bottleneck at runtime for unpredictable workloads. Working set can effectively represent some of these dynamics, and we show that combining the working set size information with memory bandwidth at runtime can lead to efficient system configurations.

4   Related Work

Current runtime memory management metrics and policies are discussed in this section.

4.1   Runtime Policies Using Memory Bandwidth Utilization

Several techniques have been employed to address the memory bottleneck, and *Dynamic Voltage and Frequency Scaling (DVFS)* of the memory controller is a primary one [4]. Higher frequency yields higher throughput but consumes more power. DVFS can reduce the memory power by 10.4% on average, 20.5% maximum for the SPEC 2006 benchmarks without compromising quality [3]. [8] uses an approximation equation (called MAR-CSE) based on the correlation of the memory access rate and the critical frequency for the minimum energy consumption. The memory access rate is the ratio of the total number of cache misses (including both instruction and data cache misses) to the number of instructions executed. MAR-CSE predicts the voltage and frequency at runtime. Although this technique does not measure the memory bandwidth directly, the memory access rate is also an indirect measure of the memory bandwidth.

4.2   Runtime Policies Using Workload Information

Recent work [10] looks into the combined effect of application compute/memory-intensity, thread synchronization contention, and nonuniform memory accesses pattern to develop a runtime energy management technique by performing DVFS on CPU cores. However, they do not consider memory bandwidth utilization and do not change the memory controller frequency.

4.3   Runtime Policies Using Reflection or Prediction

CPU DVFS has been explored extensively in literature [13] and most systems use it to meet system goals. Linux provides several governors to manage the CPU frequency at runtime (e.g., `ondemand`, `performance`, `powersave`). Recent work uses a reflective system model to predict the system behavior when different frequencies are selected [6,12].

4.4   Runtime Policies Using Task Mapping

The operating system scheduler is responsible for (1) deciding the schedule of running applications and (2) deciding which threads run on which cores. Modern systems provide heterogeneous compute resources which have different power/performance tradeoffs. The smaller cores are more power efficient but have less computational capacity than the bigger cores. Task mapping has shown energy savings of up to 51% when combined with DVFS [14].

5   Classification Methodology

The proposed approach combines the working set size and memory bandwidth by calculating their product (WBP). The objective is to find the operating frequency, which leads to the lowest energy-delay product (EDP). Based on the EDP at different values of WBP, applications are categorized into one of three classes. In this section, the WBP metric and the classification ranges are described.

The correlation between WBP and EDP is observed experimentally. Ten PARSEC benchmarks are executed with different fixed memory controller frequencies. At regular intervals (*sensing windows*) of 200 ms, the following metrics are recorded:

1. **Working Set Size**: Linux kernel 4.3 introduced idle page flags to track memory utilization. Once a process starts, the idle bits corresponding to all the virtual pages in that process are set to 1 to indicate that they have not been referenced. Whenever the process issues memory read/write requests, the idle bit corresponding to the virtual page is set to 0 by Linux kernel. A 0 implies that the page is not idle. We selected the window size as 200 ms, however exploring more window durations and feasibility of adaptive windows remain as future work. Every 200 ms, the number of 0 bits in the idle page flags are read and used to calculate the working set size as 0 as follows:

$$WorkingSetSize = \text{Number of active pages} \times \text{Size of each page}$$

2. **Memory Bandwidth**: ARM cores include logic to gather various statistics on the operation of the processor and memory system during runtime based on a Performance Monitoring Unit (PMU). The PMU provides hardware counters for different events, which are used to profile application behavior. The counter values of L2_CACHE_REFILL and MEM_ACCESS on each core are monitored to understand the memory traffic at runtime every 200 ms (Sensing Window Length = 0.2 s). Since the L2 is the last-level shared cache on the Jetson, the memory bandwidth can be calculated using these values as:

$$MemoryBandwidth = \frac{\sum_{i=1}^{activeCores} \text{L2\_CACHE\_REFILL}_{Core\_i} \times DataBusSize}{SensingWindowLength}$$

3. **Memory Power and System Power**: Nvidia drivers read the power measurements from onboard sensors connected by I2C. The separate domains for system power and memory power help isolate the energy consumed by the memory separate from the rest of the system.

4. **Latency/Delay**: The amount of time that the workload takes to complete is indicative of the compute and memory latency. The CPU governor is set to 'userspace' and the frequency of all CPU cores is set to maximum for all the experiments. Thus, changes in memory latency due to the change in memory controller frequency is reflected in the total execution time.

5.1   Classification of PARSEC Benchmarks

Our objective is to find the operating frequency that results in the lowest energy-delay product. To that effect, we are interested in finding changes in EDP across frequencies at different values of WBP. This is done by experimentally observing the average EDP (over 10 applications) of PARSEC workloads on a target embedded system described in Sect. 6.1.

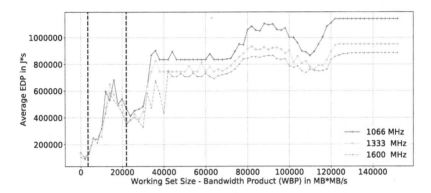

Fig. 2. Change in average EDP (energy-delay product) of PARSEC workloads across frequencies at different values of WBP (working set size - bandwidth product). (Color figure online)

The average EDP at different values of WBP for PARSEC workloads obtained experimentally are presented in Fig. 2. The different colors represent different frequencies. The PARSEC applications operate in different regions of WBP throughout execution. At low values of WBP, the EDP does not change with frequency. This is because the working set size of the application is small, and the memory requests are served from cache. Thus, operating at lower frequency does not have any effect on the EDP. As the WBP increases, memory requirement increases, and higher frequencies perform better. Frequencies lower than 1066 MHz (e.g., 800 MHz) have a very high latency whereas frequencies higher than 1333 MHz (e.g., 1866 MHz) consume too much power during the execution. Thus, they never obtain optimal EDP for any of the workloads. Hence, frequencies 800 MHz and 1866 MHz are not included in Fig. 2.

We classify applications based on their WBP profile. For each class, the goal is to select a memory controller frequency that leads to the minimum EDP. Two thresholds for WBP are selected based on the average application EDP profile at different frequencies. In this work, the operating frequency is determined statically based on the average WBP profile of workloads. However, we acknowledge the possibility of a runtime policy which checks the WBP at regular intervals to change the frequency during application execution. The classification and thresholds are proposed as follows:

1. C_1 (Small memory footprint): $0\,MB^2/s \leq WBP < 3500\,MB^2/s$ These applications have a small working set size and a low memory bandwidth. The L2

Table 1. Classification of PARSEC workloads based on average WBP (working set size - memory bandwidth product) during runtime.

Workload	WBP (in MB^2/s)	Class	EMC frequency
dedup	2100	C_1	1066 MHz
swaptions	3000	C_1	1066 MHz
bodytrack	3600	C_2	1333 MHz
ferret	3700	C_2	1333 MHz
blackscholes	5100	C_2	1333 MHz
vips	9700	C_2	1333 MHz
fluidanimate	16000	C_2	1333 MHz
canneal	22000	C_3	1600 MHz
facesim	62222	C_3	1600 MHz
streamcluster	119000	C_3	1600 MHz

cache is large enough to accommodate most of the requests to memory for this class of application. When running C_1 applications, **the system is configured at 1066 MHz**.

2. C_2 (Medium memory footprint): $3500\,MB^2/s \leq WBP < 22000\,MB^2/s$ These applications have a moderate memory requirement. The L2 cache cannot accommodate all the requests to the memory. The working set size is also considerable and generates requests which need to go to main memory. When running C_2 applications, **the system is configured at 1333 MHz**.

3. C_3 (Large memory footprint): $WBP > 22000\,MB^2/s$ These applications have a high memory requirement. Operating the system at 1600 MHz clearly gives the lowest EDP. The working set size for this class of application is large and spread out in different regions of memory. This incurs excessive cache misses and generates requests to the main memory. When running C_3 applications, **the system is configured at 1600 MHz**.

6   Evaluation

6.1   Experimental Setup

We use Jetson TX2 [1] from Nvidia, an embedded System-On-Chip (SOC) platform, to evaluate our proposed technique. The Jetson has heterogeneous compute cores (quad-core ARM Cortex A57 and dual-core Nvidia Denver2) distributed in two clusters along with an onboard 256-core Pascal GPU. Each of the clusters resides in a separate frequency domain. Jetson has a shared memory architecture, and all resources (CPU clusters, GPU) share the main memory. Jetson TX2 has an 8 GB 128-bit LPDDR4 memory and a 32 GB eMMC 5.1 for onboard storage. The Cortex cores come with: 48 KB L1 instruction cache (I-cache) per core; 32 KB L1 data cache (D-cache) per core. The Denver cores have 128 KB L1

I-cache per core; 64 KB L1 D-cache per core. All the cores share an L2 Unified Cache of 2 MB.

Jetson uses an External Memory Controller (EMC) to manage the off-chip memory traffic. The EMC has different operating frequencies ranging from 4800 KHz to 1866 MHz. The onboard ARM Cortex Real-time (R5) Boot and Power Management Processor (BPMP) changes the memory controller frequency through kernel drivers. During all the experiments, the Denver cores are switched off, and the Cortex A57 cores are configured at the highest frequency. Disabling CPU DVFA helps isolate the effect of EMC operating frequency.

6.2 Experimental Results

In Sect. 5, PARSEC benchmarks are classified into three classes, and an ideal memory controller frequency for each class is proposed. applications are executed with a fixed memory controller frequency based on class. The results are presented in Fig. 3. We expect to see lower EDP with the proposed approach when compared to techniques which do not utilize any memory information when deciding the EMC Frequency.

The average WBPs for PARSEC benchmarks are presented in Table 1. The working set size and memory bandwidth are measured using the Linux idle page tracker and L2_CACHE_REFILL PMU event counter every 200ms. The proposed static configuration uses the EDP values obtained with this method. The EDP value is compared with other static configurations (1600 MHz, 1333 MHz and 1066 MHz) which serve as baselines in Fig. 3. From the figure, we see that the proposed scheme can find the optimal configuration for eight out of ten PARSEC workloads. The proposed scheme can achieve on average 16.7% (max: 37.3%) reduction in EDP when compared to the most aggressive memory controller frequency (1866 MHz). The results are compared with an optimal scheme obtained by executing all workloads at all possible EMC frequencies and choosing the frequency that yields minimum EDP. The optimal scheme can achieve an average reduction of 17.1% (max: 39.3%) EDP when compared to the most aggressive memory controller frequency (1866 MHz).

The static method of setting the memory controller frequency is not capable of setting the optimal knob for all the applications. Benchmarks like blackscholes exhibit dynamic memory accesses patterns, as shown in Fig. 4. A static configuration is not sufficient to address these bursts of memory accesses. Therefore, it is necessary to perform DVFS adaptively during application execution. Additionally, if we consider a platform running multiple applications concurrently, the each application must be monitored and classified individually.

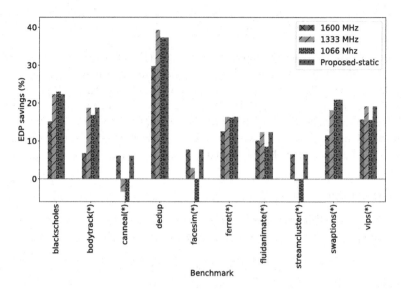

Fig. 3. EDP reduction with proposed classification using WBP compared to static-frequency baselines. Applications marked with a * have an optimal static configuration with the proposed scheme.

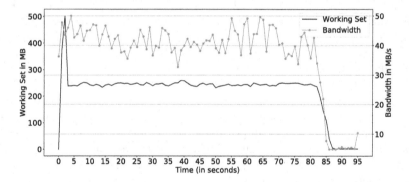

Fig. 4. Runtime memory profile of `blackscholes`. Dynamic memory access pattern calls for the exploration of a runtime policy.

7   Conclusion and Future Work

With the evolution of more heterogeneous embedded computing platforms that share a common main memory, the traditional memory bottleneck becomes even more severe in the face of balancing performance/quality and energy efficiency. In this work, we present a profiling metric, WBP (Working Set Size - Memory Bandwidth Product) that combines (1) memory bandwidth utilization and (2) working set size of running workloads. Based on the changes of EDP (energy-delay product) with frequency at different WBP, we classify applications into three categories of memory requirements. For each class, a static configuration of the memory controller frequency is determined. Our initial results show that the static configuration correctly estimates the optimal frequency for 8 out of 10 PARSEC workloads, demonstrating the promise of our approach. The static scheme of setting memory controller frequency for each class can save EDP by 16.7% on average (37.3% maximum). Although the current work uses fixed sensing windows of 200 ms, it may not be optimal, and different window sizes require exploration. Adaptive sensing window size along with runtime policies using the proposed classification technique remains as future work.

Acknowledgement. This work was partially supported by NSF grant CCF-1704859.

References

1. Nvidia Jetson TX2 Architecture. https://devblogs.nvidia.com/jetson-tx2-delivers-twice-intelligence-edge/
2. Bienia, C., Kumar, S., Singh, J.P., Li, K.: The PARSEC benchmark suite. In: PACT, New York, New York, USA, pp. 72. ACM Press (2008)
3. David, H., Fallin, C., Gorbatov, E., Hanebutte, U.R., Mutlu, O.: Memory power management via dynamic voltage/frequency scaling. In: Proceedings of the 8th International Conference on Autonomic Computing, ICAC 2011, Karlsruhe, Germany, 14–18 June 2011, pp. 31–40 (2011)
4. Deng, Q., Meisner, D., Ramos, L., Wenisch, T.F., Bianchini, R.: Memscale: active low-power modes for main memory. SIGARCH Comput. Archit. News 39(1), 225–238 (2011)
5. Denning, P.J.: Working sets past and present. IEEE Trans. Softw. Eng. 6(1), 64–84 (1980)
6. Donyanavard, B., Mück, T., Sarma, S., Dutt, N.: Sparta: runtime task allocation for energy efficient heterogeneous many-cores. In: Proceedings of the Eleventh IEEE/ACM/IFIP International Conference on Hardware/Software Codesign and System Synthesis, CODES 2016, New York, NY, USA, pp. 1–10. ACM (2016)
7. Kanev, S., et al.: Profiling a warehouse-scale computer. In: Proceedings of the 42Nd Annual International Symposium on Computer Architecture, ISCA 2015, New York, NY, USA, pp. 158–169. ACM (2015)
8. David, H., Fallin, C., Gorbatov, E., Hanebutte, U.R., Mutlu, O.: Memory-aware dynamic voltage and frequency prediction for portable devices. In: The Fourteenth IEEE Internationl Conference on Embedded and Real-Time Computing Systems and Applications, RTCSA 2008, Kaohisung, Taiwan, 25–27 August 2008, pp. 229–236. Proceedings (2008)
9. Mutlu, O., Stark, J., Wilkerson, C., Patt, Y.N.: Runahead execution: an alternative to very large instruction windows for out-of-order processors. In: Proceedings of the 9th International Symposium on High-Performance Computer Architecture, HPCA 2003, Washington, DC, USA, pp. 129-140. IEEE Computer Society (2003)
10. Basireddy, K.R., Wachter, E.W., Al-Hashimi, B.M., Merrett, G.: Workload-aware runtime energy management for HPC systems. In: 2018 International Conference on High Performance Computing & Simulation, HPCS 2018, Orleans, France, 16–20 July 2018, pp. 292–299 (2018)
11. Schaller, R.R.: Moore's law: past, present and future. IEEE Spectr. 34(6), 52–59 (1997)

12. Spiliopoulos, V., Kaxiras, S., Keramidas, G.: Green governors: a framework for continuously adaptive DVFS. In: Proceedings of the 2011 International Green Computing Conference and Workshops, IGCC 2011, Washington, DC, USA, pp. 1–8. IEEE Computer Society (2011)
13. Weiser, M., Welch, B., Demers, A., Shenker, S.: Scheduling for reduced CPU energy. In: Proceedings of the 1st USENIX Conference on Operating Systems Design and Implementation, OSDI 1994, Berkeley, CA, USA. USENIX Association (1994)
14. Wu, D., Al-Hashimi, B.M., Eles, P.: Scheduling and mapping of conditional task graph for the synthesis of low power embedded systems. IEE Proc. Comput. Digit. Tech. **150**(5), 262–273 (2003)

Tool and Method for Obtaining End-to-End Reliability Parameters of Wireless Industrial Networks

Christian Alan Krötz[1][(✉)], Max Feldman[1], Gustavo Pedroso Cainelli[1], Gustavo Künzel[2], Carlos Eduardo Pereira[1], and Ivan Müller[1]

[1] Federal University of Rio Grande do Sul (UFRGS), Porto Alegre, RS, Brazil
`christianalank@gmail.com, cpereira@ece.ufrgs.br, ivan.muller@ufrgs.br`
[2] Federal Institute of Education, Science and Tecnology of Rio Grande do Sul (IFRS), Farroupilha, RS, Brazil
`gustavo.kunzel@farroupilha.ifrs.edu.br`

Abstract. Wireless communication systems have been increasingly employed in the industry. In this context, the WirelessHART and ISA 100.11a protocols are being used due today due to the pioneering and high robustness. This work has as general objective to study the end-to-end latency of communications in wireless industrial networks. For this purpose, a tool for communication with the network gateway, with ability to extract information from the field devices and the gateway itself, is developed and used in case studies. The case studies contemplate methods to evaluate the quality of service of the network, by observing the end-to-end latency, in diverse failure situations. The faults are injected into the network and monitored by the developed tool itself. Using WirelessHART as a case study, aiming the evaluation of the applicability of these networks in the industrial processes control. The results show that the tool is capable of analyzing and obtaining the latency data of the network in a concrete manner, and its use is adequate for the most diverse studies on wireless industrial network communication.

Keywords: WirelessHART · Reliability · Robustness · Latency · Wireless networks · Industrial networks

1 Introduction

Industrial Wireless Sensor Networks (IWSNs) are gaining boost in relation to the wired technologies, as they offer benefits such as low operating cost, ease of installation, self-configuration and flexibility, which make them desirable for industrial applications [6]. As a consequence of its enormous potential, in the last decade, efforts have been made to make IWSNs technology reliable, robust, interoperable, and ready to replace traditional technologies [8]. Over time, IWSNs have been standardized and protocols such as IEEE802.15.4e, OpenWSN, WirelessHART (WH), Zigbee PRO, ISA100.11a and WIA-PA have been developed.

M. A. Wehrmeister et al. (Eds.): IESS 2019, IFIP AICT 576, pp. 77–88, 2023.
https://doi.org/10.1007/978-3-031-26500-6_7

Despite the many advantages offered by IWSNs, there are also weaknesses, mainly related to reliability and latency, which may not be suitable for use in closed loop systems, as evidenced in several studies. Different types of failures can occur in IWSNs such as, network links failure, network congestion and corrupted or lost packets [7]. End-to-end latency control is critical to many applications and services based on Networked Control Systems (NCS), which has found application in multiple areas. For example, applications that include industrial automation, mobile sensor networks, remote surgery, automated road systems and unmanned aerial vehicles [4]. Although performance measurement of wired networks has been extensively studied, measuring and quantifying wireless network performance faces new challenges and requires different approaches and techniques [2]. Regarding the NCS study, it is argued that, since performance metrics, such as latency, can be measured accurately in the lower layers of the protocol, performance evaluation is facilitated in the upper layers of the protocol. This fact motivates the creation of a method to evaluate the quality of service the network, by obtaining latencies of end-to-end communications, in several faults situations.

This work presents methods to obtain End-to-End reliability parameters from IWSNs. A tool were developed to test the proposed methods where it is possible to evaluate the temporal behavior of the network in normal operation and under fault conditions. For convenience and scope of use, WH networks are used, but the method is extensible to other protocols.

The methods and tool developed serve two fundamental purposes: first, to evaluate IWSN employability in NCS, and second, to use as a site survey system. The first one refers to obtaining the latencies, which are the main problems related to the stability of the control system, and the second refers to a tool capable of obtaining previous data the evaluation of a possible installation of this type of network, where it is possible to know if a given space/time will meet the requirements. In this sense, the tool is able to emulate typical failures, such as locks, interferences, hardware failures, among others.

The presentation of this work is organized as follows: in Sect. 2, the basic concepts used throughout the work are presented. A study on the state of the art is presented in Sect. 3, presenting the works previously performed. The implementation of the tool is described in Sect. 4. The case studies for the validation of the proposal and the presentation of the results obtained are presented in Sect. 5. The work is finalized with the conclusions on the results obtained in the Sect. 6.

2   Theoretical Foundation

The IWSNs project depends significantly on the requirements of the particular application, since different applications may have different requirements and purposes [15]. The use of IWSNs has received high attention because of its advantages over wired networks. Typical IWSNs require little infrastructure, help to improve product quality, increase production and flexibility, it is easy to install, and consequently reduce costs [6].

The WH protocol was developed with the goal of establishing a wireless communication standard for use in industrial applications. The WH is an extension of the HART [3] cabling protocol and enables full compatibility with legacy systems. Because it is a secure, time-synchronized, low-power protocol, it is suitable for industrial process control. Compatibility is defined primarily by the device description language (DDL) command structure previously developed by the HART organization [14].

The temporal evaluation refers specifically to obtaining the end-to-end latency, relevant parameter in wireless networks with multiple communications hops. The times in flows from bottom to top (uplink) and from top to bottom (downlink) are evaluated, where the largest value is the gateway (where external access to network) and the smallest value is the field device, connected directly to the plant.

The communications in the WH occur in time slots of 10 ms each [6]. The slots can be allocated through deterministic medium access mechanisms (TDMA), or shared between several nodes of the network, disputed through the mechanism CSMA-CA (Carrier sense multiple access with collision avoidance). WH adopts graph routing to deal with transmission failures through retransmissions and route diversity, and latencies are related to the scheduling and routing techniques employed. The maximum latency values are established by the scheduling of the communication so that the packets reach their destinations in known time, considering the maximum number of hops in the network and possible retransmissions. The connections between the nodes of the network are made through slots that are organized inside superframes that are repeated periodically to provide communication traffic in the network. According to the OSI (Open System Interconnection) seven-layer model, the WH contains the physical, link, network, transport layers, although the functionality of some of the layers is somewhat different from the original model.

Reliability and robustness are critical parameters in choosing a wireless communication protocol for use in industry [16]. Control and monitoring of processes in industrial environments have been changing in recent years, due to the growing advancement of research related to wireless industrial networks [5].

However, in spite of considerable efforts to provide mechanisms that increase network availability, reliability, security and maintainability, IWSNs maintains the propensity characteristic to fail due to phenomena of electromagnetic wave propagation [8].

According to [13], there are two types of failures that can occur in an IWSNs: transient failures, which generally affect communication links between network devices, and are typically caused by interference, coexistence or blocking, and permanent failures, which affect network devices, usually coming from the hardware. As an example of permanent failure, shutdown due to power failure, hardware failure or inadvertent removal of a network node can be considered, resulting in loss of communication between two pairs [9]. In this way, IWSNs must be reliable and function properly so that data can be reliably and securely delivered to their destination and with maximum latency met [1]. Some examples of typical failures of IWSNs are link failures, congestion and corrupted or lost packets due to blockages, change of communication routes or problems related to the coexistence of networks. Therefore, these failures were implemented, emulated, analyzed and will be discussed later.

3 State of the Art Analysis

In order to perform the study of the end-to-end communications latency in WH networks, and in order to evaluate and apply these networks in the control of industrial processes, a review of related articles was made.

The work develop by [16,17] developed a tool for obtaining end-to-end communication latency and insert failures in network. The former developed software allows to identify relevant questions for the verification and maintenance of WH networks, presenting as a contribution the ability to customize the tests, allowing user to evaluate data of greater interest for a specific purpose. In the case studies presented, it was possible to identify the most used routes of the network that lead to the identification of "bottlenecks", that is, network locations where latency can be increased due to routing overloads or places where the network is more susceptible to widespread failures due to local failures (blocks or hardware problems).

In order to insert network faults to carry out the case studies, [12] proposes a simulation model using Stochastic Petri Nets, in the Mobius tool, in order to evaluate WH networks in the presence of transient faults, assuming that these failures result from noisy environments that disrupt communication between devices. Later on [13], they perform the reliability assessment of the best practices indicated by the HART Communication Foundation (HCF), when the network devices are subject to permanent failures. The results presented by the authors show that best practices have different impact on the network.

The study developed by [11] approaches the problem of the analysis of assets in wireless industrial networks for the WH standard, implementing a monitoring system that allows to realize the most diverse management activities, regardless of manufacturer. Subsequently [10] presents an evaluation of the behavior of a WH network in a water level control process in a coupled tank system, using network latency and reliability as evaluation metrics, generating the results through tests real.

4 Methods and Materials

For the validation of the tool and method of analysis of the end-to-end reliability of wireless industrial networks, the following equipment was used.

Using a WH network, the tool developed uses the HART-over-IP protocol to communicate with the gateway. The gateway, in turn, communicates with the devices on the network through the WH access point. The application developed use HART commands, implemented to obtain the desired data for analysis of the network and the devices. The HART commands are encapsulated and sent to the gateway, which responds to the request, sending the requested data.

The tool interface is divided into tabs, each with a different functionality. Among these functions, it is possible to send HART commands implemented according to the WH standard: 780 (Report Neighbor Health List), 782 (Read Session List), 783 (Read Superframe List), 784 (Read Link List), 787 (Report Neighbor Signal Levels), 800 (Read Service List), 802 (Read Route List), and 840 (Read Network Device's Statistics). It also consists of the implementation of commands that calculate the latency of end-to-end communications. Use of commands to insert network failures, implemented to reflect real situations in the use of IWSNs. The tool is capable of generating a graphical topology of the network, as well as presenting a table with some network data.

4.1 Latency Analysis Strategy

To calculate the latency of the end-to-end communications of the network two special commands were implemented, one writing (command 130) and one reading (command 131) of the process variables, making use of the variable ASN Snippet, the two bytes less of the Absolute Slot Number (ASN), variable that is part of the Network Protocol Data Unit (NPDU). However, because it is a restricted variable in network segments (without user access), it was decided to make changes in the firmware of the devices for the purpose of extracting the ASN.

When the tool communicates with the gateway, which in turn communicates with a device through the access point, an ASN that is in the NPDU header is created. With the firmware change made in the device, the packet received by the device passes through the physical and link layers, arriving at the network layer, where the ASN present in the received packet is obtained. The ASN of the moment the device received the packet is also stored, and, once the timeslot has a fixed time of 10 ms, the difference between the ASNs values is calculated, obtaining a direct relation with the latency end-to-end communication between devices. These variables are forwarded to the gateway, as a process variable, through another modification in the firmware (change of process variables). The tool, by having access to these variables, can calculate the latency of the network end-to-end communications, as shown in Fig. 1.

As case studies for the validation of this work, the possible scenarios, from real WH networks, are the monitoring of a device by periodically surveying the topology and latency of the network. Once the monitoring is performed, a fault in the network is inserted through the developed tool, for example, interrupting a route through which the device communicated normally, evaluating the new topology of the network, together with the impact on the latency caused by the failure and the time to the network normalize.

With this, the tool provides relevant data for the verification of the applicability of the network in NCS, for example, providing the worst value of latency. Otherwise, the tool can be used as a site survey system for prior evaluation of a network to be installed in a plant, revealing maximum latency, "bottlenecks",

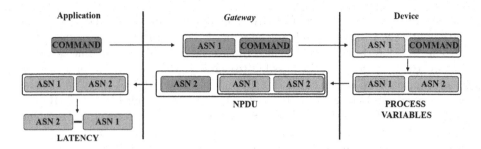

Fig. 1. Method for determining latency.

qualities of the links, all obtained automatically. Events such as hardware failures and locks are emulated and reveal what can be expected from a definitive installation. Several decisions are made in advance, in order to produce a map of the location of definitive devices, taking into account the location of repeaters. Once the definitive place of use has been evaluated, the test network is removed and replaced by commercial devices of high economic value.

5   Case Studies

For the validation of the proposal of this work, two case studies were performed that simulate real failures that occur in wireless industrial network environments, in which all the studies follow a standard for their realization. For the accomplishment of the case studies, the Wi-Analys sniffer was used for the data collection and later comparison with the data obtained by the tool. Data collection of end-to-end communications between the devices is performed for approximately two hours, starting the test until insertion of the fault and one more hour after insertion of the fault. The latency data are collected once every minute, thus producing approximately 120 samples in each case study.

The network topology is set up so that at least one device is not within reach of direct communication with the gateway, forcing the creation of a topology having at least one intermediate repeater device in communications with the target device. The latency data is always obtained in function of the device that does not have direct communication with the gateway, and the fault is inserted in an intermediate device, so that the end-to-end communications of the device can be analyzed.

5.1   Case Study 1: Disconnecting a Device from the Network

For case study 1, the command 960 (Disconnect Device). This case study emulates a device failure, where it disconnects from the network. In a real situation, this kind of fault can occur due to, which can occur due to a hardware problem, battery drained or bad contact. In this case study, the end-to-end latency between Tag 1 and Tag 1019 devices was evaluated. The Fig. 2 presents the network topology highlighting the communication routes with the target device and being the gateway represented by the Tag 1.

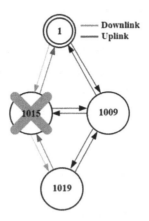

Fig. 2. Network topology of case study 1 before fault insertion.

The special commands 130 and 131 are sent periodically to obtain the end-to-end latency of the communication with the tag device 1019. After period of approximately one hour there is an average of 55 communications with the device.

A fault is inserted in the network, referring to disconnection of Tag 1015 device (command 960). The Fig. 3 presents the time diagram of the case study, denoting the period elapsed between normal operation and failure insertion.

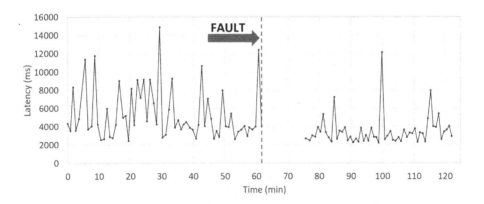

Fig. 3. Complete case study timeline 1.

Again, after approximately one more hour, a further 64 communications were collected, of which the Tag 1019 device only returned to respond after approximately 14 min.

With the disconnection of the device, a change in the topology of the network is observed (Fig. 4), changing the communication route with the Tag 1019 device.

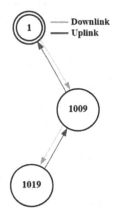

Fig. 4. Topology of the case study network 1 after failure insertion.

After data collection, a total of 119 communications were obtained, with a variation of the average latency of 12.7 s of the communications. With the data collected by the tool and checked with the sniffer data, it was possible to verify that in case study 1 the Tag 1019 device took approximately 14 min to find a new route and to respond to the requests again. After reestablishing the communications with the Tag 1019 device, it was observed that there was an improvement in the latency of the end-to-end communications between the devices, with the change in the network topology. It is possible to observe that not necessarily the topology of the network is formed aiming at a lower latency in the communications between the devices.

5.2   Case Study 2: Deleting Communications Links from a Device

In case study 2, the command 968 (Delete Link) was used. In this case study, links between devices are chosen to be deleted by the tool, to simulate signal block. In large industrial plants such as refineries, water treatment plants or chemical plants, blockages can occur when vehicles such as trucks, for example, position themselves in front of a field device. The links can be deleted and later reestablished, so that communication latency can be evaluated as well as changes in the mesh network topology.

Given the network topology in Fig. 5, sent the special commands to obtain the end-to-end latency of the communication with the tag device 1019, and sent the command 784 to obtain the communication links of the Tag device 1015.

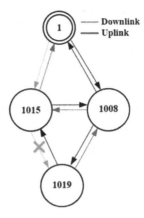

Fig. 5. Topology of the case study network 2 before failure insertion.

After one hour, there is an average of 75 communications with the device before insertion of the network failure.

The command 968 is sent to delete the communication links of the Tag device 1015 with the Tag device 1019, thereby inserting a network failure. The Fig. 6 presents the time diagram of the case study, denoting the complete period of the case study.

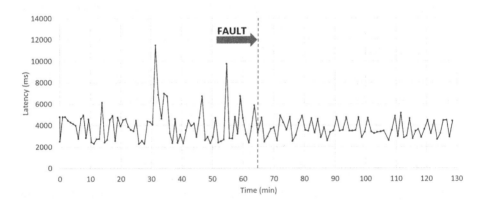

Fig. 6. Complete case study timeline 2.

As a consequence of the failure, the manager generated a new communication route with the tag device 1019 as can be seen in Fig. 7. After approximately another hour, the study was paused and 62 more communications were obtained with the Tag 1019 device.

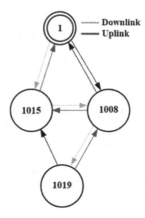

Fig. 7. Network topology of case study 2 after fault insertion.

After collecting the data, a total of 137 communications were obtained, having a mean latency variation of 9.19 s between the communications. Again, the data of the tool were collected, and these, checked with the data of the sniffer.

In this case study it is possible to verify that the change of the communication route was almost imperceptible, with a change also in the topology of the network. Being possible to emphasize that the insertion of the fault caused the sending of both downlink and uplink messages along the same path, which led to an improvement in the latency of end-to-end communication with the device.

6   Conclusions

This work explored a method for the latency analysis of the devices in the network, along with injections of failures caused by the developed tool, failures related to disconnection of network devices, loss of communication between devices and problems in the output power amplifier of a WH field device.

The tool allows analyzing and checking the characteristics of a WH network, obtaining the state of the devices on the network, communication signal quality, device nickname, device address, and graphical visualization of the network topology and presentation of statistics such as the amount and percentage of the types of links. However, the main function of the tool is to obtain end-to-end communications latency, which helps network analysis both in normal operation and in case of failure. These failures are inserted in the network by the tool, and it is possible to analyze the behavior of the network, which can provide improvements to the industrial wireless communication protocols.

The case studies presented here show the applicability of the tool in the most diverse situations that occur in the daily use of industrial wireless communication systems. First, the method to obtain the end-to-end communication latency between the devices was validated through the Wi-Analys sniffer and used for the analysis of the case studies. The case studies addressed two distinct situations of failures that may occur in the industry.

The first case study emulates a failure that can occur due to a device hardware problem causing a permanent network failure, forcing the device to disconnect from the device. In this case study it was possible to verify that the device under analysis took about 14 min to find a new route and to respond to requests again.

In the second case study the problem was addressed in the communication between two devices whose consequence is the inability to exchange information through signal block, which may happen due to some obstacle to prevent communication between the devices. Having as a result an almost unnoticeable change of communication route compared to the first case study.

Through the case studies performed using the tool to communicate with the network gateway, extracting information from the field devices and the gateway itself, it was possible to verify that in the case studies there was an improvement in the latency of the communications between the devices, even after insertion of the fault. This does not mean that the topology of the network is formed aiming at a lower latency in the communications between the devices, since there are several types of routing and scheduling algorithms that can use the same input parameters, but with different objective functions (latency, energy consumption, number of hops), specifications that are unknown, as well as the algorithms. Therefore, the main route of a communication is not necessarily based on lower latency but on other unknown criteria, such as network robustness.

References

1. Belkneni, M., Bennani, M.T., Ahmed, S.B., Kalakech, A.: Congestion control dependability assessment. In: 2018 14th International Wireless Communications Mobile Computing Conference (IWCMC), pp. 969–974, June 2018. https://doi.org/10.1109/IWCMC.2018.8450347
2. Galloway, B., Hancke, G.P.: Introduction to industrial control networks. IEEE Commun. Surv. Tutorials 15(2), 860–880, Second 2013. https://doi.org/10.1109/SURV.2012.071812.00124
3. HART, C.F.: Wirelesshart TDMA data link layer specification, HCF spec-075 revision 1.1, Parte Norma (2008)
4. Hespanha, J.P., Naghshtabrizi, P., Xu, Y.: A survey of recent results in networked control systems. Proc. IEEE 95(1), 138–162 (2007). https://doi.org/10.1109/JPROC.2006.887288
5. Machado, T., Muller, I., Winter, J., Dickow, V., Pereira, C.E., Netto, J.C.: WirelessHART network analyzer with coexistence detection. In: 12th IEEE International Conference on Industrial Informatics (INDIN), pp. 696–701, July 2014. https://doi.org/10.1109/INDIN.2014.6945598
6. Muller, I., Pereira, C.E.: Gerenciamento Descentralizado de Redes Sem Fio Industriais Segundo o Padrão WirelessHART. Universidade Federal do Rio Grande do Sul, Porto Alegre, Tese de doutorado (2012)
7. Paradis, L., Han, Q.: A survey of fault management in wireless sensor networks. J. Netw. Syst. Manag. 15(2), 171–190 (2007). https://doi.org/10.1007/s10922-007-9062-0

8. Raposo, D., et al.: An autonomous diagnostic tool for the wirelessHART industrial standard. In: IEEE 17th International Symposium on A World of Wireless, Mobile and Multimedia Networks (WoWMoM), pp. 1–3, June 2017. https://doi.org/10.1109/WoWMoM.2016.7523536

9. Saifullah, A., Xu, Y., Lu, C., Chen, Y.: Distributed channel allocation protocols for wireless sensor networks. IEEE Trans. Parallel Distrib. Syst. 25(9), 2264–2274 (2014). https://doi.org/10.1109/TPDS.2013.185

10. Santos, A., et al.: Assessment of wirelessHART networks in closed-loop control system. In: IEEE International Conference on Industrial Technology (ICIT), pp. 2172–2177, March 2015. https://doi.org/10.1109/ICIT.2015.7125417

11. dos Santos, A.C.S., Silva, I.M.D.: Ferramenta para Análise de Ativos em Redes Industriais WirelessHART. Universidade Federal do Rio Grande do Norte, Dissertação de mestrado (2015)

12. Silva, I., Guedes, L.A., Portugal, P., Vasques, F.: Preliminary results on the assessment of wirelessHART networks in transient fault scenarios. In: ETFA2011, pp. 1–4, September 2011. https://doi.org/10.1109/ETFA.2011.6059165

13. Silva, I., Guedes, L.A., Portugal, P., Vasques, F.: Dependability evaluation of wirelessHART best practices. In: Proceedings of 2012 IEEE 17th International Conference on Emerging Technologies Factory Automation (ETFA 2012), pp. 1–9, September 2012. https://doi.org/10.1109/ETFA.2012.6489649

14. smar: WirelessHART - características, tecnologia e tendências (2018). http://www.smar.com/brasil/artigo-tecnico/wirelesshart-caracteristicas-tecnologia-e-tendencias, [Online; acessado 10-Outubro-2018]

15. Wang, Q., Jiang, J.: Comparative examination on architecture and protocol of industrial wireless sensor network standards. IEEE Commun. Surv. Tutorials 18(3), 2197–2219, Thirdquarter 2016. https://doi.org/10.1109/COMST.2016.2548360

16. Winter, J.M., Lima, C., Muller, I., Pereira, C.E., Netto, J.C.: WirelessHART routing analysis software. In: Brazilian Symposium on Computing System Engineering, pp. 96–98, November 2011. https://doi.org/10.1109/SBESC.2011.21

17. Winter, J.M., Pereira, C.E.: Software de análise de roteamento de dispositivos WirelessHART. Universidade Federal do Rio Grande do Sul, Trabalho de conclusão de graduação (2010)

Architecture and Application

Towards ASIP Architecture-Driven Algorithm Development

Manil Dev Gomony$^{(\boxtimes)}$, Mihaela Jivanescu, and Nikolas Olaziregi

Nokia Bell Labs, Antwerp, Belgium
manil_dev.gomony@nokia-bell-labs.com

Abstract. Application-Specific Instruction-set Processors (ASIP) are ideal for realizing physical layer signal processing algorithms in communication systems as they offer performance similar to hard-wired datapath implementations, while providing sufficient programmability to adapt with the continuously evolving communication standards. Several design choices needs to be made while developing an algorithm for a specific signal processing function, such as the selection of the algorithm itself, choice of the mathematical operations and numerical precision, that affects the throughput, area and power consumption of ASIP implementation. Traditionally, the algorithm development and the ASIP architecture exploration is performed as separate processes resulting in large design time or a sub-optimal solution. This paper presents a simple methodology for the algorithm-ASIP designer(s) to understand the impact of various algorithmic design choices on the ASIP performance and make the right design choices at very early stage, thereby reducing the design time at least by a factor of 2.8x in algorithm research and development.

Keywords: Application-specific · Processor architecture · Design-space exploration · Signal processing · Physical layer

1 Introduction

Application-Specific Instruction-set Processors (ASIP) are custom designed processors with an architecture (and instruction-set) optimized for a limited set of applications/algorithms. Hence, ASIPs stand in a better position in terms of power, performance and area (PPA) when compared to a General-Purpose Processor (GPP), and flexibility when compared to hard-wired solutions [6]. ASIPs are ideal for realizing the physical layer signal processing algorithms in communication systems where the PPA is critical, while providing sufficient programmability to adapt according to the continuously evolving communication standards, for e.g. 5G, Wi-Fi, G.fast. Several design choices need to be made while developing a physical layer signal processing algorithm, such as the selection of the algorithm, mathematical operations and numerical precision, that affects the PPA of ASIP implementation.

Supported by Flanders Innovation and Entrepreneurship (VLAIO).

M. A. Wehrmeister et al. (Eds.): IESS 2019, IFIP AICT 576, pp. 91–100, 2023.
https://doi.org/10.1007/978-3-031-26500-6_8

The traditional algorithm-ASIP design flow shown in Fig. 1, starts with algorithm development, which includes devising the algorithm, system-level performance (e.g. SNR) estimation using high-level models (e.g. in Matlab) and bit-accurate implementation in C/C++. The ASIP architecture is then designed based on past experience and manual analysis of the algorithm, and implemented using a commercially available tool [1,2,15], that automatically generates an instruction-set simulator for throughput estimation. The area usage and power consumption of the RTL implementation of the ASIP is then evaluated using a RTL synthesis tool (e.g. Synopsys DC) for a certain technology node. The ASIP architecture is further optimized after manual analysis of the bottlenecks in the architecture, and the performance is estimated again. This manual design-space exploration process is repeated until the performance requirements are satisfied and/or an optimal solution is found, and if not a different algorithm is selected or the existing algorithm is modified and the whole design-space exploration process is repeated. In addition to the modifications on the algorithm, the designer has to explore the computational precision of the algorithm and evaluate the impact on throughput, area and power consumption to identify the optimal precision settings. The traditional design methodology takes significant amount of time as it involves several iterations involving manual implementation/modification of the ASIP architecture and its performance evaluation through synthesis.

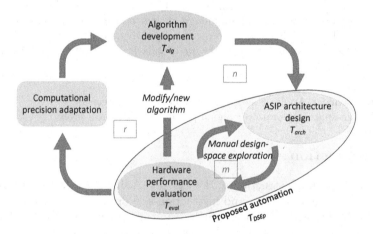

Fig. 1. Traditional Algorithm-ASIP design loop showing the different number of iterations n, m, r, required for algorithm modifications, ASIP architecture design-space exploration and computational precision exploration, respectively. The proposed methodology automates the manual iterations to reduce the overall design-time.

In this paper, we aim to close the gap between the Algorithm-ASIP design loop. The two main contributions in this paper are: 1) A simple methodology combined with a fast heuristic algorithm and an abstract cost model of ASIP to automate the early stage design-space exploration of algorithm-ASIP development process, as shown in Fig. 1, such that an algorithm-ASIP designer can make early design choices while understanding the impact on ASIP performance. 2) An evaluation of the proposed methodology under different use cases and different designer experience levels. The rest of the paper is structured as follows: Sect. 2 presents related work, Sect. 3 provides background on ASIP architecture and Sect. 4 the proposed methodology for the automated early design space exploration. In Sect. 5, we present the experimental results and the evaluation of the proposed methodology under different scenarios. Finally, we conclude the paper with future work in Sect. 6.

2   Related Work

There is already a large amount of related work [4,7,9,12] on the design-space exploration of ASIP architectures, that target the entire tool-chain for an optimal ASIP design and implementation, focusing on instruction set and datapath design, and re-targetable compiler generation. In addition, several automated framework [8,11,13] for early design-space exploration of ASIP instruction-set and data path architectures has been proposed in the past. The profiling based design methodology [3] to perform early identification of hot spots in the ASIP allows algorithm-ASIP architecture co-design. In [5], an architecture and design methodology for rapid prototyping of VLIW processors for signal processing application is proposed. To summarize, prior art on the ASIP design methodologies focus on determining the optimal ASIP architecture for multiple number of applications that would require continuous profiling with the applications and needs prior knowledge on ASIP architecture design. In addition, the applications or algorithms should be known or fixed in advance, and hence, they are not suitable to be used in the early design-space exploration by an algorithm designer during the algorithm development phase.

3   Background

The basic building blocks of an ASIP constitute Functional Units (FU), Register Files (RF), Load/Store Units (LSU), Data Memories (DM) and a Program Memory (PM), as shown in Fig. 2 [8]. The PM stores the compiled binary of the application/algorithm, which is used to generate the instructions for the FUs, RF and LSU. The FUs perform basic arithmetic and logic operations (addition, multiplication, shifting, etc.) and complex mathematical functions (square root, division, etc.). One or more FUs connected in series using pipeline registers to perform a sequence of operations using a single instruction is called an *Issue slot* [9]. The RF stores the temporary data used by the Issue slots, while the LSU keeps track of the address to the DM where the data to/from the issue slots are stored. Determining the architecture of an ASIP includes selection of the number of issue slots, type and number of FUs in each issue slot, size of RF, and number and size of DM and LSUs. The selection of these parameters has an impact on the area usage, power consumption and throughput of application execution. Note that the design-space exploration in this work focuses only on the data path elements, i.e., the FU, RF and LSU, however, we plan to include the DM in the future work.

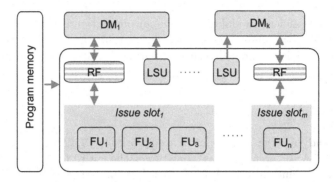

Fig. 2. Generic ASIP architecture constituting of Functional Units (FU), Register Files (RF), Load/Store Units (LSU), Data Memories (DM) and a Program Memory (PM).

4   Proposed Methodology

The proposed automated methodology, shown in Fig. 3, consists of three steps: Intermediate Representation (IR), Data Flow Graph (DFG) and Architecture (ARCH) generation.

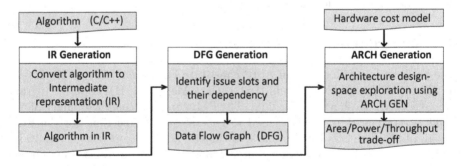

Fig. 3. Proposed automated methodology for design-space exploration includes generation of Intermediate Representation (IR) of algorithm, Data Flow Graph (DFG), and Design-space exploration using our proposed heuristic ARCH generation.

IR Generation: Starting from the algorithm implementation in C programming language, an existing C-compiler, e.g. LLVM or GCC, is used to generate the Intermediate Representation (IR) of the application program. IR represents all paths that might be traversed during the execution of a program. In IR, Static single assignment (SSA) form is used where each variable is assigned exactly once and useful for the static analysis of code. During the IR generation, we fully unroll all loops in the code. For example, the IR representation of a C-program performing two multiply-accumulate operations is shown in Fig. 4. The different storage required for the program execution, the data types and the basic operations and their dependencies can be identified easily from the IR.

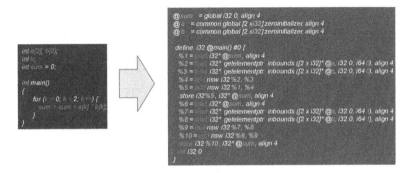

Fig. 4. Example illustration of a C implementation of a multiply-accumulate operation converted to Intermediate Representation (IR).

DFG Generation: The IR of the algorithm is analyzed to identify the FU types and width, RF sizes and width, and a *Data Flow Graph (DFG)* [10,14] is generated, as shown in step 2 in Fig. 5. In the DFG, the FUs and registers represent the nodes and the edges of the graph represents the dependencies between the FUs. The DFG represents the largest un-optimized ASIP architecture called the *best-parallel architecture.* In other words, implementing the best-parallel architecture results in the highest throughput possible for a given algorithm, but consuming the largest area and power. The data types of the variables in the IR are used to determine the size of FUs, RF and DM. Note that the IR Generation and the DFG Generation steps are similar to the prior art on ASIP design methodology, however, the main difference here is that we generate the initial best-parallel architecture after fully unrolling the loops.

ARCH Generation: Starting from the best-parallel architecture, our goal is to generate and compare the different ASIP architectures by sharing of computational resources during the execution of the algorithm. This means that the different architectures will have different area usage, power consumption and/or latency, as shown by the example illustration in Fig. 5. In the example, the two issue slots on the architecture shown on the left side is merged to a single issue slot to create the architecture on the right side. This is only possible when the operations in the issue slots are similar. As a result of merging, the architecture on the right side has lower area usage (and power consumption) but longer execution latency. Since the mapping of issue-slots on another is an NP-hard problem, we propose a heuristic algorithm *ARCH GEN* to reduce the exploration run-time. The basic idea of ARCH GEN is to optimize the DFG representing the best-parallel architecture by *shrinking* to identify Pareto-optimal architectures in terms of power, area and throughput. ARCH GEN performs shrinking in a step-by-step manner, consisting of three basic steps:

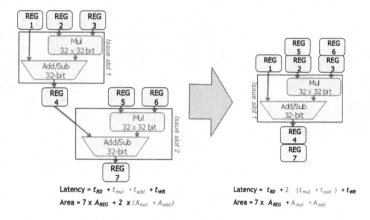

Fig. 5. Example illustration of a DFG and design-space exploration by shrinking. Two issue slots of the same type are reduced to one that results in an increase of the computational latency (decrease in throughput) and reduction in the area usage and power consumption.

Step 1: Identify and group issue slots: By parsing through the DFG, the issue slots (i.e. one ore more FUs with shared input and/or output registers as explained in Sect. 3) are identified. Issue slots of the same type are then grouped together such that the shrinking can be performed by re-use of (some of) the issue slots for the execution of the DFG. Note that the dependency information of the issue slots is retained for performing the shrinking while maintaining the execution order and to compute the throughput of execution of the DFG.

Step 2: Reduce issue slots without penalty: Depending on the algorithm, there might be two or more different paths in the DFG with different latency. In such cases, issue slots of the same type in the shorter (faster) path can be reduced (shared or re-used) during the execution to balance the latency of both paths such that the overall throughput is not affected. Note that for simplicity, we have assumed the reduction of an issue slot does not results in reduction of number of registers required to store the results of intermediate computation (as shown by registers REG 4, REG 5 and REG 6 in Fig. 5). However, including the DM in to the analysis will have an impact in the register file size, which is currently a limitation of our proposed methodology.

Step 3: Reduce issue slots with penalty: The goal of this step to generate DFG architectures with lower power and area usage by trading-off throughput. Once the latency of all the paths in the DFG is balanced without affecting the throughput (Step 2), one of the branches is randomly selected to reduce the number of issue slots. This will reduce the throughput of the execution of the DFG, but the area usage and power consumption will be lower. Step 2 is then repeated, i.e. the issue slots are reduced one-by-one from each other issue slot groups such that the latency of all paths are balanced. Step 3 is repeated until the number of issue slots in each group is reduced to one. This means that the shrinking is stopped when we reduce the DFG to an architecture with the lowest throughput.

During the shrinking Steps 2–3, the area vs. power vs. throughput trade-off of different architectures generated in each step is computed using a cost model that consists of area and power consumption estimates for the FUs, RFs and LSUs. When computing the throughput, the delay (in clock cycles) introduced by each FU is used. The cost model uses area and power consumption estimates for the FU and registers of different sizes obtained by synthesis for a specific process technology. The use of abstract cost model speeds up the design-space exploration process. Note that the absolute area usage and power consumption numbers of FUs are not very relevant and it does not reflect the real implementation measurements as our main goal is to perform a relative comparison between the different ASIP data path architectures.

5   Evaluation

We implemented the proposed methodology using LLVM compiler for the IR generation and Python scripts for IR parsing, DFG generation and design-space exploration using ARCH GEN algorithm. For the cost model, we have synthesized the basic functional units, such as adder, multiplier, divider etc., and registers for different widths (precision) using Synopsys DC and TSMC 16nm Fin-FET standard cell library at nominal operating conditions. Note that the power consumption of the different blocks are estimated assuming average switching activity of 0.125 in the synthesis tool. The Pareto-optimal ASIP architectures for different signal processing algorithms that are typically used in the physical layer of communication systems, such as Matrix multiplication, FFT, Matrix inverse, etc., were generated using the proposed methodology, and we found that the architectural design choices made were similar to those of an expert designer. As an example, the trade-off relation for a 6×6 matrix inverse operation using LU decomposition algorithm is shown in Fig. 6.

To evaluate the optimality of the proposed ARCH-GEN algorithm, we compared with an exhaustive algorithm that generates all possible issue slot combinations. For each combination of issue slots, a new architecture is generated by combining the issue slots if they are of the same type. The Pareto-optimal points of the exhaustive algorithm matched with the results of heuristic algorithm. However, the run-time of the exhaustive algorithm increases exponentially with the number of issue slots, as expected. For a DFG having above eight issue slots,

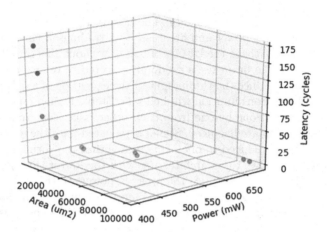

Fig. 6. Pareto optimal architecture solutions for a 6 × 6 matrix operation using LU decomposition algorithm obtained using ARCH GEN.

it was not possible to find the optimal solution even after few hours, whereas the heuristic algorithm could find the optimal solution in less than a second for algorithms having up to 70 issue slots.

We evaluated the savings in design time using the proposed methodology for both entry-level (0–2 years) and experienced (>2 years) designers. We considered use-cases of both development of new signal processing algorithm and modification of an existing algorithm and for the following scenarios (as shown in Fig. 1): Design-space exploration (DSE), Initial prototype (IP) phase of product development, and Research exploration (RE).

For a given algorithm, the time for design-space exploration is given by Eq. 1

$$T_{DSEt} = \sum_{i=1}^{m} (T_{arch(i)} + T_{eval(i)}) \tag{1}$$

where $T_{arch(i)}$ is the time taken to design and implement the ASIP hardware architecture, $T_{eval(i)}$ is the time taken to evaluate the throughput, area and power consumption of the ASIP implementation and m is the number of manual iterations needed before converging to a solution, as indicated in Fig. 1. The total design time is given by Eq. 2

$$T_{Dt} = r \times (n \times (T_{alg} + T_{DSEt})) \tag{2}$$

where T_{alg} is the time for algorithm selection and implementation, n and r are the number of times the algorithm is modified and the computational precision is modified for each algorithm, respectively. As the time for design-space exploration is less than a second, the total design time using our methodology is given by Eq. 3

$$T_{Dp} = r \times (n \times T_{alg}) + T_{arch(1)} \tag{3}$$

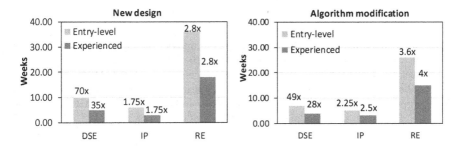

Fig. 7. Design-time speedup for an entry-level and experienced designer using the proposed automated methodology.

We found that for all cases, the design time is reduced with the proposed solution compared to the traditional approach. The speedup achieved by an entry-level and an experienced designer for both scenarios of a new algorithm design or algorithm modification, is shown in Fig. 7. As we can see, our proposed methodology results in savings of at least 1.75x in design time in all cases and with different designer experience levels. Our proposed methodology mostly benefits in research exploration for new design of an algorithm and saves over 20 weeks for a signal processing function of medium complexity, where multiple algorithms and precision configurations needs to be evaluated for ASIP implementation. Note that in addition to the savings in design time, our approach results in an optimal algorithm-ASIP implementation, whereas the manual approach might only result in a sub-optimal solution.

6 Conclusions and Future Work

We presented a simple and effective methodology to assist the algorithm-ASIP designer in understanding the impact of various algorithmic design decisions on ASIP performance. The proposed automated methodology runs in less than a second leading to a reduction in design time of at least 1.75x for designers with different experience levels and under different scenarios, benefiting mostly in research exploration of algorithms. As a future work, we would like to extend the proposed methodology to bring data memory in to the analysis and register file optimization based on data re-use to improve the accuracy of the estimation.

References

1. Cadence Design Systems Inc.: Tensilica customizable processors (2019). https://ip.cadence.com/ipportfolio/tensilica-ip/xtensa-customizable
2. Codasip Ltd.: Codasip Studio (2019). https://www.codasip.com/custom-processor/

3. Eusse, J., Williams, C., Leupers, R.: CoEx: a novel profiling-based algorithm/architecture co-exploration for ASIP design. In: 2013 8th International Workshop on Reconfigurable and Communication-Centric Systems-on-Chip (ReCoSoC), pp. 1–8 (2013). https://doi.org/10.1109/ReCoSoC.2013.6581520

4. Eusse, J., et al.: Pre-architectural performance estimation for ASIP design based on abstract processor models. In: 2014 International Conference on Embedded Computer Systems: Architectures, Modeling, and Simulation (SAMOS XIV), pp. 133–140 (2014). https://doi.org/10.1109/SAMOS.2014.6893204

5. Hoare, R.R., et al.: Rapid VLIW processor customization for signal processing applications using combinational hardware functions. EURASIP J. Adv. Signal Process. **2006**(1), 1–23 (2006). https://doi.org/10.1155/ASP/2006/46472

6. Ienne, P., Leupers, R.: Customizable Embedded Processors: Design Technologies and Applications. Morgan Kaufmann Publishers Inc., San Francisco (2007)

7. Jordans, R., Diken, E., Jozwiak, L., Corporaal, H.: BuildMaster: efficient ASIP architecture exploration through compilation and simulation result caching. In: 17th International Symposium on Design and Diagnostics of Electronic Circuits Systems, pp. 83–88 (2014). https://doi.org/10.1109/DDECS.2014.6868768

8. Jordans, R., Jóźwiak, L., Corporaal, H.: Instruction-set architecture exploration of VLIW ASIPs using a genetic algorithm. In: 2014 3rd Mediterranean Conference on Embedded Computing (MECO), pp. 32–35 (2014). https://doi.org/10.1109/MECO.2014.6862720

9. Jozwiak, L., et al.: ASAM: automatic architecture synthesis and application mapping. Microprocess. Microsyst. **37**(8 PARTC), 1002–1019 (2013). https://doi.org/10.1016/j.micpro.2013.08.006

10. Kato, T., et al.: A CDFG generating method from C program for LSI design. In: 2008 IEEE Asia Pacific Conference on Circuits and Systems, APCCAS 2008, pp. 936–939 (2008). https://doi.org/10.1109/APCCAS.2008.4746177

11. Lapinskii, V.S., Jacome, M.F., De Veciana, G.A.: Application-specific clustered VLIW datapaths: early exploration on a parameterized design space. IEEE Trans. Comput. Aided Des. Integr. Circuits Syst. **21**(8), 889–903 (2002). https://doi.org/10.1109/TCAD.2002.800451

12. Meloni, P., Pomata, S., Tuveri, G., Secchi, S., Raffo, L., Lindwer, M.: Enabling fast ASIP design space exploration: an FPGA-based runtime reconfigurable prototyper. VLSI Des. **2012**, 11:11 (2012). https://doi.org/10.1155/2012/580584

13. Pomata, S., et al.: Exploiting binary translation for fast ASIP design space exploration on FPGAs. In: 2012 Design, Automation & Test in Europe Conference & Exhibition (DATE), pp. 566–569 (2012). https://doi.org/10.1109/DATE.2012.6176533

14. Rosien, M., Smit, G., Krol, T.: Generating a CDFG from C/C++ code, pp. 200–202. STW Technology Foundation (2002). Imported from DIES

15. Synopsys Inc.: Synopsys IP designer (2019). https://www.synopsys.com/dw/ipdir.php?ds=asip-designer

Using Data Mining and Mobile Devices to Assist the Interactive Automotive Diagnostics

Leonardo P. de Oliveira, Marco A. Wehrmeister$^{(\boxtimes)}$ ⓘ,
and Andre S. de Oliveira ⓘ

Federal University of Technology - Parana (UTFPR), Av. Sete de Setembro 3165,
Curitiba, PR 80230-901, Brazil
{wehrmeister,andreoliveira}@utfpr.edu.br

Abstract. This work aims to assist the diagnostics of car defects by relating the data obtained through the vehicle telemetry with the driver's perceptions on a problem when it is perceived. Including the driver in the diagnostic process allows the engineers to identify features to be improved in the car design, even though a possible error/mistake is not apparent. Thus, the driver is seen as a new "sensor" capable of reporting his perceptions. For that, we propose an approach that includes data mining on the automaker knowledge base, the car's telemetry data obtained through an OBD device, the drivers' perception captured by a mobile device such as a Smartphone or a Tablet. The proposed *Interactive Diagnostic* approach enables a more complete preventive diagnostics in comparison with the traditional diagnostic based only on the telemetry data. In addition, the automaker receives the gathered data allowing their engineers to analyze the error/defect and fix the problem or improve the car design. The proposed approach was evaluated through some case studies. Diagnostic engineers answered a questionnaire that shows how the proposed approach influences the diagnostic process, i.e. the solution of the problem was found in fewer steps compared to the current diagnostics process. Therefore, this work advances both the state-of-the-art and the state-of-the-practice in automotive diagnostics by (i) exploring the vehicles' connectivity in the diagnostics process in an efficient way, and (ii) allowing the automobile industries to obtain more concrete information on the products they offer.

Keywords: Automotive diagnostic · Embedded software · Data mining · Mobile device · Human-computer interaction

1 Introduction

An increasing number of new functions and systems are included in modern cars in order to meet the demands coming from the market [19]. Thus, automakers must improve techniques for diagnosing problems and faults in the vehicle's Electronic Control Units (ECUs). This work addresses the problems related to malfunction caused by misunderstandings in the system project. Errors are defects

© IFIP International Federation for Information Processing 2023
Published by Springer Nature Switzerland AG 2023
M. A. Wehrmeister et al. (Eds.): IESS 2019, IFIP AICT 576, pp. 101–113, 2023.
https://doi.org/10.1007/978-3-031-26500-6_9

in the physical components of the system. Failures are detected by using Diagnostic Trouble Codes (DTCs), which are codes generated by ECUs that show malfunction on a specific system [15].

Generally, the automaker uses proprietary software[1] for the system diagnostics. The system variables are available in the vehicle via On-Board Diagnostic (OBD) interface [7]. At the car repair workshop, the access is restricted to the DTCs readings generated by the ECUs and accessed through the *Automotive Scanner*. The diagnostics specialists decode the DTCs messages, allowing them to repair the car. The customer (i.e. the driver) sees some DTCs through Malfunction Indicator Lamp (MIL) that are available on the vehicle dashboard.

When the car is in use, the diagnostics specialists are responsible for detecting errors or malfunction on the scheduled maintenance inspections; in all other situations, the driver is in charge of detecting errors. Thus, the quality level of his/her analysis depends on how much he/she knows about his/her car functioning. Malfunctions of sensors and actuators are recorded as a DTC. The DTC is immediately deleted from the system when the corresponding problem is solved. The highest priority DTCs are grouped into the *present breakdown* group. These DTCs are constantly evaluated and appear promptly in the system even when they are deleted. The group named *stored breakdowns* includes lower priority DTCs that are stored in the system only at the time the error is evidenced, i.e. if a DTC is deleted, it disappears from the system. Such a DTC reappears in the system only when the same error occurs again. Since there is no evaluation routine similar to the one used for the present breakdown DTCs [14].

A widely adopted diagnostic approach is to delete the complete DTC record from the system before any analysis of the vehicle itself. If the problem is a present breakdown, its DTC reappears, and thus, the diagnostic specialist knows exactly where the problem is. However, for stored breakdown DTCs, such an approach causes loose of information. Therefore, the specialist needs to simulate the situation described by the driver in order to make the DTC reappear. It is very common not being able to simulate the exact same situation, and thus, the problem cannot be identified and no specific repair is performed. This is a problem for the driver since such a situation increases the time necessary for the repair service to be done, i.e. from the perception of the vehicle's problem to the issue verification and repair at the car repair workshop, which may demand multiple repair service appointments. For the automaker, such a situation impacts on the return of the information on the vehicle issues and also the quality of the service perceived by the customers. According to a market survey [6], 92% of emerging market, customers want their e-mails or requests to be answered by the automaker in less than 24 h.

This work addresses the problem related to the difficulty that an automaker has to obtain information on the problems and failures that occur in its vehicles. The main goal is to improve the automotive diagnostics process by means of relating the data obtained with the telemetry scanning of the vehicle with the

---

[1] I.e. the automaker does not have access to the source code, and hence, it is difficult to adapt the software to specific needs.

driver's perceptions about a given problem. Novel diagnostic techniques should support a large number of systems that will emerge in the coming years [16]. In this sense, it is also necessary to explore the connectivity provided by both mobile devices and nowadays vehicles, in order to evolve the vehicles design and also improve the security and customer experience while driving. For that, we propose a novel approach that includes the driver in the car diagnostic process. The driver's opinion is considered, as he/she represents a new "sensor" that is able to report his/her perceptions. The goal is to improve not only the diagnostics process but also the capability of the automaker engineers to identify elements to be improved in the car design, even though if they do not present an apparent error. The proposed approach also includes data mining on the automaker knowledge base, the car's telemetry data obtained through an OBD device. An Expert System [11] was created from the knowledge obtained from a data mining process. Such a system takes the driver's perception captured by a mobile device (e.g. Smartphone or Tablet) and also the telemetry data as input, and integrates them with the knowledge obtained the automaker database. The proposed interactive diagnostic approach enables a more complete diagnostics in comparison with the traditional diagnostics based only on the telemetry data.

Real-world situations of automotive diagnostics have been used to evaluate the proposed approach. Each case study involved data from the vehicle telemetry system and information reported by the driver. Specialists of automotive diagnostics analyzed the provided data and state a solution to the given problem. Results show an improvement in the automotive diagnostics process. A decrease in the number of steps necessary to diagnose the problem has been obtained by using the proposed interactive diagnostic approach. Consequently, a decrease in the time necessary to repair the vehicle may be achieved as the number of visits to the repair workshops may decrease. This way, this work contributions are: (i) a new approach that applies the connectivity of the vehicles in the diagnostics process in an efficient way; (ii) the approach impacts positively in the diagnostic of the vehicle problems; (ii) the approach improves in information sharing among the stakeholders of the automotive industry (especially the automakers, the network of repair workshops, and the drivers), as the automakers can obtain more concrete information on the issues of products they offer.

This paper is organized as follows. Section 2 discusses some open issues in the automotive diagnostic area. Section 3 presents the proposed approach to assist the automotive diagnostics. Section 4 discusses the results obtained by applying the approach in an experiment with automotive diagnostic engineers. Finally, Sect. 5 draws some conclusions and points to future work directions.

2 Related Works

A survey on automotive diagnostics [16] presents an analysis of current state-of-the-art, the open problems and challenges in this field. The main challenge is to make the automotive diagnostics more consistent, especially in obtaining and using reliable data from the car telemetry. Although such a subject has been debated for a long time, researchers are still looking for new ways to do it. According to [16], 40% of analyzed articles address the problem of extracting data from the vehicle. Smartphones are used along with the OBD device in [10,12,21]. The smartphone is used to interface with the OBD for reading or writing data; according to [16], this is the most common approach among the analyzed papers. The data obtained from mobile device is sent through the Internet to a server or database for a wide range of services, e.g. telemetry, driver profile recognition, car status review, points of interest.

Other approaches such [5,22] and [3] use the smartphone connected to the vehicle to gather information or control some of its services. In those approaches, the driver uses voice commands to interact with the vehicle. None of these works use the OBD, the smartphone, or their integration, as tools to improve the automotive diagnostic process. On the other hand, [1] evaluates intelligent hybrid systems to predict failures based on run-time information from in-vehicle sensors e.g. automobile battery voltage, engine coolant temperature, and air fuel ratio internal combustion. Although the those results can be somehow used in automotive diagnostics for preventive maintenance, that work does not discuss it. The so-called loggers are industrial-grade solutions available on the market to equip specific vehicles with in order to gain intelligence to detect a specific problem. Combining information obtained from the loggers with an interview of the driver is considered state-of-the-art for the inspection of suspicious problems. However, important pieces of information may be lost in this process. The longer the delay between the interview and the logger data acquisition, the greater the likelihood that the driver forgets to report something.

Unlike the mentioned works, this work proposes a novel automotive diagnostic approach that employs the data extraction via the integrated use of OBD and mobile devices. Therefore, this work proposes a novel diagnostic model in which telemetry data is obtained via the OBD device, however, the driver is inserted as a new filter in the vehicle i.e. new a "sensor" in the process. Obtaining the information from the driver when he/she is driving may assist the diagnostics. An expert system (built based on an automaker issues database) captures the driver's perception on the car issue and combines such information with the telemetry data gathered through the OBD device. Such information is recorded and sent to the automaker, enabling its engineers to access valuable information which would be lost in the traditional automotive diagnostic process.

3   Interactive Approach to Assist Automotive Diagnostics

3.1   Overview

The proposed automotive diagnostics approach was developed to assist the engineers/technicians throughout the diagnostics process by using the vehicle telemetry data, driver's perception, and a computer system to capture, process and send information to the automaker. Such a computational system can be seen as an interface between the driver and the vehicle. It provides valuable information to be used in the car diagnostics. Obtained data is sent to the automaker as the problems occur in the vehicle. The system is able to guide the driver in the diagnostic process even when he/she does not have in-depth knowledge about the vehicle operation. Figure 1 shows an overview of the system architecture.

When the driver notices an unusual situation in the vehicle, he/she triggers the interactive diagnostic software on the mobile device and starts the data gathering. The driver interacts with the *Interactive Diagnostics Software Assistant* (IDSA) through text or voice commands. IDSA is responsible for: (a) identifying the keywords in the driver's description, and (b) requesting the relevant telemetry data. Upon receiving a command, IDSA requests the reading of the DTCs data that are stored in some vehicle's ECUs. For that, an OBD device is connected to the vehicle communication system. Once the data is collected, e.g. DTCs data and driver's perception, IDSA sends the data (via the Internet) to a server, which is physically located at the automaker.

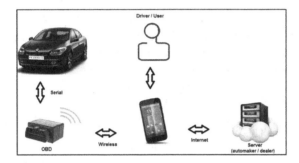

Fig. 1. Car-Driver-Automaker interface system

3.2 Applying Data Mining on the Automaker Knowledge Base

To assist in the automotive diagnostics, a classifier was created in order to categorize an automotive problem based on the driver's speech. Artificial intelligence [23] and data mining [4] techniques, specifically the decision tree [9] have been employed. The data from real customer claims obtained from automaker's knowledge database was used to train the classifier. The automaker collects data from customer claims. An employee makes a phone call to customers who bought cars within the period of 3–6 months. The customer reports the problems he/she perceived in the vehicle. This speech is named "customer verbalization" and is transcribed in the exact same sentences as the customer spokes. Such a verbalization is saved in the automaker knowledge database.

The created classifier complies with the method currently applied by the automaker. This way, the classifier uses a set of keywords defined for each problem class. Every time a keyword appears in the analyzed text, its counter is increased. After the analysis of the text, the problem class with the highest score represents the problem reported in the customer's speech. This is a simple yet efficient approach (see Table 1).

The initial step is to discover the characteristics of each class, the keywords that identify each group, and the characteristics that differentiated them. For this, all customer verbalizations stored in the automaker database were analyzed. The keywords analysis consisted of reading the verbalizations and identifying the words that are linked to the problem classes that appear in the database. As usual in the training of classification algorithms, the database was divided in the proportion of 70% samples for training data and 30% samples for validation. It is important to mention that this work focuses only on two problem classes (multimedia and motor) as a demand from the automakers. However, the latter will not be presented here because they are protected under a non-disclosure agreement. For the multimedia, the following groups and related keywords were identified: (a) *Hands-free (hf)*: mobile, smartphone, phone, speech, voice, answer, talk and dial agenda; (b) *Sound Quality (sq)*: sound box, speaker, sound, sound system, echo, noise, squeak, volume; (c) *Reception (rr)*: station, radio station, radio stations, tuning, tuning, tuning; (d) *Bluetooth (bt)*: connect, Bluetooth, connection; (e) USB: usb, pen drive; (f) *Antenna (an)*: antenna, little antenna; (g) *GPS (gp)*: GPS, address, location, map. The selected relevant keywords are neither among the most frequent, nor among the least frequent [18], i.e. the keywords are on an intermediate area among the most cited words.

The next step was to implement the algorithm that identifies the problem classes based on the occurrences of the keywords. The algorithm counts each word contained in the verbalization. At the end of the analysis, the group of words that contains the highest number of occurrences defines the problem class that is reported on the verbalization. For example, for the verbalization *"The vehicle has a problem with the sound system. I hear a constant wheezing when I'm at speeds above* 100 km/h", the result of the analysis is 0-hf 2-sq 0-rr 0-bt 0-usb 0-an 0-gps. Thus, this verbalization is classified as "Sound quality" and represents a complaint about the sound quality in the vehicle.

The proposed classifier were compared with *Decision Tree* and *Neural Network*. Two distinct implementations for each technique were assessed. The results are presented in Table 1. A slightly better result was achieved by the proposed classifier. Such a result might be due to linear independence of the data used by the classifiers. However, it is important to highlight that the other algorithms might achieve better results on more complex classification problems, i.e. when the classification is less intuitive in comparison to the one presented here.

Table 1. Classifiers performance

	Accuracy
Decision Tree (R) [13]	82.35
Decision Tree (Weka) [8]	89.8
Neural Network (R) [2]	91.08
Neural Network (Weka) [8]	96.7
Proposed Classifier	98

3.3   Interactive Diagnostics Software Assistant

The *Interactive Diagnostics Software Assistant* (IDSA) is a Android App that executes on a mobile device, e.g. smartphone or tablet, and implements a guided diagnostics process. The IDSA aims to integrate the driver, the vehicle, and the automaker's server. The gathered data, i.e. telemetry data and the driver's perception, is sent to the automaker via Internet. The automaker's cause/effect knowledge base was used to create a diagnostics decision tree. This decision tree drives the questions that are presented to the driver when IDSA is activated.

The IDSA ensures that the driver reports the vehicle problems when he/she perceives them while using the vehicle, i.e. he/she is a new "sensor" the diagnostics process. When the driver selects the diagnostic function, he/she has two options: (i) choose to register a complaint; and (ii) search for a error/fault in the vehicle. Figure 2 illustrates the process of recording driver perceptions.

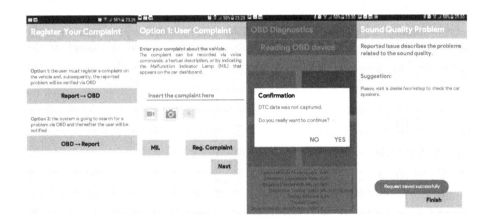

Fig. 2. IDSA screenshots for recording the driver's perceptions

The driver has to register his/her perceptions of the car in the *Claim Register screen*. The driver may choose to record two types of perceptions: (i) *Conventional*: he/she registers a complaint that is not linked to any dashboard indicator light icons; and (ii) *Indicator Light*: he/she indicates which indicator light is linked to his/her complaint. The complaint is registered after the typing process or voice capturing. IDSA presents the *Diagnostic screen* in which the system searches for DTCs by reading data from the CAN network via the OBD device. Thereafter, the driver is directed to the *Comments screen* in which he/she is instructed to act on the reported problem. Finally, the driver finishes the diagnostic process and send the gathered data to the automaker's server via Internet.

On the other hand, the IDSA can also look for an error or fault within the system. Thus, the IDSA checks the vehicle variables in order to find them. If the IDSA identifies something unusual, it reports the error/fault to the driver so that he/she can issue his/her perception, which, in turn, will later be sent to the automaker's server. The process is a different: IDSA shows the *Diagnostic screen*, thereafter the *Complaint screen*, and the remaining process is the similar.

The IDSA uses a OBD-java-API library [17] in order to identify automatically the communication protocol used in the vehicle and to send and interpret the desired commands. The mobile device connects to an OBD-II dongle via Bluetooth, which, in turn, communicates with the vehicle ECUs and extracts the data from the car communication bus.

The automaker's server was developed following the *Representation State Transfer* (REST) paradigm. The data exchanged between the system components are structured with the JSON format. This architecture allows the driver to record his/her notifications, and also the automaker to store highly relevant information on the vehicles usage. Such key information might be lost when the DTCs are erased when the car arrives at any repair workshop for a repair service.

The automaker server-side services must be scalable and capable of processing and analyzing a large amount of data, in order to provide a feedback to the driver that needs some assistance. Although we acknowledge that big data techniques must be employed for these sort of server-side services, this work is limited to the development of a notifications acknowledge system as a proof of concept. In the future work we will investigate how to deal and process with such an enormous amount of driver and vehicle data within an acceptable time frame.

4   Evaluation and Results

4.1   Overview

The proposed approach was evaluated through some experiments. Three case studies was performed. They are based on real cases registered by the automaker in which some problems occur during the diagnostics/solving process due to the lack of detailed information.

By using the created IDSA prototype, it was possible to simulate three situations: (a) the driver makes a notification, the IDSA searches the information in the vehicle telemetry system; (b) the IDSA detects a DTC and then asks the driver for additional information on his/hers perception; and (c) the diagnostics of a problem without an associated DTC nor system variable that evidences it but with information on the driver's perception. In all situations, IDSA sends such data to the server as a lest step. Due to space constraints, this paper discusses only the situations (a) and (c).

Each case study includes data from the vehicle and information reported by the driver. Automotive diagnostics experts were interviewed. These experts answered to questionnaires that contained the case studies data. The goal was to evaluate how much the information obtained from the driver can influence the analysis of the diagnostics experts.

A set of questions was selected from the automakers' knowledge base for each case study. A technical interviewer should ideally ask the driver these questions when he/she arrives at the car repair workshop. In the proposed approach, the

IDSA asks these questions at the moment the problem is detected (by the car or by the driver). Thus, the automaker and the car repair workshop receives in advance a report on the vehicle. Thus, the diagnostics staff can anticipate the analysis. Two questionnaires were created. The first one provides only the text of the driver complaint and also the options to solve the problem. This questionnaire simulates how the problem is currently handled in the car repair workshops. The second questionnaire provides the information generated by the IDSA in addition to the driver complaint text. In this case, the IDSA asks questions related to the classified problem, restricting the number of possible diagnoses and making the diagnostics more effective.

The questionnaires were applied to 40 professionals related to the diagnostics process, e.g. engineers, quality analysts, technical receptionists, and mechanics. To ensure the validity of the responses and to avoid bias in the answers, each professional answered only one questionnaire that was randomly selected. The impact of the proposed approach on the diagnostics process was measured by comparing the results obtained through both questionnaire. Thus, a diagnostics approach is considered more efficient whether it reduces the number of steps for the analyst to perform the correct procedure.

4.2 Issue Evidences Captured Through DTC

This case study evaluates how the proposed approach assists the diagnostics in a situation in which the driver selects the option to look for a problem in the vehicle, and then the IDSA encounters a DTC. The driver is then asked about the problem, and the information is sent to the automaker's server via Internet.

In this case study, the problem is a poor coupling of the vehicle's electrical harness. When the car passes on a rough ground, the harness is cracked causing the injection light to come on. The driver notices the MIL indicator on the dashboard and commands the IDSA to search for a possible vehicle fault. The IDSA encounters the DTC number C01061 which indicates failure of the collector pressure sensor. Then, the driver is directed to a screen on which he/she must answer: (1) How often does the injection light rise? Options: a-Continually, **b-Intermittent**, c-Never; (2) In what situation of direction does it occur? Options: a-Sloped ground, **b-Wavy ground**, c-Plane, d-All; (3) The problem occurs with: Options: a-Cold Engine, b-Hot Engine, **c-Both**. The responses provided by the driver are indicated in bold-face. The goal is to refine the problem and guide the analyst to the correct diagnostics. The driver's responses and the detected DTC provides additional data to the diagnostics. The interviewees had the following options to chose as an action to perform: A - Carrying out a driving test; B - Analyze the collector pressure sensor; C - Analyze the injection calculator; D - Analyze the conformity of the vehicle's electrical harness; and E - Other method not mentioned. Which one? - discursive option. The action that solves the problem is to analyze the vehicle's electric harness (i.e. option D).

A total of 40 interviewees were split into groups of 20 persons. The first group answered the questionnaire without the additional information provided by the driver through the IDSA. The result is the following: 03 interviewees chose to analyze the electric harness, i.e. the correct action, as the first action to be performed; 08 interviewees chose to perform such an action as the second action; whereas 05 as the third action and 03 as the fourth action. One interviewee does not choose to perform this action. In other words, 80% of the experts who answered the questionnaire without the extra information would take 2 steps or more to solve the problem, and one expert would not identify the problem.

On the other hand, The second group answered the questionnaire that includes the additional information coming from the IDSA. These analysts perform better: 14 interviewees chose to analyze the electric harness as the first action, while 01 chose do it in the second step, 03 in the third step, and 01 in the fourth step. One interviewee does not choose to analyze the electric harness. Therefore, 70% of the experts would solve the problem in the first action, i.e. there is an improvement in the number of correct actions as the first step.

This experiment indicates that the interviewees decided to analyze the vehicle's electric harness as the first action due to the access to the extra information. Thus, the IDSA assisted the diagnostics process since the correct diagnostics was identified more rapidly for the majority of the interviewees in the second group. Even considering that the improvement was only in one step, for the customer's reality, this implies fewer visits to the car repair workshop, and thus, his/her vehicle is repaired more quickly.

4.3   Issue Without Associated DTC Data

The second case study presents a problem related to the existence of a strange noise that occurs when the driver presses lightly on the brake pedal. The solution is to change the brake caliper wheel pins. This is an undetectable situation for the IDSA since the problem does not have an associated DTC. Such a situation can only be diagnosed through the driver report. The driver reports the existence of a noise that bothers him/her during driving. When the driver hears the unpleasant sound, he/she registers the perception in the IDSA. Then, the IDSA asks some questions and presents relevant information about the classified problem.

The driver registers his/her perception by saying "Only when I slow down it makes some noise, just the noise, nothing else. I think it's a regular noise. With the engine on, on movement. I don't know in what gearbox it is". The keyword identified by the IDSA is "noise" because it was repeated three times. The word "gearbox", which is repeated once, is a key word for another problem. IDSA classifies the problem as "Noise and Vibration" since there is a prevalence of keywords linked to this class. No DTCs are found, and thus, the IDSA cannot find an apparent problem in the vehicle that could evidence the perceived noise.

This diagnostics situation is highly dependent on driver's information. Thus, the analyst needs details on which conditions the noise appears in order to find a solution. Such an information will help the diagnostic expert in the process of simulating the issue. Therefore, IDSA directs the driver to a screen, in which he/she must answer the following questions: (1) In which part of the vehicle does the noise concentrate? Options: **a-Front**, b-Rear, c-Center); (2) Does the noise occur inside or outside the passenger compartment? Options: **a-Inside**, b-Outside; (3) What is the sort of noise? Options: a-Bass, **b-Sharp**; (4) In which situation does the noise occur?: Options: a-When pushing abruptly on the brake, **b-When pushing lightly on the brake**, c-On a rough ground, d-During acceleration. Responses provided by the driver are indicated in bold-face. The interviewees had the following options to chose as an action to perform: A - Check engine cushion; B - Perform driving test; C - Check brake caliper bracket pins; D - Check for gap in front suspension linkage. Action that solves the problem is checking brake caliper easel pins (option C).

Likewise the previous case study, the interviewees in groups of 20 persons. The first group answered the questionnaire without the additional information provided by the IDSA. As a result, 15 interviewees, i.e. 75%, chose to conduct a driving test as the first action to check the existence of the noise reported by the driver. The correct measure to solve the problem was discovered by the experts in the third action on average. Only 2 interviewees performed the correct analysis in the first diagnostics step. In the second group, the interviewees had access to the additional information provided by the IDSA, and hence, 85% performed the correct analysis in the first diagnostics step and whereas others in the second step. This is the most significant improvement achieved in the experiments since all experts found a solution in one or two steps, and hence, it evidenced that the additional information influences the analysis process. Considering similar issues, this result may indicate that in 85% of the situations, the driver would leave the car repair workshop with problem solved on the first visit. This is a very relevant case study as the technician is currently unable to identify this sort of malfunction easily. This difficulty was demonstrated in the first group as the majority decided to perform a driving test aiming to reproduce the very same situation reported by the driver. However, due to the lack of details or information, such a test cannot always reproduce the reported problem.

5   Conclusions and Future Works

This work proposes an approach to assist in the automotive diagnostics by combining the vehicle telemetry data obtained through an OBD device with the driver's perception captured through a mobile device. Gathered data is also sent to a server located at the automaker facility, enabling improvements in the vehicle itself and its related processes. Moreover, the automaker may explore the information provided by both the driver and the vehicle to enrich the diagnostics process performed at the car repair workshop. The proposed interactive diagnostics approach allows: (i) a reactive analysis performed by the car repair workshop, and (ii) the automaker to be proactive and foresee the problems that may occur with its vehicles. These issues were demonstrated in case studies performed to evaluate the proposed approach. The diverse nature of problems in vehicles was demonstrated: from detectable problems (those with DTCs) to other problems that are difficult to diagnose since the systems cannot detect them directly.

The results indicated that integrating the information from both the driver and the vehicle improves the diagnostics process. The proposed approach led to a decreased number of actions needed to identify the problem. The most remarkable improvement was obtained in the case study that represents a problem that cannot be directly detected by the telemetry system. Without the information provided by the driver, the diagnostics experts need at least three steps to identify the cause of a noise-related problem. In the car diagnostics context, each step represents a new visit of the driver to the car repair workshop, and hence, additional time spent without the problem being solved. Due to the driver's information captured by the Interactive Diagnostics Software Agent, 85% of diagnostics experts were led to the correct action in the first analysis step.

The proposed approach improves the diagnostics process from the point of view of both the automakers and car repair workshops. Although this work has focused on problems related to multimedia and the motor, the created classifier and its training process, can be repeated to include other problem classes, thus increasing the IDSA ability to detect errors. Identifying and handling an increased number of problem classes are important to minimize their impact on driver usage of the vehicle. A fewer number of days for discovering defects may represent significant savings on the financial resources spent on the vehicles repairing and on the company brand image.

A market trend is for the vehicles to become connected, autonomous, and self-diagnosable [20] by letting the driver (i.e. the car's owner) in a passive role on the control of the car. This study has evaluated not only the possibility of "reintegrating" the driver into the diagnostics process, but also to assesses how the information provided by him/her could improve the diagnostics. As future work, we propose to use other methods aiming to obtain the driver's perception, e.g. a device directly embedded and connected to the car, thus eliminating the need of an external mobile device. For a commercial application, it may be necessary to replace the mobile device by the vehicle's multimedia system.

References

1. Almeida, D.M., et al.: Hybrid time series forecasting models applied to automotive on-board diagnostics systems. In: International Joint Conference on Neural Networks (IJCNN), pp. 1–8 (2018)
2. Bergmeir, C.: Package 'RSNNS' - The R Project for Statistical Computing (2015)
3. Cerón, M., Fernández-Carmona, M., Urdiales, C., Sandoval, F.: Smartphone-based vehicle emission estimation. In: Rocha, Á., Guarda, T. (eds.) ICITS 2018. AISC, vol. 721, pp. 284–293. Springer, Cham (2018). https://doi.org/10.1007/978-3-319-73450-7_28
4. Cho, Y., et al.: A personalized recommender system based on web usage mining and decision tree induction. Expert Syst. Appl. 23(3), 329–342 (2002)
5. Gao, A., Wu, Y.: A design of voice control car base on SPCE061A single chip. In: IEEE Workshop on Electronics, Computer and Applications, pp. 214–217. IEEE (2014)
6. Gill, N., Winkler, M.: Cars Online 2014 - Generation Connected. Capgemini Study (2014). https://www.capgemini.com/wp-content/uploads/2017/07/cars_online_2014_final_web_group_1.pdf

7. Godavarty, S., et al.: Interfacing to the on-board diagnostic system. In: Proceedings of 52nd Vehicular Technology Conference, vol. 4. IEEE (2000)
8. Hall, M., et al.: The WEKA data mining software: an update. ACM SIGKDD Explor. Newsl. **11**(1), 10–18 (2009)
9. Han, J., Pei, J., Kamber, M.: Data Mining: Concepts and Techniques. Elsevier (2011)
10. Händel, et al.: Smartphone-based measurement systems for road vehicle traffic monitoring and usage-based insurance. IEEE Syst. J. **8**(4), 1238–1248 (2014)
11. Hayes-Roth, F., Waterman, D.A., Lenat, D.B.: Building Expert Systems. Addison-Wesley Longman Publishing Co., Inc., Boston (1983)
12. Hong, J.H., Margines, B., Dey, A.K.: A smartphone-based sensing platform to model aggressive driving behaviors. In: Proceedings of the SIGCHI Conference on Human Factors in Computing Systems, pp. 4047–4056. ACM (2014)
13. Hothorn, T., Hornik, K., Strobl, C., Zeileis, A., Hothorn, M.T.: Package 'Party'. Package Reference Manual for Party Version 0.9-998 **16**, 37 (2015)
14. Isermann, R.: Fault-Diagnosis Systems: An Introduction from Fault Detection to Fault Tolerance. Springer, Heidelberg (2006). https://doi.org/10.1007/3-540-30368-5
15. Lawrenz, W.: CAN System Engineering: From Theory to Practical Applications, 1st edn. Springer, Heidelberg (1997)
16. Oliveira, L.P., et al.: Systematic literature review on automotive diagnostics. In: Brazilian Symposium on Computing Systems Engineering SBESC, pp. 1–8. IEEE (2017)
17. Pires, B.: OBD-II Java API (2017). https://github.com/pires/obd-java-api
18. Silla, C.N., Jr., Kaestner, C.A.: Estudo de métodos automáticos para sumarizaçao de textos. Simpósio de Tecnologias de Documentos, pp. 45–49 (2002)
19. Staron, M.: Automotive Software Architectures: An Introduction. Springer, Heidelberg (2017)
20. Sugayama, R., Negrelli, E.: Veículo conectado na rota da indústria 4.0. Blucher Eng. Proc. **3**(1), 48–63 (2016)
21. Suresh, V., Nirmalrani, V.: Android based vehicle diagnostics and early fault estimation system. In: Proceedings of International Conference on Computation of Power, Energy, Information and Communication (ICCPEIC), pp. 417–421. IEEE (2014)
22. Wang, Z., et al.: Design of an Arduino-based smart car. In: 2014 International SoC Design Conference (ISOCC), pp. 175–176. IEEE (2014)
23. Witten, I.H., Frank, E., Hall, M.A., Pal, C.J.: Data Mining: Practical Machine Learning Tools and Techniques. Morgan Kaufmann, Burlington (2016)

Algorithm and System C

An Untimed SystemC Model
of GoogLeNet

Emad Malekzadeh Arasteh$^{(\boxtimes)}$ and Rainer Dömer$^{(\boxtimes)}$

Center for Embedded and Cyber-Physical Systems, University of California Irvine,
Irvine, USA
{emalekza,doemer}@uci.edu

Abstract. Deep learning and convolutional neural network (CNN) have been shown to solve image classification problems fast and with high accuracy. However, these algorithms tend to be very computationally intensive and resource hungry, hence making them difficult to use on embedded devices. Towards this end, we need system-level models for analysis and simulation. In this report, we describe a newly designed untimed SystemC model of GoogLeNet, a state-of-the-art deep CNN using OpenCV library. The SystemC model is automatically created from a Caffe model using a generator tool. We successfully validate the functionality of the model using Accellera SystemC 2.3.1 simulator. Then, we use RISC (Recoding Infrastructure for SystemC) to speed up the simulation by exploiting thread-level parallelism and report extensive experimental results.

Keywords: System-level modeling · Parallel discrete event simulation · Deep learning · Convolutional neural network · SystemC

1 Introduction

Computer vision (CV) as a scientific field aims to gain understanding of images and video. CV covers a wide range of tasks, such as object recognition, scene understanding, human motion recognition, etc. One of the core problems in visual recognition is image classification. Image classification is the problem of assigning a descriptive label to an input image from a fixed set of categories. Deep learning and convolutional neural network (CNN) have been shown to solve this hard image classification problem fast and with acceptable precision.

Early work on CNN dates back to 1989 with the LeNet network for handwritten digit recognition [7]. However, the early 2010s s started a new era for CNN applications by the introduction of AlexNet [5] for image classification. Growth of computing power, availability of huge datasets that can be used for training, and rapid innovation in deep learning architectures have paved the way for the success of deep learning techniques in recent years [11].

A CNN mainly consists of alternating convolution layers and pooling (subsampling) layers. Each convolution layer extracts features in the input by

© IFIP International Federation for Information Processing 2023
Published by Springer Nature Switzerland AG 2023
M. A. Wehrmeister et al. (Eds.): IESS 2019, IFIP AICT 576, pp. 117–129, 2023.
https://doi.org/10.1007/978-3-031-26500-6_10

applying trainable filters to the input. Later, the convolved feature is fed to an activation function, for example a Rectifier Linear Unit (ReLU) to introduce nonlinearity and obtain activation maps. Each pooling layer downsamples the activation maps to reduce computation and memory usage in the network. Features extracted from previous convolution and pooling layers are fed to a fully connected layer to perform classification. Typically, a softmax activation function can be placed following the final fully connected layer to output the probability corresponding to each classification label. For example, LeNet-5, a CNN for digit recognition, as depicted in Fig. 1, contains three convolution layers, two sub-sampling layers, and one fully connected layer [8].

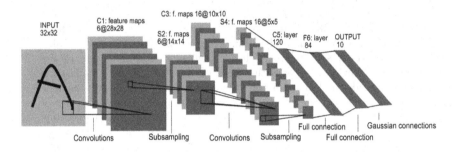

Fig. 1. Architecture of LeNet-5, a CNN for digits recognition [8]

In this paper, we develop an untimed SystemC model of GoogLeNet [12], a state-of-the-art deep CNN. Following the top-down specification approach for a classical system on chip design [1,2], our goal is to separate communication parts from computation parts. To achieve this, we exploit the fact that a neural network is a directed graph where the nodes are different layers in the network and edges connect neighboring layers.

Latest trends in cutting edge deep neural network architectures like ResNeXt (2016) [13], FractalNet (2016) [6], DenseNet [3] (2017), etc. show a substantial increase in the number of multiple parallel connections between layers in the network. This comes with a high level of thread-level parallelism, which parallel simulators can take advantage of for faster simulations.

The rest of this paper is organized as follows: Sect. 2 describes high level structure of GoogLeNet. Section 3 describes SystemC modeling details of each layer and the overall GoogLeNet model. Section 4 presents sequential and parallel simulation results with an analysis of valuable observations. At last, Sect. 5 concludes this case study.

2   GoogLeNet Structure

GoogLeNet is a deep CNN for image classification and detection that was the winner of the ImageNet Large Scale Recognition Competition (ILSVRC) in 2014 with only 6.67% top-5 error [12]. GoogLeNet was proposed and designed with computational efficiency and deployability in mind. The two main features of GoogLeNet are (1) using 1×1 convolution layer for dimension reduction and (2) applying network-in-network architecture to increase representational power of the neural network [12].

GoogLeNet is 22 layers deep when only layers with learned parameters are considered. The total number of layers (independent building blocks) is 142 distinct layers. The main constituent layer types are convolution, pooling, concatenation, and classifier. GoogLeNet includes two auxiliary classifiers that are used during training to combat the so-called vanishing gradient problem. The detailed types of layers inside GoogLeNet and the number of each type of layers are summarized in Table 1.

Table 1. GoogLeNet layer summary

Layer type	Count
Convolution	57
ReLU	57
Pooling	14
LRN	2
Concat	9
Dropout	1
InnerProduct	1
Softmax	1
Total	142

Our focus for now is on inference by using the proposed neural network architecture, and not the training for fine-tuning network parameters or suggesting improved network architecture. Therefore, our model does not include the two auxiliary classifier layers.

A schematic view of GoogLeNet is depicted in Fig. 2. An image is fed in on the left, and processed by all layers. Then, a vector with probabilities for the set of categories comes out on the right. The index of a class with a maximum probability is looked up in a table of synonym words that outputs the class of the object in the image, i.e. "space shuttle".

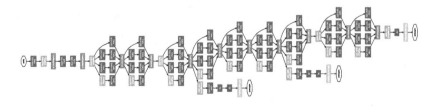

Fig. 2. GoogLeNet network with all the bells and whistles [12]

To get pre-trained network parameters, we have used the Caffe (Convolutional Architecture for Fast Feature Embedding) model zoo. Caffe is a deep learning framework originally developed at University of California, Berkeley, and is available under BSD license [4]. The GoogLeNet Caffe model comes with (1) a binary file `.caffemodel` that contains network parameters, and (2) a text file `.prototxt` that specifies network architecture. Including weights and bias values, there are a total of 5.97 million learned parameters in GoogLeNet.

We also use another text file listing 1000 labels used in ILSVRC 2012 challenge that includes a synonym ring or synset of those labels.

3   SystemC Modeling of GoogLeNet

We now describe how we design a SystemC model of GoogLeNet.

3.1   Reference Model Using OpenCV

Our SystemC model of GoogLeNet is implemented based on an original model using OpenCV 3.4.1, a library of computer vision functions mainly aimed for real-time applications written in C/C++ [10]. The OpenCV library was originally developed by Intel and is now free for use under the open-source BSD license. OpenCV uses an internal data structure to represent an n-dimensional dense numerical single-channel or multi-channel array, a so called `Mat` class. Therefore, our model uses the `Mat` data type to store images, weight matrices, bias vectors, feature maps, and class scores. This becomes practical while interacting with various OpenCV APIs.

Furthermore, OpenCV provides an interface class, `Layer`, that allows for construction of constituent layers of neural networks. A `Layer` instance is constructed by passing layer parameters and is initialized by storing its learned parameters. A `Layer` instance computes an output `Mat` given an input `Mat` by calling its `forward` method. We refer to this class as OpenCV `layer` for the rest of this paper. OpenCV also provides utility functions to load an image and read a Caffe model from `.prototxt` and `.caffemodel` files.

3.2   Modeling Goals

Given the OpenCV primitives, we set three design goals in the early stage of model development as follows:

1. *Generic layers*: Since GoogLeNet is composed of only a handful of layer types, the layers shall be parameterized by their attributes using a custom constructor. For example, a pooling layer shall be parameterized by its type (max-pooling or average pooling), its kernel size, its stride, and the number of padding pixels.

2. *Self-contained layers*: Each layer shall implement the functionality it requires without the need of an external scheduler to load its input or in case load its parameters. For example, a convolution layer shall have a dedicated method to load its parameters (weight matrix and bias vector) used only at the time of construction.

3. *Reuseable and modular code*: Since most CNNs share a common set of layers, the code shall be structured in a way to enable the feeding of any kind of CNN with minimum effort. For example, the layer implementation shall be organized as code template blocks and the SystemC model shall be autogenerated using only the network model defined by Caffe model files.

Note that these goals will allow us to easily generate a SystemC model also for other Caffe CNNs. At the same time, the models generated will have a well-organized structure that enables static analysis. Specifically, this allows us to perform parallel simulation with RISC [9], as described in Sect. 3.6 below.

3.3   Layer Implementation

Each layer in the CNN is defined as a sc_module with one input port and one output port. Ports are defined as sc_port and are parameterized by our own defined interface classes, mat_in_if and mat_out_if. These user-defined interfaces are derived from sc_interface and declare read and write access methods with a granularity of Mat. The choice of Mat for a granularity of port parameterization simplifies the design by focusing on the proper level of abstraction at this stage of modeling. As an example, the module definition of the first convolution layer conv1_7x7_s2 is shown in Listing 1.1.

As shown in lines 41–53 of Listing 1.1, each module has several attributes that are all defined as data members inside the class definition. For example, a convolution module is defined by its name, number of outputs, number of pixels for padding, kernel size, and number of pixels for stride. If a layer also has learned parameters, two Mat objects are defined as member variables to store the weight matrix and the bias vector. In that case, their values are initialized at the time of module construction. For example, a convolution module has a designated load method that reads pre-trained Caffe model files and stores weight and bias values in the weights and bias member variables.

```
1   class  conv1_7x7_s2_t  :  sc_core :: sc_module
2   {
3
4   public :
5       sc_core :: sc_port <mat_in_if>   blob_in ;
6       sc_core :: sc_port <mat_out_if>  blob_out ;
7
8       SC_HAS_PROCESS( conv1_7x7_s2_t );
9
10      conv1_7x7_s2_t ( sc_core :: sc_module_name n_ ,
11          String  name_ ,
12          unsigned  int  num_output_ ,
```

```
13        unsigned int pad_,
14        unsigned int kernel_size_,
15        unsigned int stride_,
16        unsigned int dilation_,
17        unsigned int group_) :
18      sc_core :: sc_module(n_),
19      name(name_),
20      num_output(num_output_),
21      pad(pad_),
22      kernel_size(kernel_size_),
23      stride(stride_),
24      dilation(dilation_),
25      group(group_),
26      weights(4, weight_sz, CV_32F, weight_data),
27      bias(4, bias_sz, CV_32F, bias_data)
28    {
29        load();
30        SC_THREAD(main)
31    }
32
33    void load();
34    void main();;
35    void run(std::vector<Mat> &inpVec,
36        std::vector<Mat> &outVec);
37
38  private:
39
40    String            name;
41    unsigned int      num_output;
42    unsigned int      pad;
43    unsigned int      kernel_size;
44    unsigned int      stride;
45    unsigned int      dilation;
46    unsigned int      group;
47    static const int  weight_sz[4];
48    unsigned int      weight_data[64*3*7*7];
49    static const int  bias_sz[4];
50    unsigned int      bias_data[64];
51    Mat               weights;
52    Mat               bias;
53
54  };
```

Listing 1.1. Conv1_7x7_s2 module definition

Each module has also a main thread that continuously reads its input port, computes results, and writes those to its output port. Data processing is handled by the run method. Here, we rely on OpenCV to perform the computations. The run method creates an instance of OpenCV layer and calls its forward method by passing references to input Mat and output Mat objects.

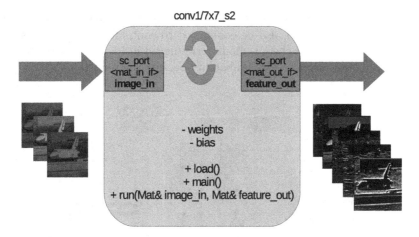

Fig. 3. Convolution layer

As an example, Fig. 3 illustrates the module defining the first convolution layer in GoogLeNet. The input to the module is a `Mat` object containing 3 color channels of 224×224 pixels of the input "space shuttle" image and the output is another `Mat` object containing 64 feature maps with the size of 112×112 pixels.

3.4   Netspec Generator

Since each convolution layer consists of different parameters, writing module declarations by hand is an error-prone and tedious task. Moreover, declaring all modules and queues in the top level GoogLeNet module, instantiating them with the correct parameters, and binding queues to neighboring modules is also a laborious task. Therefore, we develop a generator tool to automatically extract the network architecture from a textual protocol buffer `.prototxt` and the network learned parameters from binary protocol buffer `.caffemodel`. The generator, called **netspec**, is written in Python and uses Python interface to Caffe library, `pyCaffe`, in order to read `.caffemodel` and `.prototxt` files to construct its internal data representation of the neural network. `Netspec` then uses this data structure to generate SystemC code for all convolution modules and the top level GoogLeNet module with all interconnecting FIFO channels.

3.5   Validation by Simulation

A top level test bench validates our GoogLeNet SystemC model against the reference OpenCV implementation. The test bench instantiates our SystemC GoogLeNet module which contains all modules inside the network with all the interconnecting queues as Design under Test (DUT). It also instantiates a stimulus module to feed the design with images of size 224×224 with three color channels, and a monitor module to read the final class scores and output the label with the maximum probability (Fig. 4). To measure the performance of the model, our test bench can also be configured to continuously feed in a stream of images. In that case, a checker module is plugged inside the monitor to check the correct classification and its probability against the reference model.

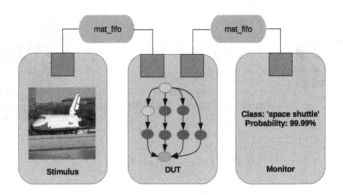

Fig. 4. Top-level test bench

3.6   Modular Source File Structure and Build Flow

Following good practices of SystemC coding, we place each module definition in a header file .hpp and the corresponding module implementation in a .cpp file. Also, to explore parallelism existing in the GoogLeNet system level model using RISC, we decide to split the implementation into two separate .cpp files. One .cpp file contains only methods that directly call OpenCV APIs ⟨*module_name_cv.cpp*⟩ and the other only contains the **main** method implementation that does not directly interact with OpenCV APIs ⟨*module_name.cpp*⟩. This prevents RISC from unnecessarily analyzing and instrumenting the code inside the OpenCV library, by only feeding object files generated from CV parts and not including OpenCV library source code.

First .caffemodel and .protoxt files are fed to the **netspec** tool to generate code for convolution modules and the overall GoogLeNet module. Once these modules are generated, all ⟨*module_name.cpp*⟩ and ⟨*module_name_cv.cpp*⟩ files are passed to the GNU compiler to generate the object files. Then, the object files are passed all together to the GNU linker with OpenCV and SystemC libraries to obtain the final executable. Running the executable requires the Caffe model files to load convolution modules with weights and bias values and also a synset file to read the class names.

The build flow specifically for RISC requires minimum effort due to our early decision to split the OpenCV source code from the model source code. Since RISC prefers all the source code in a single file, all header files and implementation files are merged into one file. This flattened source code, with object files generated from the OpenCV part of the modules, is then fed to RISC which then generates a multithreaded parallel executable.

4   Experimental Results

Our untimed SystemC model of GoogLeNet compiles and simulates success-fully with Accellera SystemC 2.3.1. For parallel simulation, we also compile and simulate the model using RISC V0.5.1 to speed up simulator run time. Both simulation results match the OpenCV reference model output.

4.1   Performance Setup

We use two different computer platforms to benchmark the simulations. The specifications of each platform are shown in Table 2. We name platforms based on the number of logical cores visible to the operating system. The number of logical cores is double the number of physical cores when hyper-threading technology (HTT) is enabled.

To have reproducible experiments, the Linux CPU scaling governor is set to 'performance' to run all cores at the maximum frequency, and file I/O opera-tions i.e. *cout* are minimized. SystemC 2.3.1 and OpenCV 3.4.1 are built with debugging information[1].

Moreover, the OpenCV library can be built with support for several paral-lel frameworks, such as POSIX threads (pthreads), Threading Building Blocks (TBB), and Open Multi-Processing (openMP), etc. We build OpenCV with the support for pthread to run in multithreaded mode and also without support for pthread to run only on a single-thread. Lastly, the stimulus module is configured to feed 500 images with size of 224×224 pixels to the model.

Table 2. Platform specification

Platform name	4-core host	8-core host	16-core host	32-core host
OS	CentOS 7.6	CentOS 7.6	CentOS 6.10	CentOS 6.10
CPU Model name	Intel E3-1240	Intel E3-1240	Intel E5-2680	Intel E5-2680
CPU frequency	3.4 GHz	3.4 GHz	2.7 GHz	2.7 GHz
#cores	4	4	8	8
#processors	1	1	2	2
#threads per core	1	2	1	2

---

[1] OpenCV has built with -O0 flag meaning (almost) no compiler optimizations.

4.2 Simulation Results

For benchmarking, we measure simulation time using Linux */usr/bin/time* under
CentOS. This time function provides information regarding the system time,
the user time, and the elapsed time. Measurements are reported for sequential
SystemC simulation using Accellera SystemC compiled with POSIX threads.
Parallel simulation is performed using RISC simulator V0.5.1 in non-prediction
(NPD) mode. Tables 3, 4, 5 and 6 show the measurements for each simulation
mode on the four different platforms using the single-thread and multithreaded
OpenCV. In case of parallel simulations, we set the maximum number of concurrent threads allowed by the RISC simulator to the number of available logical
cores on each platform.

Table 3. Measurement results on 4-core host (HTT off)

Time (s)	Single-thread		Multithreaded	
	Accellera	RISC	Accellera	RISC
User time	627.19	651.59	680.01	664.02
System time	1.55	1.11	34.26	18.26
Elapsed time	629.49	253.29	199.44	234.36
CPU utilization	99%	257%	358%	291%
Speedup	1x	2.48x	3.15x	2.68x

Table 4. Measurement results on 16-core host (HTT off)

Time (s)	Single-thread		Multithreaded	
	Accellera	RISC	Accellera	RISC
User time	912.79	921.95	1164.69	960.48
System time	34.76	42.19	705.22	134.25
Elapsed time	947.93	275.29	154.45	260.7
CPU utilization	99%	350%	1210%	419%
Speedup	1x	3.44x	6.13x	3.63x

4.3 Analysis

Table 3 allows the following observations:

1. **RISC introduces thread-level parallelism**
   RISC is faster than single-thread OpenCV with Accellera and it speeds up
   simulator run time up to 2.48x on the 4-core machine.

Table 5. Measurement results on 8-core host (HTT on)

Time (s)	Single-thread		Multithreaded	
	Accellera	RISC	Accellera	RISC
User time	621.49	961.44	1164.13	1046.39
System time	1.52	1.28	84.06	34.85
Elapsed time	622.68	254.07	184.09	232.57
CPU utilization	100%	378%	678%	464%
Speedup	1x	2.45x	3.38x	2.67x

Table 6. Measurement results on 32-core host (HTT on)

Time (s)	Single-thread		Multithreaded	
	Accellera	RISC	Accellera	RISC
User time	911.98	1177.02	2124.87	1299.86
System time	35.31	52.76	1838.35	224.84
Elapsed time	947.7	273.27	155.72	274.29
CPU utilization	99%	450%	2544%	555%
Speedup	1x	3.46x	6.08x	3.45x

2. **OpenCV parallelism is even faster than RISC**
   We observe that multithreaded OpenCV speeds up simulator run time using
   Accellera up to 3.15x on the 4-core machine. Therefore, thread-level parallelism in OpenCV primitives is more efficient than thread-level parallelism at
   SystemC level.
3. **Combining OpenCV and RISC parallelism does not deliver the best
   speedup**
   Since RISC and OpenCV threads unknowingly from each other compete for
   resources, exploiting parallelism in RISC and OpenCV at the same time does
   not increase the speedup. For example, multithreaded OpenCV using RISC
   (2.68x) performs worse than multithreaded OpenCV using Accellera (3.15x)
   on the 4-core machine.
4. **RISC performance improves slightly with OpenCV parallelism**
   RISC gains small speedup by also using parallelism in OpenCV. For example,
   RISC speeds up multithreaded OpenCV (2.68) in comparison with single-
   thread OpenCV (2.48x).

   Table 4 supports observations 1 through 4 as well. It also allows for the following observation:

5. **Performance does not scale by the number of cores**
   Quadratic increase in the number of cores only leads to double increase in
   performance. Relative good speed up to 3.15x on the 4-core machine does not

scale to 16-core machines and only gets 6.13x speedup compared to sequential single-thread simulator run time.

Table 5 and 6 use hyper-threading technology (HTT) and allow for the following observations:

6. **HTT is ineffective for this application**
   Enabling HTT slightly improves speedup from 3.15x on the 4-core machine without HTT to 3.38 on the 4-cores with HTT (8-cores). In case of 16-cores to 32-cores, performance has not improved at all.
7. **HTT substantially increases user and system time**
   We observe that the user and system times increase significantly with HTT turned on. At this point, the origin of this time increase is unclear for us. We will investigate this further in more detailed future research.

In summary, Fig. 5 shows the speedups for different sources of parallelism: single-threaded OpenCV using **RISC**, multithreaded **OpenCV** using Accellera and multithreaded **OpenCV** using **RISC**. The illustration shows a significant speedup using parallelism introduced by RISC and multithreaded OpenCV. It also demonstrates that combining OpenCV and RISC parallelism does not provide a remarkable speedup.

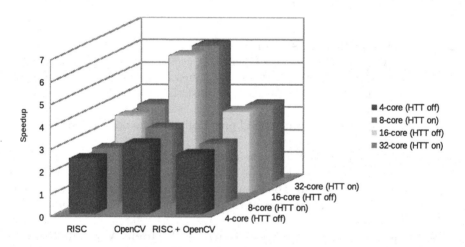

Fig. 5. Speedup comparison on different platforms based on the source of parallelism

5   Conclusion

In this report, we have described an untimed SystemC model of GoogLeNet using OpenCV 3.4.1 library. We also developed a tool to automatically generate SystemC code from Caffe model files. We successfully simulated the generated model using Accellera SystemC 2.3.1 and RISC V0.5.1.

Experimental results show significant simulation speedups using RISC, as well as using multithreaded OpenCV. Results also show that combining OpenCV and RISC parallelism did not deliver significant speedup.

References

1. Gerstlauer, A., Dömer, R., Peng, J., Gajski, D.D.: System Design: A Practical Guide with SpecC. Kluwer (2001)
2. Grötker, T., Liao, S., Martin, G., Swan, S.: System Design with SystemC. Kluwer (2002)
3. Huang, G., Liu, Z., van der Maaten, L., Weinberger, K.Q.: Densely connected convolutional networks. In: 2017 IEEE Conference on Computer Vision and Pattern Recognition, CVPR 2017, pp. 2261–2269. IEEE Computer Society (2017)
4. Jia, Y., et al.: Caffe: convolutional architecture for fast feature embedding. arXiv preprint arXiv:1408.5093 (2014)
5. Krizhevsky, A., Sutskever, I., Hinton, G.E.: ImageNet classification with deep convolutional neural networks. In: NIPS (2012)
6. Larsson, G., Maire, M., Shakhnarovich, G.: FractalNet: ultra-deep neural networks without residuals. CoRR abs/1605.07648 (2016)
7. Le Cun, Y., et al.: Handwritten digit recognition: applications of neural network chips and automatic learning. Commun. Mag. **27**(11), 41–46 (1989)
8. LeCun, Y., Haffner, P., Bottou, L., Bengio, Y.: Object recognition with gradient-based learning. In: Shape, Contour and Grouping in Computer Vision. LNCS, vol. 1681, pp. 319–345. Springer, Heidelberg (1999). https://doi.org/10.1007/3-540-46805-6_19
9. Liu, G., Schmidt, T., Cheng, Z., Mendoza, D., Dömer, R.: RISC Compiler and Simulator, Release V0.5.0: Out-of-Order Parallel Simulatable SystemC Subset. Technical report CECS-TR-18-03, CECpS, UCI (2018)
10. OpenCV Tutorials, Load Caffe framework models. https://docs.opencv.org/3.4/d5/de7/tutorial_dnn_googlenet.html. Accessed 11 May 2019
11. Sze, V., Chen, Y., Yang, T., Emer, J.S.: Efficient processing of deep neural networks: a tutorial and survey. Proc. IEEE **105**(12), 2295–2329 (2017)
12. Szegedy, C., et al.: Going deeper with convolutions. In: IEEE Conference on Computer Vision and Pattern Recognition, CVPR 2015, pp. 1–9 (2015)
13. Xie, S., Girshick, R.B., Dollár, P., Tu, Z., He, K.: Aggregated residual transformations for deep neural networks. CoRR abs/1611.05431 (2016)

An Efficient Lightweight Framework for Porting Vision Algorithms on Embedded SoCs

Apurv Ashish$^{(\boxtimes)}$, Sohan Lal, and Ben Juurlink

Technische Universität Berlin, Berlin, Germany
apurv.ashish@campus.tu-berlin.de, {sohan.lal,b.juurlink}@tu-berlin.de

Abstract. The recent advances in the field of embedded hardware and computer vision have made autonomous vehicles a tangible reality. The primary requirement of such an autonomous vehicle is an intelligent system that can process sensor inputs such as camera or lidar to have a perception of the surroundings. The vision algorithms are the core of a camera-based Advanced Driver Assistance Systems (ADAS). However, most of the available vision algorithms are x86 architecture based and hence, they cannot be directly ported to embedded platforms. Texas Instrument's (TI) embedded platforms provide Block Accelerator Manager (BAM) framework for porting vision algorithms on embedded hardware. However, the BAM framework has notable drawbacks which result in higher stack usage, execution time and redundant code-base. We propose a novel lightweight framework for TI embedded platforms which addresses the current drawbacks of the BAM framework. We achieve an average reduction of 15.2% in execution time and 90% reduction in stack usage compared to the BAM framework.

Keywords: Embedded systems · Computer vision · Autonomous systems · ADAS · TI TDA2xx

1 Introduction

Advanced Driver Assistance Systems (ADAS) can fully or partially assist a human during the driving process. The rapid rise of ADAS in the automotive industry is a prime example of the transforming capabilities of embedded vision technology. As shown in Fig. 1, the recent years have seen unprecedented growth in the field of embedded vision systems which has transformed it from being a research-oriented field to real industrial use-case. The significant increase in applications implementing embedded vision systems has been fuelled by the recent improvements in the area of embedded hardware [7], and availability of accurate and robust algorithms.

In principle, an ADAS can be implemented with different types of sensors such as radar, lidar or camera, however, considering the current trends,

© IFIP International Federation for Information Processing 2023
Published by Springer Nature Switzerland AG 2023
M. A. Wehrmeister et al. (Eds.): IESS 2019, IFIP AICT 576, pp. 130–141, 2023.
https://doi.org/10.1007/978-3-031-26500-6_11

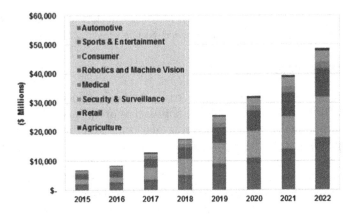

Fig. 1. Growth in embedded vision based applications [1]

camera-based applications are gaining more popularity [2]. The compute-intensive algorithms needed to process the camera inputs require specifically designed embedded hardware for delivering real-time performance. However, these algorithms cannot be ported on embedded platforms out of the box because most of the significant vision libraries such as OpenCV are x86 architecture based. Moreover, embedded platforms may use specific algorithm standards such as Texas Instrument's XDAIS standard [17] and proprietary compilers which are not standard compliant as GCC compilers. Furthermore, the limited memory constraints and specialised SIMD requirements are other factors which are not addressed in x86 algorithm development. Therefore, the commonly available algorithms have to be adapted before they can be ported on an embedded platform.

The TI's TDA2xx [11] platform, which is also the target platform for evaluation in this paper, provides a Block Accelerator Manager (BAM) framework [16] for porting of x86 algorithms on embedded platforms. The BAM framework provides abstraction and improves programmability, however, the BAM framework also has a few drawbacks such as graph-based execution, more complexity (exposed interfaces) and limited DMA functionalities which influence the porting time of the algorithms as well as the runtime of a ported algorithm.

In this paper, we propose and develop a new lightweight framework aiming to rectify the drawbacks of the BAM framework. The term lightweight essentially refers to the conceptual gravity of the framework, i.e., the reduced number of exposed interfaces and the required code changes during the process of algorithm porting. The proposed framework significantly reduces execution time and stack usage of an ported application.

In summary, following are the main contributions of the paper.

- We propose a novel lightweight framework for porting computer vision algorithms on embedded platforms.
- We address several drawbacks of the BAM framework such as graph-based execution, best block search.

– Our framework provides an average 15.2% reduction in execution time and 90% reduction in stack usage compared to the existing BAM framework.

2 Related Work

There exists a myriad of approaches to port vision algorithms on embedded platforms [3–6,8,14,18]. These diverse approaches are primarily dictated by the spectrum of different available processing platforms and different programming models associated with these platforms. The use of ARM-based architectures allows the use of standard programming models, however, they are not well suited for compute-intensive applications. Hence, the use of Graphics Processing Units (GPUs) or vector processors is encouraged to accelerate compute-intensive applications to achieve higher energy efficiency. However, GPUs do not support real-time operating systems (RTOS) or similar frameworks which makes it challenging for scheduling of hard real-time applications such as ADAS [9].

An ADAS application consists of different algorithms as building blocks and performance optimization strategies for the individual algorithms have been thoroughly investigated [10,12]. In [10], Nieto et al. propose a design and development methodology in the form of an iterative cycle which enables development of quick prototypes and further optimising and tuning specific aspects of the algorithms. Apart from the algorithm optimization, the "time to market" aspect has also been given fair attention. The difficulty of implementing an entire ADAS application on the hardware has led to hybrid solutions, where software and hardware implementations are combined to obtain the desired performance [5,6,14,18].

In [8], Kocić et al. propose a methodology for porting of ADAS applications on heterogeneous platforms based on the computational requirement of different algorithms. They propose a method of decoupling an application such as a face-detection application into different parts depending on the type of computational requirements and algorithm-specific optimizations. The pixel manipulation part of the application, for example, colour space conversion is ported on SIMD cores (GPUs), whereas face-detection algorithms are implemented on DSP cores.

J. Perez proposes porting of the brake-by-wire application to an embedded platform using a directed acyclic graph (DAG) [3]. The DAG is used to present the schedule of the application threads to six processing elements and the dataflow between the application threads, enabling task and temporal parallelism. Gostovic et al. propose a similar approach for porting of vision algorithms on an embedded platform [4]. They port an object detection algorithm to TI TDA2xx platform using a DAG. The DAG is used to model the data-flow between different computation nodes as well as the input and output nodes. TI provides Block Accelerator Manager (BAM) framework to expedite the process of porting vision algorithms on its embedded platforms [16]. We observe that the BAM framework has several drawbacks such as graph-based execution which leads to higher stack usage.

In contrast to the above-mentioned works, we propose an efficient lightweight framework for porting of vision algorithms on embedded platforms that rectifies several drawbacks of the existing BAM framework.

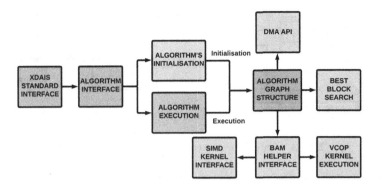

Fig. 2. Block diagram of BAM framework (adapted from [16])

3 Background

3.1 TDA2XX System-on-Chip

TI's TDA2xx [11] is a high-performance System-on-Chip (SoC) based on TI's open multimedia applications platform architecture. The architecture is specifically designed for front camera and surround view applications. The embedded vision engine [13] (EVE) subsystem in TDA2xx platform is a programmable vector processing engine, best suited for pixel manipulation operations such as color space conversion. TDA2xx platform supports four independent EVE subsystems.

EVE subsystem consists of an ARP32 scalar core, a vector coprocessor (VCOP) SIMD unit, and an Enhanced DMA (EDMA) controller. The ARP32 is a 32-bit scalar core and functions as the subsystem controller. The critical features of the scalar core include the control and coordination of EVE's internal interactions and interaction with other subsystems in the TDA2xx SoC. The VCOP is a SIMD engine with built-in loop control and address generation functionality. The EDMA block is the local DMA unit for the EVE subsystems. The EDMA unit is used for transferring data blocks between system memories (typically SDRAM and/or L3 SRAM) and internal EVE memories (data buffers).

3.2 Block Accelerator Manager Framwork

To expedite the process of porting algorithms on EVE subsystem, TI provides Block Accelerator Manager (BAM) framework. Figure 2 shows the block diagram of the BAM framework. The prime objective of the BAM framework is to simplify and speedup the porting of vision algorithms on TI's embedded platforms. The BAM framework achieves this objective by performing block-based image processing rather than processing full image frame in a single execution. The block-based processing is particularly suited to the needs of embedded platforms. Further, the BAM framework provides abstraction of the data movement and vector programming with the implementation of the directed acyclic graph.

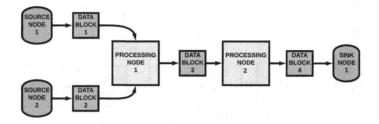

Fig. 3. Graph based execution (adapted from [16])

As shown in Fig. 2, the entire framework is subdivided into two parts: XDAIS interface and algorithm interface. The XDAIS interface is designed to enable multiple algorithms to coexist and share system resources. The co-existence of various algorithms is ensured by preventing 'hard-coded' use of critical system resources such as memory, DMA, and other accelerators. The XDAIS interface also enables a client application to query the algorithm specific requirements.

The algorithm-specific exposed interfaces are used by a client application for the execution of the algorithm. As shown in Fig. 2, the algorithm initialization interface is used by the client interface for the initialization of an algorithm's graph structure. In the algorithm initialization, the reference to specific APIs or functions is assigned to different nodes of the graph as designed by a programmer. The execution interface is used by the client application to call the graph structure at the time of execution. The algorithm-specific computation code is executed on the vector co-processor which supports a C-variant programming model. The computation code is called through a wrapper rather than an explicit call to the algorithm's computation function. As shown in Fig. 2, the helper functions basically initialize and execute the computation code. The input and output DMA transfers are realized by the source and sink nodes of the directed acyclic graph.

As shown in Fig. 3, the DAG represents the source/sink nodes for data input/output and processing nodes where the actual computation takes place. The source and sink nodes are programmed in standard C implementation which controls the TI's EDMA (Enhanced Direct Memory Access) unit. The processing nodes are implemented using Kernel-C, the TI's vector core programming language which handles actual algorithmic computation. Further details about the BAM framework can be found in [16].

4   Proposed Framework

Figure 4 shows the block diagram of the proposed framework called Efficient-BAM (E-BAM). The framework is designed to address drawbacks of the BAM framework as explained later. The proposed approach offers the same level of abstraction as provided by the BAM framework. We introduce substantial architectural changes to enhance the porting mechanism of vision algorithms on

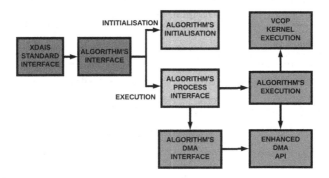

Fig. 4. Block diagram of the proposed framework (Color figure online)

TDA2xx platform which results in improved runtime performance. In the following subsections, we describe the main architectural changes to the existing BAM framework as well as the motivation for these changes. The green blocks in Fig. 4 highlights the major architectural changes in the proposed framework.

4.1 Modular Execution Model

The abstraction provided by the BAM is achieved primarily through a graph creation which results in higher stack memory usage because the graph structure is stored in the EVE on-chip memory during execution. Further, the graph object is referenced for every image block, which results in the call overhead. Hence, the graph creation adds to the overall execution time of an application.

In the proposed framework, instead of creating a wrapper such as a graph structure for the DMA operation, memory allocation and kernel execution, we perform these operations explicitly but in separate modules. This approach ensures lower stack usage, which is required to store the graph object and removes the latency due to repeated calls to the graph object. It also makes code more transparent and easy to extend due to its modular nature.

4.2 Enhanced DMA API

The block-based processing requires image blocks to be repeatedly fetched, processed and written back to the external memory. The BAM framework provides two basic functions, i.e., auto-increment and scatter-gather DMA. We extend DMA API with new features such as short inline functions, link transfer and chain transfer [15]. In general, an application may require repeated DMA transfers and the inline functions provide considerable improvement as it reduces the considerable function call overhead. The transfer use cases such as the transfer of input blocks between predefined memory location benefit from the link transfer feature because it removes the requirement of repeated parameters update. Similarly, the chain transfer feature automatically triggers the next transfer event after completion, hence, reducing the overhead of triggering a new transfer event.

Table 1. Qualitative comparison

Key features	BAM	E-BAM
Graph creation	Online	No graph creation
Best block search	Runtime	Offline
DMA	Generic TI DMA library	Enhanced DMA API

4.3   Best Block Search

In block-based image processing, dimensions of a block can have a significant effect on the performance of the application. The BAM framework offers a block optimization method, which deduces the optimum block dimensions, keeping valid memory allocation during the process. However, the drawback with this approach is the expensive processor cycles spent in search of optimal block dimensions during run-time.

In the best block search algorithm for the E-BAM framework, we initialize the block width and height of an image segment with the values of 16 and 8 respectively. The choice of this value is influenced by the SIMD width of the vector processor. In order to find optimum dimensions, we iteratively increase block dimensions and calculate the required memory size. When the required memory size exceeds the available memory, the block dimensions in the previous iteration are accepted as optimum block dimensions. This process ensures that all the data fits in the available memory without leaking or overwriting each other. Since the memory size of the EVE subsystem and image size are known before hand, the offline computation of the best block is justified. Further, since the ping-pong buffers in the EVE subsystems have only one read and write port, we ensure that the input and output blocks are not written back to the same buffer, thereby eliminating the waiting time before the block is read or written back to the buffer.

Table 1 shows the summary of key features of BAM and E-BAM frameworks. In the BAM framework, graph initialization takes place during runtime of an application, however, in the E-BAM framework, the graph structure is not used. On contrary, the E-BAM framework uses a mix of modular and sequential programming to provide the same level of abstraction with improved runtime performance. The best block search feature required for deducing the optimum block dimensions is calculated during the execution of an application, however, in the E-BAM framework, the best block search is performed offline. The BAM framework uses the generic TI DMA library with basic functionalities, whereas the E-BAM framework is equipped with the customized DMA API which supports additional features such as short in-line functions, link and chain transfers.

5   Experimental Setup

To evaluate our proposed framework, we use TI TDA2xx as the test platform. For benchmarking of the baseline BAM and proposed framework (E-BAM), we choose image pyramid generation as the test application. The choice of the image pyramid generator for evaluation is justified considering its complexity, intensive computation and DMA requirements. We perform benchmarking for the BAM and E-BAM frameworks using two different test vectors at three different frequencies (535, 600 and 650 MHz) for the TDA2xx platform. Although, the number of cycle count provides an accurate measure of the execution time, we present our results for three different frequencies as it reflects the practical use case where the TDA2xx platform can be operated at three different frequencies. We present execution time which is the average of five consecutive test runs for each test vector. Moreover, the timing measurement for TDA2xx platform is done in total number of processor cycles which can account even small variations.

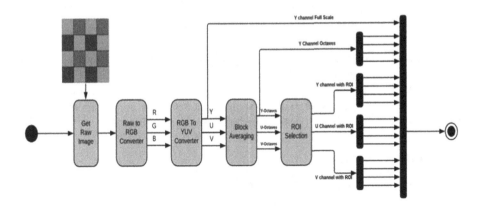

Fig. 5. Pyramid generation application

As shown in Fig. 5, the pyramid generation from raw camera input comprises of three different algorithms, all executing in parallel with the output of the first algorithm (RAW to RGB conversion) serving as the input for the second algorithm (RGB to YUV conversion) and the output of the second algorithm as the input for the third algorithm (Block Average). The application also requires synchronization of data-block movement to/from the external memory. The image pyramid application is also suitable for measuring the DMA overhead in both frameworks since it requires intensive DMA operations due to 17 different output images to be written back to off-chip memory.

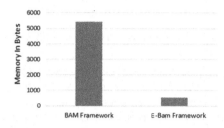

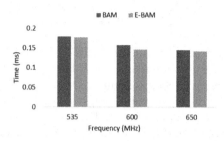

Fig. 6. Stack usage comparison   **Fig. 7.** DMA overhead

6   Experimental Results

We compare our efficient lightweight framework (E-BAM) with the existing BAM framework. We provide quantitative comparison of stack usage, execution time at algorithm level as well as at application level.

6.1   Stack Usage

Figure 6 shows the stack usage in bytes of E-BAM and BAM frameworks. We see that the proposed framework reduces 90% stack usage compared to the BAM framework. The significant reduction in the stack usage is the result of not using graph-based execution. The reduction in stack usage is very important as it opens up possibilities for processing of larger block dimensions.

6.2   DMA Overhead

The DMA overhead is the time which processor spends while waiting for completion of input or output block transfer. Figure 7 shows the proposed framework reduces the DMA transfer time compared to the BAM framework. The improvement is largely due to the improved DMA API with short inline function calls and additional features such as link transfer that we implemented for customized DMA transfers.

6.3   Execution Time at Algorithm Level

Figure 8 and Fig. 9 show the execution time of individual algorithms for BAM and E-BAM frameworks at 600 MHz. We see that all three algorithms (Raw to RGB, RGB to YUV and Block Average) achieve significant reduction in execution time compared to the BAM framework. The average reduction in execution time for the three algorithms is approximately 12%. The considerable reduction in execution time is due to the reduced complexity in the handling of kernel computation code in the E-BAM framework. The BAM framework involves function calls to BAM helper functions which act as an interface between the kernel computation code and the executed function. However, in the E-BAM, we initialize and call the kernel computation function explicitly.

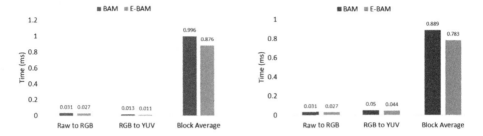

Fig. 8. Execution time for test vector 1   **Fig. 9.** Execution time for test vector 2

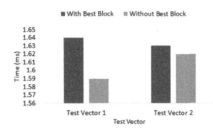

Fig. 10. Overhead of best block search

6.4   Best Block Search Overhead

As shown in Fig. 10, the best block search algorithm incurs a significant amount
of overhead in the BAM framework. The results shown in Fig. 10 are the average
of five consecutive runs for the same algorithm on two different test vectors
with platform running at 600 MHz. The execution without the best block search
is performed with the block dimensions of 256×16 (width $\times$ height), which
is calculated manually. The best block search increases the overall execution
time. The best block search can also lead to variation in the execution time
due to different amount of time incurred to search the best block, which can
be problematic to model in a time-budget based hard real-time system. The E-
BAM algorithm does not suffer from the overhead and execution time variation
since the best block is computed offline.

6.5   Execution Time at Application Level

Figure 11 and Fig. 12 show the execution time of the entire application (including the initialization, algorithmic computation and DMA transfer) for BAM
and E-BAM frameworks at three different frequencies. Again, we see that the
proposed framework reduces the execution time for different frequencies. The
average reduction in execution time is about 15.5% and 14.9% for the first and
second test vector, respectively. On average the proposed framework delivers an
average reduction in execution time of 15.2% compared to the BAM framework.
In addition to the reduced complexity in the handling of kernel computation code

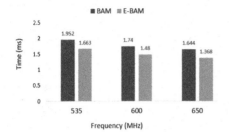
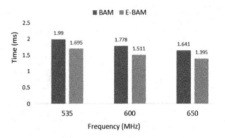

Fig. 11. Execution time for test vector 1   **Fig. 12.** Execution time for test vector 2

and enhanced DMA API, the removal of additional overhead due to repeated calls to graph object also contributes to the reduced execution time of the E-BAM framework.

7   Conclusions

The recent improvements in the performance of embedded hardware and accuracy of artificial vision systems have made autonomous vehicles a reality. However, different hardware architectures, programming models and varying use cases make porting and optimization of vision algorithms on embedded platforms an uphill task. The BAM framework provides a significant improvement in terms of programmability and abstraction for porting of vision algorithms on TI platforms, however, it has several drawbacks. We propose a novel lightweight framework E-BAM for porting of vision algorithms on TI platforms. We optimize the BAM framework by removing graph-based execution, shifting the best block search to offline and customizing the DMA API which supports additional features such as link transfers. Our proposed framework reduces average execution time by 15.2% along with 90% reduction in the stack usage compared to the existing BAM framework.

References

1. Computer Vision Hardware and Software Market to Reach $48.6 Billion by 2022 (2016). https://www.tractica.com/newsroom/press-releases/computer-vision-hardware-and-software-market-to-reach-48-6-billion-by-2022/
2. Global Automotive Camera-based ADAS Market 2018–2022 (2018). https://www.researchandmarkets.com/reports/4516968/global-automotive-camera-based-adas-market-2018
3. Gonzales-Conde Perez, J.L.: Analysis of Task Scheduling for Multi-Core Embedded Systems (2013)
4. Gostovic, M., Pranjkic, M., Kocic, O., Maruna, T.: Experience from porting complex algorithms on heterogeneous multi-core systems. In: IEEE 7th International Conference on Consumer Electronics-Berlin (ICCE-Berlin), pp. 235–238 (2017)

5. Hsiao, P.Y., Yeh, C.W.: A portable real-time lane departure warning system based on embedded calculating technique. In: IEEE 63rd Vehicular Technology Conference, VTC, vol. 6, pp. 2982–2986 (2006)
6. Jeng, M.J., Guo, C.Y., Shiau, B.C., Chang, L.B., Hsiao, P.Y.: Lane detection system based on software and hardware codesign. In: 4th International Conference on Autonomous Robots and Agents, ICARA, pp. 319–323. IEEE (2009)
7. Kisacanin, B., Bhattacharyya, S.S., Chai, S.: Embedded Computer Vision. Springer, Heidelberg (2008)
8. Kocić, O., Simić, A., Bjelica, M.Z., Maruna, T.: Optimization of driver monitoring ADAS algorithm for heterogeneous platform. In: 24th Telecommunications Forum (TELFOR), pp. 1–4. IEEE (2016)
9. Maghazeh, A., Bordoloi, U.D., Eles, P., Peng, Z.: General Purpose Computing on Low-Power Embedded GPUs: Has it Come of Age? (2013)
10. Nieto, M., Vélez, G., Otaegui, O., Gaines, S., Van Cutsem, G.: Optimising computer vision based ADAS: vehicle detection case study. IET Intell. Transport Syst. 10(3), 157–164 (2016)
11. Nikolic, Z., Agarwal, G., Williams, B., Pearson, S.: Ti Gives Sight to Vision-enabled Automotive Technologies. Texas Instruments, Technical report (2013)
12. Poudel, P., Shirvaikar, M.: Optimization of computer vision algorithms for real time platforms. In: 42nd Southeastern Symposium on System Theory (SSST), pp. 51–55. IEEE (2010)
13. Sankaran, J., Hung, C.Y., Kisačanin, B.: EVE: a flexible SIMD coprocessor for embedded vision applications. J. Signal Process. Syst. 75(2), 95–107 (2014)
14. Stein, G.P., Rushinek, E., Hayun, G., Shashua, A.: A computer vision system on a chip: a case study from the automotive domain. In: IEEE Computer Society Conference on Computer Vision and Pattern Recognition-Workshops, CVPR, p. 130 (2005)
15. TI: KeyStone Architecture Enhanced Direct Memory Access (EDMA3) Controller (2015). http://www.ti.com/lit/ug/sprugs5b/sprugs5b.pdf
16. TI: BAM Algorithm Framework User Guide (2019). http://www.ti.com/tool/processor-sdk-tdax. Linux and RTOS Processor SDK for Vision V3.06.00
17. Torud, S.: A Technical Overview of eXpressDSP-Compliant Algorithms for DSP Software Producers (2002). http://www.ti.com/lit/an/spra579c/spra579c.pdf
18. Velez, G., Cortés, A., Nieto, M., Vélez, I., Otaegui, O.: A reconfigurable embedded vision system for advanced driver assistance. J. Real-Time Image Proc. 10(4), 725–739 (2015)

Analysis

IoT Assistant for People with Visual Impairment in Edge Computing

Manoel José S. Júnior$^{(\boxtimes)}$, Horácio F. Oliveira, and Raimundo S. Barreto

Institute of Computing - Federal University of Amazonas, Manaus, Brazil
{manoel.junior,horacio,rbarreto}@icomp.ufam.edu.br

Abstract. We advocate that technology can make it possible to develop devices capable of recognizing people and objects, mainly with the aid of machine learning, computer vision, and cloud computing. Such devices can be used in the daily life of a visually impaired person, providing valuable information for guiding their steps, providing a better quality of life. This paper proposes an architecture that uses computer vision and applies deep learning techniques to an Internet of Things (IoT) assistant for people with visual impairment. Considering that an IoT device is a limited device, it's used edge computing to improve the proposed architecture so that the device may be updated over time. The recognized object is converted into Text To Speech (TTS), allowing the user to listen to what has been recognized and also the distance from the user to the object. Unrecognized objects are sent to the cloud, and the device receives a re-trained network. The proposed architecture has been implemented using known and proved technologies such as Raspberry Pi 3, USB camera, Ultrasonic Sensor module, You Only Look Once (YOLO) algorithm, Google-TTS, and Python. Experimental results demonstrate that our architecture is feasible and promising.

Keywords: IoT · Machine learning · Edge computing · Computer vision

1 Introduction

Accessibility is the design of products, devices, services, or environments for people with disabilities in such a way that it guarantees the safety and physical integrity of people with special needs or reduced mobility, thus ensuring the right to come and go, and even to enjoy the same environments as a person without special need [3]. Accessibility usually can be viewed as the ability to access, but focused on enabling access for people with disabilities, or special needs, or enabling access through the use of assistive technology.

Recent advances have changed the way humans have lived. Computational devices have evolved to provide a better user experience in all areas of knowledge. However, there is a class of people who can benefit from technology to increase the quality of life and thus to live a healthy, normal life.

© IFIP International Federation for Information Processing 2023
Published by Springer Nature Switzerland AG 2023
M. A. Wehrmeister et al. (Eds.): IESS 2019, IFIP AICT 576, pp. 145–154, 2023.
https://doi.org/10.1007/978-3-031-26500-6_12

According to [1], it is predicted that there would be about 38.5 million people blind in 2020 (out of a total global population of 7.7 billion), equivalent to approximately 5 percent of the population. Most of these people live in confinement, without interaction with the outside world, because they can not move around due to the absence of adequate support.

Despite the existence of several technologies, such as GPS and ultrasonic sensor, that enable a walking stick to measure the distance to objects, there is an opportunity to improve accuracy detection and inform what is the object type ahead of the user, such as a person, a dog, a hole, and so on.

The Internet of Things, or IoT, is a system of interrelated computing devices, objects, animals or people that are provided with unique identifiers and the ability to transfer data over a network without requiring human-to-human or human-to-computer interaction. This includes everything from cellphones, glasses, coffee makers, washing machines, headphones, lamps, wearable devices, and almost anything else you can think. Nowadays, IoT devices are capable of performing sophisticated detection and recognition tasks to provide interactions between humans and their physical environment.

The inclusion of Deep-learning on IoT devices often demands real-time requirements. For example, a security camera that does object-recognition tasks usually requires a detection latency of less than 500 ms to capture and respond to target [14].

Considering that an IoT device is a limited device, it's used edge computing to improve the proposed architecture, in such a way that the device can be updated over time. The recognized object is converted into speech, allowing the user to listen to what has been recognized and also the distance from the user to the object. Unrecognized objects are sent to the cloud, and the device receives a re-trained network.

The remainder of this paper is organized as follows. In the next section, the related work is presented. Our proposed system is then explained in Sect. 3. We show and discuss the implementation of the system in Sect. 4. The results and future work are described in Sect. 5. Finally, in Sect. 6 the conclusions and future work is presented.

2   Related Work

There are other projects aimed to help people with visual impairment. For instance, the approach described by Choudhury et al. in [6] shows the transformation of images in Braille using You Only Look Once (YOLO) algorithm. However, there are other faster ways to guide a person without the need to interpret signals. In [12], a prototype uses algorithms to detect real-life symbols, such as a bathroom, a subway, or a snack bar. However, it does not help the user reaching these locations safely during the route. Several objects and obstacles can cause accidents in your percussion. In contrast, Alam et al. used various technologies to find the location within a closed environment, but visually impaired people need devices that enable their interaction with the outside environment [7].

In our proposed architecture, the glasses allow an outdoor experience, giving more freedom and quality of life to the user of the device. It is also possible to receive guidance quickly without the need for interpretation. This work also adds value to the work [12], being able to find the obstacles present in the path of the visually impaired.

Therefore, in comparison with the above studies, it is possible to observe that much work has already been done. However, what highlights this project is that this proposal aims to identify the distance of objects, then converting video in real time in speech format (TTS). Also, objects present in the user route that was not identified is sent to the cloud. In the cloud, a neural network retrains the model and returns an update of the software, so the device becomes more robust and customized to the user. All of this is possible using resources for IoT, Machine Learning, and Cloud Computing. In the next section, the proposed model is discussed in details.

3   System Proposed

The model presented allows the use of two sensors: an ultrasonic sensor to measure the distance and the camera to capture images.

The captured distance is converted into voice, using Google Text to Speech (TTS). The photo captured by the camera goes through a resizing process to be inserted in an already trained network that receives the photo and goes through a classification process using the YOLO algorithm. YOLO is a neural network-based object detection algorithm. It receives an image as input and returns another picture with boxes around possible objects known to the already trained network. These objects then receive a label. Joseph Redmon created an implementation of this study, called darknet, developed in C language and CUDA [2].

The model uses this already trained network that covers a variety of objects. To better present the strategy, one unidentified object was used. Because it is impracticable to train this network in computational constrained IoT devices, the concept of edge computing is used, allowing near, local, cloud-based devices to take care of the processing job.

He Li has demonstrated in his work that it is possible to implement machine learning on IoT devices with the help of edge computing to share computing resources, not overloading devices since they have processing, memory and power limitations [8]. Based on this principle, the unidentified object can be shared with a PC with greater processing power (edge device) and, then, this object goes through a process of deep learning matching.

The most widely used neural networks for processing deep learning workloads are Convolutional Neural Network (CNNs), which convert unstructured image data into structured object label data. Generally, CNNs work as follows: first, a convolution layer scans the input image to generate a feature vector; second, an activation layer determines which feature in the vector must be activated for the image under inference; third, a layer of pooling reduces the size of the resource vector [14].

The training result is a file with changed weights. After finishing the training, the device is notified that there is an update to be made. When the user accepts the update, the device can identify the previously unidentified object.

4   Implementation of the System Design

4.1   Architecture

In Fig. 1 it is possible to see the division of architecture in 3 main parts. The first part is the input of the system. A Raspberry-based device represents the second part of system (the software components used in the design), and the third part is the output of the system.

The system receives as input the images provided by the USB camera, which is represented by the label 1 in the figure. The distance of the nearest object is then informed by the ultrasonic sensor represented by label 2 of the figure.

In the center of the image, represented by the label 3, is the Raspberry device. The implementation uses the *Raspbian version 2019-04-08-raspbian-stretch-full*, this version contemplates Python v3 by default. Python was used to create the state machine and to do the integration of the modules. *Numpy, Pandas*, and *Keras* is used to do some manipulation and testing. Also, the *Jupyter notebook* had a key role in the information sharing to simulate edge computing.

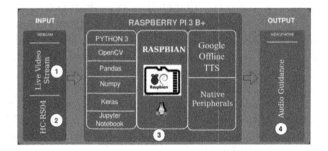

Fig. 1. Block diagram.

4.2   Software Design

The state machine developed to provide the user with the option of choosing a mode of use, it is represented by a finite automaton, where each state represents an option, as shown in Fig. 2.

(a) *Instruction*: represented by the symbol *q0*, the device initiates in it when it is turned on, we call initial state. Here the device speaks the available options, giving the user the options to choose which mode to use.

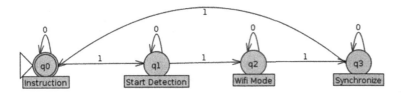

Fig. 2. State machine of system

(b) *Start Detection*: this state, represented by the symbol *q1*, is responsible for triggering the camera to capture the frames for analysis of the algorithm and to measure the distance of the objects. In the next, step the detection algorithm is started. If the object is recognized, the object name and distance from the nearest object is sent to the speech synthesizer. If the object has not been identified, the image is stored, and the speech synthesizer only receives the distance from the object. Even though the object has not been identified, the user is informed that there is an unidentified object and how far away it is, as shown in Fig. 3.

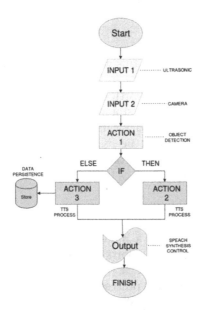

Fig. 3. Detection cycle

(c) *Wi-Fi Mode*: this state, represented by the symbol *q2*, is the mode of connectivity, responsible for searching for wireless networks. The device identifies which Wi-Fi networks are available and uses the text to Speach, to indicate the SSIDs available for the user to connect manually. SSID is the acronym for "service set identifier." The choice for a WI-FI network and the password, were defined directly from the code at the time of implementation. To make this feature available to the user, we map a strategy that is described in the Sect. 5

(d) *Synchronize*: represented by the symbol *q3*, if the device is connected to the internet, in this state, the unidentified images are sent to the server. The cloud or receive neural network updates, ensuring synchronization (see Fig. 4).

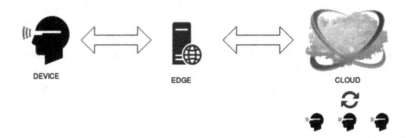

Fig. 4. Synchronize

If the device never connects to the network, it will not be possible to add new objects to be recognized. In this way the architecture would not work and not reach the expected goal.

Another key point that is worth highlighting: the proposed architecture allows communication and cloud storage, which is to say if we have multiple such devices around the world, they can share the experience of the other user. This also allows the device that needs to upgrade, does not necessarily need to retrain its network, because in the cloud, there may already be a request previously made by another user.

4.3 Hardware Design

Raspberry Pi 3 Model B + is a mini-PC that runs Linux distributions like Raspbian and Ubuntu but also supports other operating systems like Windows 10 IoT and custom versions of Linux. It has a BCM2837B0, Cortex-A53 (ARMv8) 64-bit SoC @ 1.4 GHz Broadcast processor. 1 GB of LPDDR2 SDRAM. 2.4 GHz and 5 GHz IEEE 802.11b/g/n/ac Wireless LAN, Bluetooth 4.2, BLE.

Was used a Logitech C270 HD model camera for live streaming. A powerful feature of the Raspberry Pi is the GPIO (general purpose input/output) pin line along the top edge of the board. A 40-pin GPIO header is found on all current Raspberry Pi cards [4]. The GPIO was used to add buttons and connect the ultrasonic sensor. Although raspberry provided input and output (IO) interfaces, it was necessary to develop hardware to feed the ultrasonic modules separately and add resistors because of the voltage difference. It is possible to see in Fig. 5 the developed circuit board.

Fig. 5. First prototype

In Fig. 6, there are two buttons. The first button allows you to select the usage mode (*Instruction, Start Detection, Wi-fi Mode,* or *Synchronize*). The second button is the confirmation button. To improve usability, braille translations are placed next to the buttons.

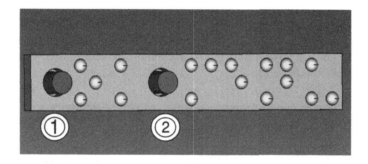

Fig. 6. Buttons with braille translations.

5   Results and Future Work

5.1   Accuracy Test

In this section, the architecture validation is showed. The first experiment was to perform the detection algorithm on an object known by the network. The time for this operation was 29 s, with 93% accuracy.

Then the same test was performed, but for an unidentified object. The time for this operation was 33 s. We noticed that when the object is not identified, the network takes a little longer to reply.

With the unidentified object collected, was calculated the time to send the image to the edge with a resolution of 600 × 480 pixels. The time spent on sending the image was of 4 s. The quality of the connection at the time of the upload was 7.02 Mbps.

With the image at the edge, the training time was 5 min, taking into account the configuration of the device with GPU of 12 GB-RAM.

Returning re-training network, the time to upgrade the device was 4 minutes, for a 300 MB size file, and the quality connection at that time was 9.95 Mbps for download. The results can be seen in Fig. 7.

TEST	Time	Accuracy
Known object	29 seconds	93%
Unknown object	35 seconds	0%
Send image to Edge	4 seconds	
Download network weights	4 minutes	
New object added	30 seconds	80%

Fig. 7. Test result.

On the left of Fig. 8, the photo of the eagle is an example of the system, at the opposite end we have a hole in the middle of the street, this was the image used to retrain the network.

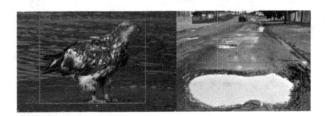

Fig. 8. Comparison.

We also did distance experiments based on the specification of the ultrasonic sensor. Its range of action is of 2 cm to 4 m. It was observed with some experiments ranging from 1 to 4 m, As can be seen in Fig. 9.

The accuracy testing of the YOLO algorithm shows 80 to 100% accuracy for objects recognized by the network. With the addition of new objects, accuracy remained at the same margin of success.

5.2   Problems Occurred

Since we did not have a computer with good performance to retrain the network in edge, we had to use the cloud to simulate this environment. Another problem

Fig. 9. Ultrasonic module accuracy test.

was encountered during developed the prototype. The response time was between 12 to 14 min to identify an object. It was circumvented the problem by using the raspberry GPU, decreasing response time considerably to 10 to 30 s. With this result, it was identified that the optimization of the operating system, can improve even more the response time.

5.3 Future Work

As a future work, we will implement voice recognition to integrate with *TTS* allowing the user can not only know the available *Wi-Fi* networks, but he can also speak the name of the network to which he wants to connect, desired network password.

6 Conclusion

This paper examined an architecture that uses computer vision and applies deep learning techniques to an IoT device.

The combination of technologies has shown that some substantial resources can be shared to achieve a common good.

He also showed that the advancement of technology could benefit people with visual limitations, bringing a better quality of life and interaction with the outside world.

Also, it has been demonstrated that these smart devices can be improved over time and adaptable to the routine of their users, making the device unique and personal.

All the tests performed presented good experimental results, thus demonstrating that our architecture is feasible and promising.

Acknowledgement. This research was partially supported by Priority Program for the Training of Human Resources - CAPDA/SUFRAMA/MDIC, under the terms of Federal Law n° 8.387/1991.

References

1. The Lancet Global Health. https://www.thelancet.com/journals/langlo/article/PIIS2214-109X(17)30293-0/fulltext. Accessed 19 Apr 2019
2. Joseph Chet Redmon. https://pjreddie.com/darknet/yolo/. Accessed 18 Apr 2019
3. United Nations - Convention on the Rights of Persons with Disabilities. https://www.un.org/development/desa/disabilities/convention-on-the-rights-of-persons-with-disabilities.html. Accessed 21 May 2019
4. Raspberry Organization. https://www.raspberrypi.org/documentation/usage/gpio/. Accessed 23 Apr 2019
5. Heya, T.A., Arefin, S.E., Chakrabarty, A., Alam, M.: Image processing based indoor localization system for assisting visually impaired people. In: 2018 Ubiquitous Positioning, Indoor Navigation and Location-Based Services (UPINLBS), Wuhan, pp. 1-7 (2018)
6. Choudhury, A.A., Saha, R., Shoumo, S.Z.H., Tulon, S.R., Uddin, J., Rahman, M.K.: An efficient way to represent braille using YOLO algorithm. In: 2018 Joint 7th International Conference on Informatics, Electronics & Vision (ICIEV) and 2018 2nd International Conference on Imaging, Vision & Pattern Recognition (icIVPR), Kitakyushu, Japan, pp. 379–383 (2018)
7. Alam, M.M., Arefin, S.E., Alim, M.A., Adib, S.I., Rahman, M.A.: Indoor localization system for assisting visually impaired people. In: 2017 International Conference on Electrical, Computer and Communication Engineering (ECCE), Cox's Bazar, pp. 333–338 (2017)
8. Li, H., Ota, K., Dong, M.: Learning IoT in edge: deep learning for the internet of things with edge computing. IEEE Netw. $32(1)$, 96–101 (2018). https://doi.org/10.1109/MNET.2018.1700202
9. Lan, F., Zhai, G., Lin, W.: Lightweight smart glass system with audio aid for visually impaired people. In: TENCON 2015–2015 IEEE Region 10 Conference, Macao, pp. 1–4 (2015)
10. Fadlullah, Z.M., et al.: State-of-the-art deep learning: evolving machine intelligence toward tomorrow's intelligent network traffic control systems. IEEE Commun. Surv. Tutorials $19(4)$ 2432–2455, Fourthquarter 2017
11. Verhelst, M., Moons, B.: Embedded deep neural network processing: algorithmic and processor techniques bring deep learning to IoT and edge devices. IEEE Solid-State Circ. Mag. $9(4)$, 55–65, Fall 2017
12. Rani, K.R.: An audio aided smart vision system for visually impaired. In: 2017 International Conference on Nextgen Electronic Technologies: Silicon to Software (ICNETS2), Chennai, pp. 22–25 (2017)
13. Yao, S., et al.: Deep learning for the internet of things. Computer $51(5)$, 32–41 (2018)
14. Tang, J., Sun, D., Liu, S., Gaudiot, J.: Enabling deep learning on IoT devices. Computer $50(10)$, 92–96 (2017)
15. Mahdavinejad, M.S., Rezvan, M., Barekatain, M., Adibi, P., Barnaghi, P., Sheth, A.P.: Machine learning for internet of things data analysis: a survey. Digital Commun. Netw. $4(3)$, 161–175 (2018)
16. Mendki, P.: Docker container based analytics at IoT edge video analytics usecase. In: 2018 3rd International Conference On Internet of Things: Smart Innovation and Usages (IoT-SIU), Bhimtal, pp. 1-4 (2018)

Analysis of Low Cost Sensors Applied to the Detection of Obstacles in High Voltage Towers

Guido Szekir Berger, Matheus Fellype Ferraz, Álvaro Rogério Cantieri, and Marco Aurélio Wehrmeister[✉] [iD]

Federal University of Technology - Paraná (UTFPR), Curitiba 80230-901, Brazil
{berger,mferraz}@alunos.utfpr.edu.br, alvaro.cantieri@ifpr.edu.br, wehrmeister@utfpr.edu.br

Abstract. In several applications involving autonomous navigation of robotic systems, the selection of the applied sensors is a criterion of extreme importance, allowing the correct identification of obstacles within a safe detection range. Thus, the characterization of the sensors becomes a necessary step in identifying the terms of use and limitations of the different devices analyzed, in order to focus on the correct choice for different applications and scenarios of use. This paper discusses a study about the use and characterization of various ultrasonic sensors and low cost laser sensors applied to the detection of components commonly used in high voltage towers, which have distinct properties and geometries, for means of evaluating a possible use in future autonomous systems through unmanned aerial vehicles. Based on the results obtained, it was possible to identify the characteristics of use of the analyzed sensors in a controlled environment and in an uncontrolled environment, providing vital information for the correct choice of sensors applied to autonomous navigation in high voltage towers scenarios.

Keywords: Ultrasonic sensor · Laser sensor · Power lines components · Sensors properties

1 Introduction

Technological trends on Unmanned Aerial Vehicles (UAVs) indicate that increasingly high-risk operations must be less trusted to human pilots and progressively more to the autonomous capabilities dictated by a reliable sensory system embedded to an UAV, through which the environment around the aerial vehicle is perceived in order to complete its mission [6]. Therefore, any type of robot should have the ability to perform a reliable detection of obstacles and to act in a timely manner to prevent static or dynamic obstacles found in unknown environments [5]. Different technologies can be employed for distance measurements in complex environments. State-of-the-art technologies such as laser scanner sensors

© IFIP International Federation for Information Processing 2023
Published by Springer Nature Switzerland AG 2023
M. A. Wehrmeister et al. (Eds.): IESS 2019, IFIP AICT 576, pp. 155–166, 2023.
https://doi.org/10.1007/978-3-031-26500-6_13

from manufacturers SICK, Velodyne and Hokuyo offer a good resolution and area of operation, but at a high cost, also requiring the UAVs to be medium or large due to their weight and demanding a high computational performance [8].

Accordingly, an approach involving low cost sensors, such as ultrasonic (US) and laser sensors, can be presented as an attractive alternative applied to sensory systems embedded to UAVs to detect obstacles in electric distribution lines scenarios. The investigation of the laser and US sensors as to their distribution, opening angle, quality of measurements on different object geometries and environmental influences should be investigated in order to obtain parameters of choice of the best types of sensors suitable for high voltage line inspection. In this context, the presented experiment aims to evaluate each proposed sensor in different environmental conditions and to identify their characteristics and behaviors towards commonly used high voltage tower parts. Besides, the conducted tests generated generated results that are estimates of the use of different types of sensors on different types of parts, usually used in high voltage towers, making it possible to establish a relation with the use of these sensors in future robotic navigation systems on UAVs applied to high voltage towers. The structure of this article consists of Sect. 2, where the methodology found in the literature on the use and influences of US and laser sensor architecture are presented. The characteristics of the US and laser sensors are discussed in Sect. 3, and Sect. 4 displays methods adopted to conduct the experiments. Section 5 presents the results obtained and in Sect. 6, final considerations are discussed.

Related Works. Achieving a robust, low-cost sensing system capable of detecting all obstacles present in highly complex scenarios is a difficult task that requires knowing the environment at all times. Many of the collision avoidance systems are directly related to the use of two-dimensional laser range measurement sensors, which are normally used as scanning sensors due to wide performance range. However, laser sensors fail under conditions of high solar incidence and require diffuse reflection to detect objects, unlike US sensors that are not affected by interference from external environments or even under foggy conditions [13]. On the other hand, US sensors have the disadvantage of being susceptible to errors due to variations in air temperature [11] and reading errors consequent to the angle of actuation [2]. Nevertheless, in order to solve most of the detection problems related to laser and US sensors, the combination of these devices is presented in the literature as an advantageous solution for detection of obstacles. The work conducted by Niwa, Watanabe and Nagai, revealed the need to identify the best working angles for ultrasonic sensors to be used in unmanned aerial vehicles, exploring the limitations of using the HC-SR04 ultrasonic sensors and, through the results, indicating the feasibility of its application in UAVs for obstacle detection [9]. Also seen in the contribution by Singh and Borschbach, several interference characteristics of US sensors were explored in outdoor environments. As a result, it was possible to identify some causes of external factors such as angulation, influence of movement and atmospheric pressure so that future sensorial systems can compose an architecture in robotic units to detect obstacles [12]. Approaches involving the characterization of different types of sensors, especially the US and laser sensors, have resulted in the creation of efficient detection and autonomous navigation systems with low cost sensors. As seen in Gageik, Müller and Montenegro, the use of SRF02 ring-architected sensors in a UAV was explored with the intention of detecting obstacles in a 360° range. The results showed that the behavior of 12 ultrasonic sensors when tested on dynamic objects, in this case a moving wall, allowed the UAV to maintain a distance of 1m from the obstacle. However, the system presented very limited detection results in addition to the adoption of a ring distribution whose operating angles generated problems in distance readings. As final observations, the author identifies a real need to use laser-type sensors to compose a more robust detection system [4]. To circumvent the problems, another work carried out by Gageik, Müller and Montenegro, used a low-cost sensory system embedded to an UAV that was composed of several types of sensors, among them 16 laser sensors and 12 US sensors, disposed in a ring architecture and acting as a system detection for collision avoidance. Hence, the final results provided a low-cost sensor architecture which presented operational capabilities of detection and diversion of obstacles, such as people and walls, proving to be a reliable and cheaper system than state-of-the-art systems, in addition to being of easy implementation and low computational load [4]. In the research conducted by Krämer and Kuhnert, different types of approaches related to the interference generated around the electromagnetic field on different types of US sensors were discussed. Besides, as the impact generated by the rotations of the motors near the sonars was evaluated, a scanning laser sensor was implemented, whose range and detection capacity contributed to the effectiveness of the work [8]. Considering that several contributions using US and laser sensor architectures require results that prove their real applicability, the characterization of different sensors incorporated as a unit of detection and prevention of obstacles in UAVs should be considered as a step of extreme importance, which provides a perspective of different types of sensory technologies and their effective application in different scenarios [14].

2   Characteristics of Ultrasonics and Laser Sensors

US sensors have excellent characteristics of versatility as they operate at low power consumption, offer great ranges of performance, and are not affected by light and dust, resulting in a sensor that is extremely useful for outdoor use. In addition, US sensors can measure transparent objects such as glass, which means that the color of the object does not interfere, further increasing the use of US sensors in external navigation systems [6]. However, these sensors are susceptible to reading errors due to variations in air temperature, and the angle of incidence and low directionality, respectively [15]. The operation mode of US sensors is based on a method called Time of Flight (TOF) that works by emitting a high frequency sound pulse by means of an emitter. When colliding with an object, the sound wave is reflected, returning to the ultrasonic sensor receiver. Based on the period of time between the pulse sent and the received pulse, the distance between the sensor and the object [7] is calculated as shown in Eq. (1).

$$Distance = Speed_{sound} * Time/2 \tag{1}$$

However, when more than one US sensor is operating in close proximity, it may occur that one sonars receives the echo of another signal emitted by adjacent sonars, resulting in incorrect readings of distances due to disturbance caused by neighboring sound waves [2]. This phenomenon is known as crosstalk and occurs in almost all types of US sensors, usually in systems that are composed of multiple sensors that adopt the ring architecture, whose goal is to completely cover a given robotic architecture. Environments that have a smooth surface may also contribute to crosstalk reading errors due to wave reflections generated by US sensors [3].

US sensors depend on the speed of sound to calculate the time between the emission of the sound wave and the received echo at the receptor. On the other hand, the speed of sound used in the linear equation applied to ultrasonic sensors may be modified in function of the environment conditions, such as temperature and humidity, to which the sensors are exposed. Consequently, the reading data are affected by inaccuracies caused by variation of environmental conditions. According to the International Standard Atmosphere (ICAO), the speed of sound is 340 m/s under standard environmental conditions (20 °C temperature with 0% humidity and 101.3 kPa). Nonetheless, as the temperature rises, the speed of sound increases approximately 0.6 m/s for each 1 °C. This fluctuation can be observed in the system represented in Eq. 2, where c is the speed of sound (331.4 @ 0 °C), T is the temperature (°C) and H is the value of the environmental relative humidity [11].

$$c = 331.4 + (0.606 * T) + (0,0124 * H) \tag{2}$$

In this context, the implementation of temperature sensors operating collectively to the US sensors is a way to compensate for the disturbances caused by climate change and to grant greater precision in the acquisition of distance readings [11]. As for the laser sensors, their operation method is similar to that of the US sensors, where a pulsating laser beam is emitted and reflected on an object, the time between the emission and the return of the reflected pulse is calculated [1]. Different types of sensors can be applied to detect obstacles, however, rotary sensors of LIDAR (Light Detection and Ranging) type have been outstanding in terms of reading stability and present high degree of applicability, in addition to their low cost.

Laser sensors present greater range of actuation than US sensors, allowing 360° detection of the space surrounding them. Classical methods of detection and prediction of obstacles based on computational vision strategies use a high computational load, which for sensors like YDLidar this is not a problem since it does not depend on that quantity of processing power [10].

3   Choice of Sensors

To achieve the objective of this contribution, different techniques to investigate characteristics of multiple types of ultrasonic and laser sensors must be approached. Thus, information regarding opening angle range, evaluation of performance in internal and external environments, accuracy and measurement errors must be identified. The final composition of the sensors should identify with precision all the objects studied and analyzed in different scenarios. The choice of sensor models, presented in Table 1, is based on their detection range, which should be at least 2 m, a distance that is considered as the minimum necessary to safely detect the components present in a high voltage towers. The cost of the sensors was also considered in order to validate only sensors that are available in the market at a low cost, as presented in Table 1.

Table 1. List of sensors used.

Sensor	Range	Resolution	Current	Price
HC-SR04	2–400 cm	0,3 cm	15 mA	1$
RCW-0001	1–450 cm	1 mm	2.8 mA	1$
US-15	2–400 cm	0,5 mm	2.2 mA	2$
US-16	2–300 cm	3 mm	3.8 mA	2$
VL53L0X	0–200 cm	1 mm	19 mA	5$
VL53L1X	0–400 cm	1 mm	16 mA	15$
YDLidar X4	0–10 m	1 mm	380 mA	99$
LidarLite V3	0–40 m	1 cm	135 mA	130$

4   Experimental Methods

The schematic presented in Fig. 1 illustrates the configurations adopted to conduct the indoor tests, in which, see Fig. 1, the analyzed sensors are positioned in a 15 cm height from the test table and the detected parts (P1–P8) are moved in 10 cm intervals over a 1 mm accuracy measuring tape. As the performance of the sensors are susceptible to environmental conditions, a humidity and temperature sensor (DHT11) was coupled to the US sensory systems in order to compensate variations and the tests happened in diffuse sunlight. Therefore, the assessment was based on different configurations for the US sensors, which were (a) individually with no angle variation, (b) individually with 0°, 15°, 25° and 35° angle apertures and (c) in pairs with 0°, 15°, 25° and 35° angle apertures. Besides, the YDLidar used a 10° setup instead of the default 360° scan.

As stated previously, the objective of this article is to evaluate each sensor used in indoor and outdoor experiments and to identify their characteristics and behaviors towards 7 pieces that commonly compose a high voltage tower as presented in Table 2. In addition, a steel plate (P8) was also evaluated due to its

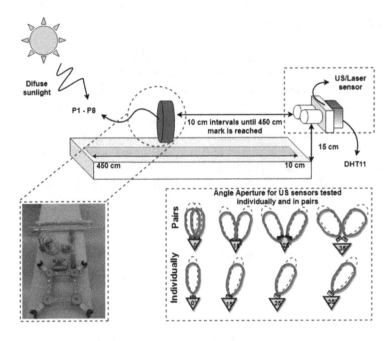

Fig. 1. Experimental procedures.

easy-to-detect geometric shape, which will provide an estimate of the maximum performance of all the sensors used.

The controller board used to process all US sensors data was the Arduino Mega 2560, and the values read were transmitted via serial output to a computer. For every 10 cm covered by the parts used in the tests, 45 samples were taken. For the YDLidar sensor, a raspberry Pi 3B + controller board was selected, through which the developed code stored all its reading information.

Table 2. Components of high voltage towers used during the experiments.

Component	Abbreviation
Aluminum cable 91 AAC	P1
Aluminum cable 61 AAC	P2
Aluminum cable OPGW	P3
Glass insulator	P4
Connector bracket	P5
Vibration damper	P6
Spacer damper	P7
Steel plate	P8

After acquiring preliminary results, the sensors were tested in an external environment, only those that obtained the best results in terms of linearity in the detection of obstacles were selected. It is important to highlight that the studied sensors are low cost elements, which results in the presence of few inaccurate responses. Thus, one of the purposes of this work is to report the functional characteristics of the studied sensors, including their imprecision, as a function of the acquired values from the tested objects.

5 Experimental Results

5.1 Average Obstacle Detection

For sensors that compose obstacle detection systems, a preliminary response of their maximum and minimum operating range becomes essential to estimate their influences and accuracy during operation. In this context, the results, as seen in Fig. 2, reveal the average distance that can be detected on components P3 and P4 towards all sensors used in this experiment within a range of 50 cm to 450 cm. In this preliminary assessment, certain components such as P4 can be detected on a range up to 400 cm by laser sensors and 300 cm by most of the US sensors, which are considered relatively safe distances within an obstacle prediction scenario. In the case of piece P3, several failures were identified, indicating that for a sensory system that must detect cables or lines distributed along an power line, these sensors have unsatisfactory results.

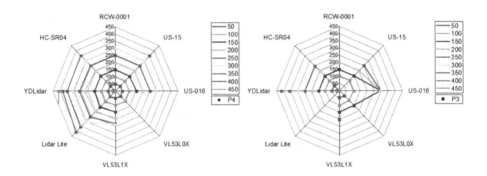

Fig. 2. Average distance of parts P4 and P5.

5.2 Out of Range

The reliability of the sensor to detect obstacles is directly related to the amount of real data samples captured in order to understand the complexity of the scenario in which it is acting. To evaluate the amount of real numerical information generated, 30 samples for each 10 cm covered by the sensors were acquired, identifying the reading error rate, i.e. the amount of "Out of Range" reported when attempting to detect objects, as shown in the Fig. 3.

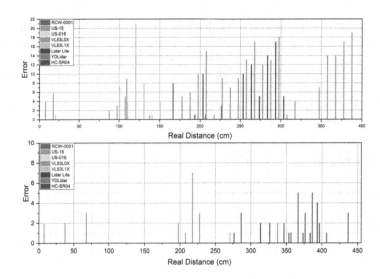

Fig. 3. Number of distance reading errors. on top result of errors in P5 and down P8.

Therefore, this analysis indicates the degree of reliability for each sensor on detecting different materials. Obstacles like the P8 piece presented low repeatability of reading errors. For smaller parts such as P5, several detection failures were identified, especially by the US015 sensor.

5.3 Mean Angular

The evaluation of sensors with respect to their maximum angulation range is important as there is a limit of detection for each type of US sensor. Objects that are outside this range are not detected by the sensor and therefore may represent an accident within an autonomous system. Even in cases where several ultrasonic sensors are being used close to each other, problems related to crosstalk may occur. For this purpose, the general mean responses obtained from each US sensor were investigated individually on opening angles of 15°, 25° and 35°. These angular apertures were controlled by a stepper motor to grant a high degree of angular accuracy, as displayed in Fig. 4.

Subsequently, the same metrics were performed with two US sensors alongside each other (Fig. 5), applying the same angular variation to identify perturbations regarding their proximity during operation. The comparison of responses obtained in tests performed by the sensors individually and by side-by-side revealed problems associated with crosstalk.

The comparison of angular measurements between individually tested and paired US sensors shows that at angles greater than 25° severe distortions in distance measurements occurred, and, based on the proximity between sensors and their angle of aperture, the Crosstalk phenomena is pointed out. In the evaluations of different angles, the results that conferred the best effect with

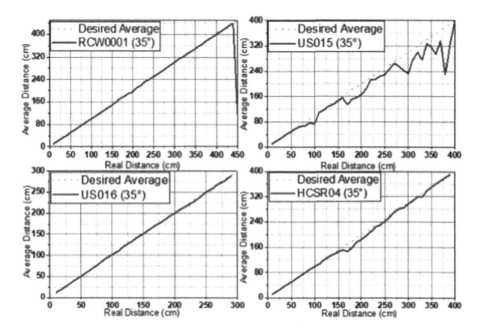

Fig. 4. Angular measurements on individually tested US sensors on P8 object.

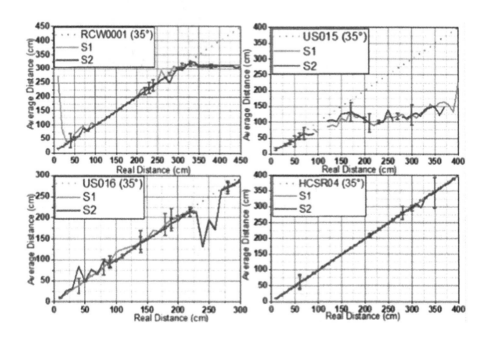

Fig. 5. Angular measurements on US sensors tested in pairs on P8 object.

greater angulation opening were determined by 25° and the sensor that presented the best results was the HC-SR04 sensor and the worst result was given by the US-015.

5.4   Influence on External Environment

Estimating the influence of external environmental conditions on the sensors and analyzing how much their accuracy is affected is extremely important to evaluate the usefulness of the sensory system. To test the external influence, the sensory unit was coupled to an UAV with the sensors that presented the best results based on their generated responses to all the materials tested. On a servo motor, a VL53L1X sensor with two HC-SR04 sensors were placed in a 25° angle and an amount of 400 samples were acquired from a wall in an external environment, performing a scan of 180° and covering intervals of 50 cm until reaching the maximum range of 4 m. In this context, it was possible to evaluate the performance of these sensors when being used in scanning an external environment, as Fig. 6 shows.

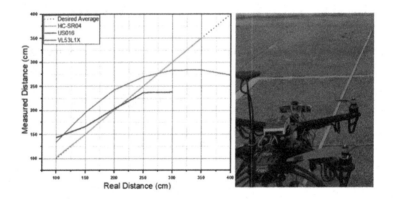

Fig. 6. Average responses generated by the influence of the external environment.

As seen in Fig. 6, the VL53L1X presented a fall in the readings e low linearity due to exposition to external environments, proving its ineffectiveness in a real inspection scenario. On the other hand, the HC-SR04 obtained satisfactory results, since it acquired a great margin of linearity even with constant movement provided by the servo motor, differently from the US-016 sensor, that presented the worst responses in this scenario. When tested in the ground, the YDLidar presented promising results in detection (Fig. 7), obtaining a sample amount of 800 reading points for each meter of distance from the wall with a aperture of 10°, culminating in a total distance of 10 m.

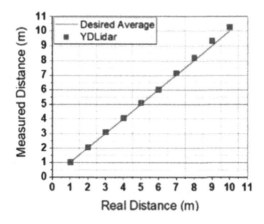

Fig. 7. Average responses generated by YDLidar in external environment.

6   Conclusion

The studies conducted in this work resulted in the conclusion that low cost sensors can be used to detect components of a high voltage tower. Among the US sensors, the HC-SR04 sensor presented the best responses, by maintaining linearity as it collected data correspondent to the distances from the obstacles even with constant movement created by the servo motor. Moreover, it was verified that when the US sensors were disposed close to each other, satisfactory responses from RCW-0001, US-016 and HC-SR04 were obtained in a maximum aperture of 25°. It was established that materials P1, P2 and P3 are the most difficult parts to detect, since they presented responses with values lower than 3 m. As a suggestion for future works, the application of ultrasonic sensors that actuate with a large range could generate better results in the case of the materials cited, but it is important to consider that the actuation spectrum for US sensors is a cone, in order to obtain a actuation area without sunlight interference, differently from the laser sensors. Based on the responses presented by the laser sensors, the YDLidar conferred full detection capabilities in both the internal and external environments, in addition to the lowest quantity of "Out of Range" values, and the high degree of precision when fixed on a determined target. The responses obtained in this contribution can be applied to future projects in sensor architectures, in order to test it in an UAV used to monitor high voltage towers and to gather conclusive information regarding the characterization of the low cost sensors utilized in high voltage tower inspections.

References

1. Adarsh, S., Kaleemuddin, S.M., Bose, D., Ramachandran, K.I.: Performance comparison of infrared and ultrasonic sensors for obstacles of different materials in vehicle/robot navigation applications. In: IOP Conference Series: Materials Science and Engineering, vol. 149, no. 1 (2016). https://doi.org/10.1088/1757-899X/149/1/012141

2. Arbor, A.: Using coded signals to benefit from ultrasonic sensor crosstalk. In: IEEE International Conference on Robotics and Automation, pp. 2879–2884 (2001)
3. Chandrashekar, L.: Characteristics of sonar sensors for short range measurement. Int. J. Eng. Res. Technol. (IJERT) **3**(11), 340–344 (2014)
4. Gageik, N., Müller, T., Montenegro, S.: Obstacle detection and collision avoidance using ultrasonic distance sensors for an autonomous quadrocopter. Int. J. Eng. Trends Technol. **17**(2), 1–6 (2012)
5. Holz, D., Nieuwenhuisen, M., Droeschel, D., Schreiber, M., Behnke, S.: Towards multimodal omnidirectional obstacle detection for autonomous unmanned aerial vehicles. ISPRS - Int. Archives Photogram. Remote Sens. Spatial Inf. Sci. XL-1/W2(September), 201–206 (2013). https://doi.org/10.5194/isprsarchives-xl-1-w2-201-2013
6. Ishihara, M., Shiina, M., Suzuki, S.N.: Evaluation of method of measuring distance between object and walls using ultrasonic sensors. J. Asian Electr. Veh. **7**(1), 1207–1211 (2009). https://doi.org/10.4130/jaev.7.1207
7. Khoenkaw, P., Pramokchon, P.: A software based method for improving accuracy of ultrasonic range finder module. In: 2nd Joint International Conference on Digital Arts, Media and Technology 2017: Digital Economy for Sustainable Growth, ICDAMT 2017 (1), pp. 10–13 (2017). https://doi.org/10.1109/ICDAMT.2017.7904924
8. Krämer, M.S., Kuhnert, K.D.: Multi-sensor fusion for UAV collision avoidance. In: International Conference on Mechatronics Systems and Control Engineering, pp. 5–12 (2018). https://doi.org/10.1145/3185066.3185081
9. Niwa, K., Watanabe, K., Nagai, I.: A detection method using ultrasonic sensors for avoiding a wall collision of quadrotors. In: 2017 IEEE International Conference on Mechatronics and Automation, ICMA 2017, pp. 1438–1443 (2017). https://doi.org/10.1109/ICMA.2017.8016028
10. Oh, J., Choe, D., Yun, C., Kim, J., Hopmeier, M.: Towards the development and realization of an undetectable stealth UAV. In: Proceedings - 3rd IEEE International Conference on Robotic Computing, IRC 2019, pp. 459–464 (2019). https://doi.org/10.1109/IRC.2019.00097
11. Shin, S., Kim, M.H., Choi, S.B.: Ultrasonic distance measurement method with crosstalk rejection at high measurement rate. IEEE Trans. Instrum. Meas. **68**(4), 972–979 (2019). https://doi.org/10.1109/TIM.2018.2863999
12. Singh, N.A., Borschbach, M.: Effect of external factors on accuracy of distance measurement using ultrasonic sensors. In: Proceedings - International Conference on Signals and Systems, ICSigSys 2017, pp. 266–271 (2017). https://doi.org/10.1109/ICSIGSYS.2017.7967054
13. Wu, X., Cai, Y., Chen, Y., Wang, K.: Transmission line unmanned aerial vehicle obstacle avoidance system incorporating multiple sensing technologies. In: Journal of Physics Conference Series, vol. 1069, no. 1, pp. 1–6 (2018). https://doi.org/10.1088/1742-6596/1069/1/012025
14. Xie, X., Liu, Z., Xu, C., Zhang, Y.: A multiple sensors platform method for power line inspection based on a large unmanned helicopter. Sensors (Switzerland) **17**(6), 1–17 (2017). https://doi.org/10.3390/s17061222
15. Zhmud, V.A., Kondratiev, N.O., Kuznetsov, K.A., Trubin, V.G., Dimitrov, L.V.: Application of ultrasonic sensor for measuring distances in robotics. In: Journal of Physics: Conference Series, vol. 1015, no. 3 (2018). https://doi.org/10.1088/1742-6596/1015/3/032189

Monitoring of an Artificial DNA in Dynamic Environments

Mathias Pacher$^{(\boxtimes)}$ and Uwe Brinkschulte

Johann Wolfgang Goethe-Universität, 60629 Frankfurt am Main, Germany
{pacher,brinks}@es.cs.uni-frankfurt.de

Abstract. In the last decade, bio-inspired techniques like self-organization and emergence have been in the focus of several research projects to deal with the challenge to develop, to configure and to maintain highly distributed and embedded systems. In biology the structure and organization of a system is coded in its DNA, and several dynamic control flows are regulated by the hormone system. We adapted these concepts to embedded systems using an artificial DNA (ADNA) and an artificial hormone system (AHS). Based on these concepts, highly reliable, robust and flexible systems can be created. These properties predestine the ADNA and AHS for the use in future automotive applications.

We showed in recent publications several examples for the use of the ADNA/AHS approach dealing with automotive applications running on the processors of a single distributed system of processors. We also showed how to adapt the ADNA/AHS approach so that different systems using the ADNA can merge at run-time if these systems come in communication range and form a new system including the ADNAs of both systems. In this contribution, we present and evaluate a way to monitor the ADNA and its tasks. This can be used to realize paywalls or security mechanisms for the ADNA.

Keywords: Artificial DNA · Artificial hormone system ·
Self-organization · Dynamic merger and separation · Monitoring

1 Introduction

In the last decade, bio-inspired techniques like self-organization and emergence have been in the focus of several research projects to deal with the challenge to develop, to configure and to maintain highly distributed and embedded systems. They are a promising approach to handle real-world applications such as control tasks in cars which may suffer from processor or task failures and must adapt to a changing environment. In biology, the structure and organization of a system is coded in its DNA. The dynamic control flows are regulated by the hormone system. We adapted these concepts and developed the Artificial DNA (ADNA) by which the blueprint of the structure and organization of an embedded systems can be described. The ADNA can be stored in every processor of the

© IFIP International Federation for Information Processing 2023
Published by Springer Nature Switzerland AG 2023
M. A. Wehrmeister et al. (Eds.): IESS 2019, IFIP AICT 576, pp. 167–178, 2023.
https://doi.org/10.1007/978-3-031-26500-6_14

system. The tasks described by the ADNA are distributed to the processors in a self-organizing way by an artificial hormone system (AHS). The combination of ADNA and AHS allows to create very robust and flexible systems providing self-X features like self-configuration, self-optimization and self-healing. We have already demonstrated these features in previous publications [3] using an autonomous self-balancing robot vehicle.

We showed in [12] that the concept of ADNA and AHS can successfully be applied to a dynamic environment of distributed systems which merge and separate at run-time. Merging different systems of distributed processors makes sense

- if the processors of one system offer functionalities which are not offered by the other system or
- if the processors of one system offer these functionalities but promise a better performance in terms of execution time, reaction time, needed memory space or power consumption or
- if processors of a system fail and some of its tasks can run on the other system's processors in order to guarantee graceful degradation.

If tasks of other systems run on processors of the own system, it is mandatory to monitor them as they use the computing power of the own processors. Thus, it is reasonable to let the other system's owner pay for using the computing power. Another reason is to guarantee security of the own system, i.e. to prevent the other systems ADNA to harm the functionality of the own system. In this paper, we show

1. ways to adapt the ADNA and AHS to run such a monitoring task on the own system and
2. an evaluation of this task.

The conception of both the ADNA and the AHS is presented in Sect. 3. The architecture of the ADNA/AHS system for dynamic environments is presented in Sect. 4. In Sect. 5 we discuss the evaluation results while Sect. 6 concludes this paper.

2   Related Work

Our approach relies on self-organization in automotive applications and embedded systems and have been explained in detail in [1,3]. Other approaches on this topic have been addressed especially at the ESOS workshop [4]. None of the presented approaches at ESOS deals with self-organization using DNA-like structures.

Several authors in [10] emphasize the necessity of redundant processors and sensors in future autonomous cars, however, they do not propose such a fine-grained approach as possible by the ADNA. In [7] a redundancy scheme for processors in automotive applications is proposed where a voting algorithm is used to determine the validity of results of redundant processors. This is different from our approach which improves the exploit of redundancy using the ADNA.

To realize DNA-like structures, we have to describe the building plan of an embedded system in a compact way so it can be stored in each processor core. Therefore, we have adapted well known techniques like netlists and data flow models (e.g. the actor model [9]) to achieve this description. However, in contrast to such classical techniques our approach uses this description to build the embedded system dynamically at run-time in a self-organizing way. The description acts like a DNA in biological systems. It shapes the system autonomously to the available distributed multi/many-core hardware platform and re-shapes it in case of platform and environment changes (e.g. core failures, temperature hotspots, reconfigurations like adding new cores, removing cores, changing core connections. etc.). This is also a major difference to model-based [11] or platform-based design [14], where the mapping of the desired system to the hardware platform is done by tools at design time (e.g. a Matlab model). Our approach allows very high flexibility and robustness due to self-organization and self-configuration at run-time while still providing real-time capabilities.

In [13] the concept of trust is used in self-organizing systems as a mechanism to enable agents to decide if they execute tasks for other agents. Self-aware computing systems (SACS) [8] are a new research topic and deal with modeling systems and their environments. The models help to interact with and to manipulate the environment according to user-specified goals. None of these approaches deals with DNA-like structures at run-time.

3   Conception of the Artificial Hormone System and DNA

This section briefly describes the concept of the artificial DNA and the underlying artificial hormone system (AHS). For detailed information see [1,2,5].

3.1   Artificial DNA

The approach presented here is based on the observation that in many cases embedded systems are composed of a limited number of basic elements, e.g. controllers, filters, arithmetic/logic units, etc. This is a well known concept in embedded systems design. If a sufficient set of these basic elements is provided, many embedded real-time systems could be completely built by simply combining and parametrizing these elements. Figure 1 shows the general structure of such an element. It has two possible types of links to other elements. The *Sourcelink* is a reactive link, where the element reacts to incoming requests. The *Destinationlink* is an active link, where it sends requests to other elements.

Each basic element is identified by a unique Id and a set of parameters. The sourcelink and the destinationlink of a basic element are compatible to all other basic elements and may have multiple channels.

The Id numbers can be arbitrarily chosen, it is important only that they are unique. Figure 2 gives an example for a PID controller which is often used in

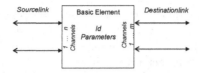

Fig. 1. Structure of a basic element (task)

Fig. 2. Sample basic element

closed control loops. This element has the unique Id = 10 and the parameter values for P, I, D and the control period. Furthermore, it has a single sourcelink and destinationlink channel.

Embedded systems can be composed by using these basic elements as building blocks. Figure 3 shows a very simple example of a closed control loop based on basic elements. An actor (defined by its resource id, e.g. a motor) is controlled by a sensor (also defined by its resource id, e.g. a speed sensor) applying a constant set-point value. If we consider the closed control loop to be the *function* of the embedded system, it is divided by the ADNA into *tasks*: the basic elements.

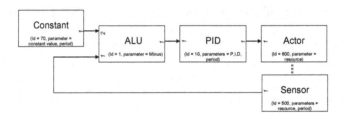

Fig. 3. A closed control loop consisting of basic elements

If a sufficient set of standardized basic elements with unique Ids is available, an embedded system will no longer be programmed, but composed by connecting and parametrizing these elements. The building plan of the system can be described by a compact netlist containing the basic elements, its parameters and interconnections. This netlist can be stored in each processor of the system. It therefore represents a digital artificial DNA (ADNA) which allows to partition and build the system at run-time. Detailed examples and a very memory efficient format to store an ADNA are presented in [1, 2].

3.2   Building the System from Its ADNA by the AHS

Using the ADNA the system is divided into functions (e.g. control functions, closed control loops, data processing, filtering, etc.) and tasks (the basic elements of a function). Each processor has a local copy of the ADNA and therefore knows all these functions, tasks and their interconnections. It passes this information to the local instance of its artificial hormone system (AHS). The AHS is a completely decentralized mechanism to assign tasks to distributed computing nodes, see [5]. It uses artificial hormones (emulated by short messages) to find the most suitable computing node for each task based on node capability, load and tasks interconnection. It can also detect failing nodes and tasks by missing hormone values. So all basic elements of the ADNA are assigned as tasks at run-time by the AHS to the available processors. These elements are then interconnected according to the ADNA. This means the functions build themselves at runtime in the best possible way on the available processor resources. In case of a processor failure the basic elements are autonomously reassigned and reconnected to other processors as long as there is enough computing power left. Assignment and reassignment of tasks is done in real-time (with a time complexity of $\mathcal{O}(n)$, where n is the number tasks) as proven in [5] and demonstrated by a self-balancing robot vehicle in [2]. The ADNA therefore enables an extremely robust and fine-grained distribution of functions to processors. A function is not bound to a single processor but can be split among several processors on the task (basic element) level. In case of processor failures only the affected basic elements are automatically moved to other processors. Additionally, the importance of basic elements can be derived from the ADNA and used to operate the most important parts if not enough computation power is left to assign all tasks. A detailed description of building a system from the ADNA and complex examples can be found in [2].

3.3   Application of the ADNA and AHS Concept to Automotive Systems

In automotive applications the system functions (anti-locking brake, traction control, stability control, engine control, driving assistants, infotainment, etc.) are executed by the car's processors, the ECUs (electronic control units). To enable advanced concepts like autonomous driving, many of these systems require fail-operational behavior. So a highly robust design is necessary. In classical approaches, a function is usually mapped to an ECU (e.g. anti-locking brake to the anti-locking brake ECU). To provide fail-operational behavior, critical ECUs have a backup ECU (1:1 redundancy). In more advanced approaches like e.g. the AutoKonf project [6], several ECUs share a single backup ECU (p:1 redundancy) to reduce the overhead. These approaches apply redundancy on the *function level*. In contrast, the self-healing process of the ADNA and AHS concept provides redundancy on the *task (basic element) level*. This enables a very fine-grained and efficient use of the available ECU resources.

It is simple to see that the failure probability of a $p:1$ redundancy approach like in the AutoKonf project with q failing ECUs is

$$P(q) = \begin{cases} 1 - \frac{(k-q)!}{k!} \cdot \frac{(a-1)!(p+1)^{q-1}\left((a-q)(p+1)+qr\right)}{(a-q)!} & \text{if } q \leq a \\ 1 & \text{else} \end{cases}$$

where $k = n + a$ is the number of ECUs with n being the basic number of ECUs and $a = \lceil \frac{n}{p} \rceil$ being the redundant ECUs. $r = (n \bmod p) + 1$ is the number of remaining ECUs is n is not a multiple of p.

The failure probability of the ADNA/AHS approach can be computed much easier as there are only two choices: Either there are enough ECUs to run all tasks; the failure probability is 0 then, or there are not enough ECUs to run all tasks; the failure probability is 1 then. Figure 4 compares the failure probability of a 1:1 redundancy approach with ADNA-based redundancy using $k = 2n$ (12 ECUs each) and a conventional 2:1 redundancy approach with ADNA-based redundancy using $k = 1.5n$ (9 ECUs each). The 1:1 and 2:1 redundancy approaches produce a failure probability greater than 0 if more than a single ECU fails and converge to 1. They reach the failure probability 1 when four (2:1 redundancy) and seven (1:1 redundancy) ECUs fail. The redundancy due to the ADNA-based redundancy behaves much smoother: Their failure probabilities are 0 up to four ($k = 1.5n$) and seven ($k = 2n$) failing ECUs and then jump to 1. Therefore, it makes sense to apply the ADNA/AHS concept to the automotive area. This is especially interesting in the context of the approach of this paper as the number of fully functional ECUs may dynamically be increased.

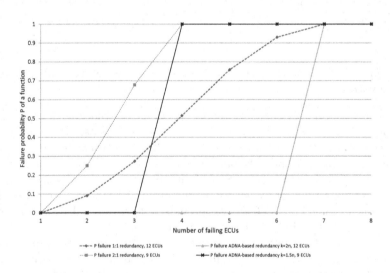

Fig. 4. Fail-operational limits of different redundancy configurations

4   Architecture of the ADNA/AHS Approach for Dynamic Environments

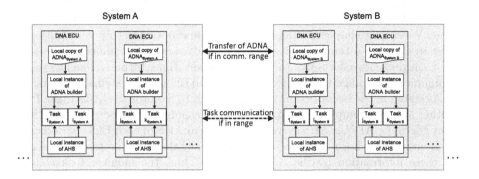

Fig. 5. Architecture

Figure 5 shows the architecture of the ADNA/AHS approach in dynamic environments. Each ECU of system A has a local copy of the system's ADNA. Therefore, their ADNA builders can parse the ADNA and segment it into tasks. It also derives the communication relations between these tasks as well as timing, logging and all other relevant parameters to run the application. Each instance of a basic element becomes a task in the embedded system. Then, the AHS tries to assign tasks to the most suitable ECU. The suitability is indicated by specific hormone levels. With the ADNA, the suitability of an ECU for a task can be derived automatically by the ADNA builder from the Id of the basic element in the ADNA representing the task and the features of the ECU. As an example, a basic element with Id = 10 (PID controller) performs better on a ECU with better arithmetic features while memory is less important. So the appropriate hormone levels can be calculated automatically by the ADNA builder and assigned to the AHS. More details on the ADNA building in a single system are presented in [1]. The same building process also performs in system B.

If the systems get in communication range (e.g. by C2C or C2X communication), they exchange their ADNAs, thus enabling the other system to process and run the other ADNA and building up a new system running the tasks of both ADNAs.[1] This enables to run tasks on the best suited currently available ECUs thus increasing the quality of task execution (by e.g. increasing the computation frequency in a closed control loop) on the one hand and to enable the execution of the ADNA despite massive failures of a system's ECUs on the other hand.

---

[1] Therefore, the ADNAs of the different systems needs to be tagged to distinguish between tasks of different ADNAs. This is indicated in Fig. 5 by the indices of the ADNAs.

The exchange of ADNA can be implemented in two different ways: The first option is that all systems are pre-programmed with the ADNAs of each system, however, the ADNA from each other system is deactivated by the ADNA builder. It activates the ADNA from another system if and only if the other system is in communication range. The second option is that each system possesses only its own ADNA and transmits it to another system if this is in communication range. We chose to implement and analyze the first option in this contribution in order to evaluate if the concept of ADNAs in dynamic environments is feasible and to neglect side-effects like the ADNA transfer time. If the systems leave the communications range they deactivate or delete the other systems' ADNAs.

As stated in the introduction, a system needs to monitor the tasks taken from another system to implement e.g. payment mechanisms. We focus on how these tasks affect the ADNA/AHS system. As the local AHS of each ECU periodically sends suppressor hormones for each taken task, the monitor task can access the these information by the AHS interface. Thus, the monitor task collects information

- on which of the own system's ECUs tasks of other systems are running,
- how many task re-allocations are caused by taking tasks of another system and
- the ECU load affected by the other system's tasks.

It is important that the monitor task remains static on a single ECU of the own system. If the monitor task did not run on the own system's ECUs, we could not guarantee for its proper execution. The limitation of the monitor task running on the own system's ECUS is guaranteed by not exporting its ADNA to any other system. Otherwise it were not able to monitor the tasks while it is re-allocated. There are two ways to locate a task on an ECU so that it is not affected by task re-allocation: The first way is to set the hormone values of all ECUs so that only a single ECU can take the monitor task. This is a simple solution which, however, has two severe disadvantages: First, it contradicts the ADNA/AHS concept which enables self-optimization and self-healing. Second, if the ECU running the monitor task fails, monitoring itself will fail.

Therefore, the more appropriate solution is to introduce inhibitor hormones which are a special kind of suppressor hormones. If the monitor task is allocated by an ECU the local AHS sends inhibitor hormones to all ECUs. This inhibitor suppresses the other ECUs eagerness to run the monitor task. But in case the ECU running the monitor task fails, the inhibitor hormone is not sent any more. This leads to a re-allocation of the monitor task but it prevents the monitor task from re-allocation due to small variations in the hormone levels. Figure 6 illustrates the way inhibitor hormones work.

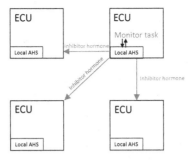

Fig. 6. Realizing a static monitoring task by inhibitor hormones

5   Evaluation

An automotive scenario may be as shown in Fig. 7: The ECUs of the cars may run the ADNA shown in Fig. 8. Here, each line describes a task used to control the cars. The numbers in the brackets describe the communication relations between the tasks and the remaining numbers describe the task's timing parameters. In the lines 1 to 3 the position of the steering wheel is used to control the angle of the front wheels. Lines 4 up to 12 describe how to use the brake pedal position to determine the brake force while lines 13 up to 22 describe how the throttle pedal position is used to compute the engine force. In line 23 a special task is activated to check if all ADNA basic blocks are executed; the binary result is shown by an actor described in line 24. Line 25 includes the monitor task.

The grey circles in the figure indicate the field strength of their wireless communication network. As it does not overlap yet, the cars are not able to communicate, however, if they overlap, the cars are in communications range.

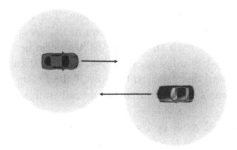

Fig. 7. Dynamic scenario

The evaluation shows a scenario where the red car is driving and after some time two third of its ECUs fail. As a result, several tasks from the red car's ADNA fail because the computing power of its ECUs does not meet the needed

```
SystemId = 1
 1 = 500 (1:2.1)                         502 100   // Sensor:      Get Steering Wheel Position
 2 =  14 (1:3.1)                         2         // Offset:      Add offset to achieve 1..3 range (this
allows to detect and ignore 0 output as invalid)
 3 = 600                                 511       // Actor:       Set Steering Actor
 4 = 500 (1:5.1 1:6.1 1:7.1 1:8.1)       500 50    // Sensor:      Get Brake Pedal Position
 5 =  46 (1:9.1)                         0         // Gate+:       Disable brake when wheel is not turning
 6 =  46 (1:10.1)                        0         // Gate+:       Disable brake when wheel is not turning
 7 =  46 (1:11.1)                        0         // Gate+:       Disable brake when wheel is not turning
 8 =  46 (1:12.1)                        0         // Gate+:       Disable brake when wheel is not turning
 9 = 600                                 513       // Actor:       Brake Actor Rear Left
10 = 600                                 514       // Actor:       Brake Actor Front Left
11 = 600                                 515       // Actor:       Brake Actor Rear Right
12 = 600                                 516       // Actor:       Brake Actor Front Right
13 = 500 (1:14.1)                        501 100   // Sensor:      Get Throttle Position
14 = 600                                 510       // Actor:       Engine Power Actor
15 = 500 (1:16.1)                        504 50    // Sensor:      Get Wheel Ticks Left Rear
16 =  13 (1:5.2)                         1 50 0    // D:           Differentiate to detect if wheel is
turning
17 = 500 (1:18.1)                        505 50    // Sensor:      Get Wheel Ticks Left Front
18 =  13 (1:6.2)                         1 50 0    // D:           Differentiate to detect if wheel is
turning
19 = 500 (1:20.1)                        506 50    // Sensor:      Get Wheel Ticks Right Rear
20 =  13 (1:7.2)                         1 50 0    // D:           Differentiate to detect if wheel is
turning
21 = 500 (1:22.1)                        507 50    // Sensor:      Get Wheel Ticks Right Front
22 =  13 (1:8.2)                         1 50 0    // D:           Differentiate to detect if wheel is
turning
23 = 998 (1:24.1)                        100       // DNA Checker: Check DNA complete
24 = 600                                 517       // Actor:       Show DNA complete
25 = 996                                 1 1 2     // Invoice:     Compute other DNAs running on own system
```

Fig. 8. ADNA to enable simple driving functions of a car

computing power. However, the red car meets other cars each 6 s and is in communication range with them for 4.5 s and can use their ECUs in this time. Figure 9 shows the cumulated results of the monitoring tasks of the oncoming cars. We present the time a gate task and a sensor task (measuring the throttle position) spent on ECUs of another system as well as the number of ECU hops of these tasks on another system. The monitor task run about 10000 AHS cycles (1 AHS cycles takes 50 msec), so the evaluation took about 8 minutes. The figure shows that the sensor task has initially been executed by the own system's ECUs. However, from about 1900 AHS cycles (which is about a minute after the start of the evaluation) the sensor task is moved to another system each time another car comes in communication range. This task is not executed any more if no other car is in communication range. The effects of the sensor task being executed only if another car is in communication range is shown in Fig. 10: The speed of the red car with the failing ECUs periodically decreases because the motor control input is missing. However, this shows that the ADNA/AHS system provides graceful degradation because if the ECUs of other system could not be used, the red car's motor control would fail completely and the car would stop.

The other monitored task is a gate task and we see that executed on the own system's ECUs most of the time. If there are not enough ECUs to take all tasks of the ADNA, the AHS decides which task to skip on internal parameters. Therefore, the monitor tasks show such a different behaviour for the sensor and the gate tasks. In future versions of the ADNA/AHS we plan to implement a priority scheme for the tasks, so that the AHS skips firstly low prior tasks. This enables the user to control the task failure behaviour in case of reduced ECU computing power.

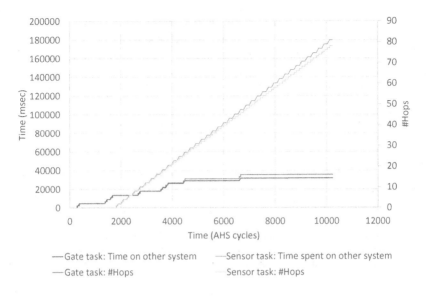

Fig. 9. Result of monitor task

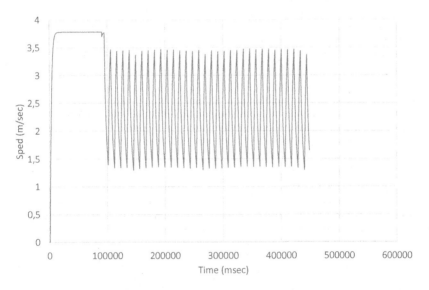

Fig. 10. Speed of damaged car

6   Conclusion

We showed in this paper that other systems' tasks can run on an ADNA/AHS system, thus increasing its dependability. However, monitoring these tasks is mandatory for payment and security reasons. We showed that the own monitor task can be located on a single ECU by using special inhibitor hormones. The evaluation showed that the monitor task can observe parameters like execution duration and number of task hops using the AHS system.

The evaluation also shows that it is mandatory to provide a priority scheme for the tasks supported by the AHS in future work. We can then guarantee that important tasks like engine control or brake control are either not moved away from their current processors or they are reallocated at first which decreases their down time.

References

1. Brinkschulte, U.: An artificial DNA for self-descripting and self-building embedded real-time systems. Concurrency Comput. Pract. Experience **28**(14), 3711–3729 (2016)
2. Brinkschulte, U.: Prototypic implementation and evaluation of an artificial DNA for self-describing and self-building embedded systems. In: 19th IEEE International Symposium on Real-time Computing (ISORC 2016). New York, UK, 17–20 May 2016
3. Brinkschulte, U.: Prototypic implementation and evaluation of an artificial DNA for self-descripting and self-building embedded systems. EURASIP J. Embed. Syst. **2017**(1), 1–16 (2017). https://doi.org/10.1186/s13639-016-0066-2
4. Brinkschulte, U., Pacher, M., Muller-Schloer, C. (eds.): Proceedings of the workshop on embedded self-organizing systems, San Jose, USA (2013)
5. Brinkschulte, U., Pacher, M., Renteln, A.: An artificial hormone system for self-organizing real-time task allocation in organic middleware. In: Organic Computing. UCS, pp. 261–283. Springer, Heidelberg (2009). https://doi.org/10.1007/978-3-540-77657-4_12
6. German Federal Ministry of Education and Research: Projekt AutoKonf. http://autokonf.de/. Accessed 23 May 2019
7. Yi, C.H., Kwon, K., Jeon, J.W.: Method of improved hardware redundancy for automotive system, pp. 204–207 (2015)
8. Kounev, S., Kephart, J.O., Milenkoski, A., Zhu, X.: Self-aware Computing Systems, 1st edn. Springer Publishing Company, Incorporated, Cham (2017)
9. Lee, E., Neuendorffer, S., Wirthlin, M.: Actor-oriented design of embedded hardware and software systems. J. Circuits, Syst. Comput. **12**, 231–260 (2003)
10. Maurer, M., Gerdes, J.C., Winner, B.L.H.: Autonomous Driving - Technical Legal and Social Aspects. Springer, Berlin (2016)
11. Nicolescu, G., Mosterman, P.J.: Model-Based Design for Embedded Systems. CRC Press, Boca Raton (2010)
12. Pacher, M., Brinkschulte, U.: Towards an artificial DNA for the use in dynamic environments. In: 22nd IEEE International Symposium on Real-Time Computing (ISORC 2019), Valencia, Spain, May 2019
13. Reif, W., et al. (eds.): Trustworthy Open Self-Organising Systems. AS, Springer, Cham (2016). https://doi.org/10.1007/978-3-319-29201-4
14. Sangiovanni-Vincentelli, A., Martin, G.: Platform-based design and software design methodology for embedded systems. In: IEEE Design and Test, vol. 18, no. 6, pp. 23–33 (2001)

Design and Analysis of an Online Update Approach for Embedded Microprocessors

Patrick Uven[1]([✉]), Philipp Ittershagen[2], and Kim Grüttner[2]

[1] Carl von Ossietzky University Oldenburg, Oldenburg, Germany
patrick.uven@dlr.de
[2] OFFIS – Institute for Information Technology, Oldenburg, Germany
kim.gruettner@dlr.de

Abstract. Software updates are already used in many systems for fixing bugs and for improving or extending their functionality. For many embedded systems with strong requirements on their availability, software updates are still not used because an update cycle usually causes a down time of the system. For servers in data centers with high availability requirements, so-called live patching solutions exist for many years. Live-Patching allows updating the software without affecting the availability of the system (i.e. no restart is required). In this work, we propose the application of live patching on small embedded microprocessors. We present a proof-of-concept implementation on a Xilinx MicroBlaze processor and compare the properties of our implementation, w.r.t. the amount of transmitted update data, memory requirements and update cycle duration against a state-of-the-art full-memory update.

Keywords: Online update · Live patching · Xilinx MicroBlaze

1 Introduction

Autonomous, dynamically changing cyber-physical systems (CPS) will permeate all areas of work and life in the future - e.g. industry 4.0; autonomous, cooperative driving; highly automated medical devices; smart grid controls; inter-modal transport systems and many more. These systems will support or perform various safety-related control tasks under conditions that will change during operation (e.g. new traffic infrastructures for highly automated vehicles, new communication technologies, new sensor technologies or security mechanisms, extended deployment scenarios, etc.). As these conditions are generally not (completely) known at the time of system development, the continuous system evolution of CPS after commissioning is of central importance. In particular, the ability to continuously incorporate experiences from the operation of systems in the field

This work is part of the Step-Up!CPS project and was funded by the German Ministry of Education and Research (BMBF) under grant agreement no. 01IS18080A.

M. A. Wehrmeister et al. (Eds.): IESS 2019, IFIP AICT 576, pp. 179–188, 2023.
https://doi.org/10.1007/978-3-031-26500-6_15

into the further development of CPS (swarm data collection as well as continuous updating) and to design systems in such a way that improvements can be introduced into CPS promptly is crucial.

In contrast to smartphones and PC operating systems, where regular updates are part of everyday life, updates of highly dependable CPS place significantly higher demands on the architectures of these systems. Considering dependability as a measure of a system's availability, reliability and its maintainability we can see that updates support maintainability and online updates (i.e. updating the system while it remains operational) support availability.

This work considers the design and analysis of an online update approach for an embedded microprocessor. Our contributions consist of

1. a modular software live patching approach (called append update) for online updates of functions at run-time (i.e. an update without stopping the system),
2. a proof-of-concept implementation of the append update approach on a Xilinx Zynq MPSoC, which demonstrates updating a Xilinx MicroBlaze processor system initiated from the ARM based processing system, and
3. an analysis and a comparison against a state-of-the-art offline update approach.

This paper is structured as follows. The next section presents an overview of related work in the area of software update techniques. Section 3 describes the full and append (live patching) update approaches, which is followed by a proof-of-concept implementation on a Xilinx MicroBlaze microprocessor system in section Sect. 4. Section Sect. 5 evaluates our approach and compares the full and append update approaches. The paper closes with a conclusion in Section Sect. 6.

2   Related Work

Existing commercial solutions in the automotive sector (e.g. encrypt [9], Infineon [3], as well as SWUpdate [2], libostree [6] or Mender [1] for embedded Linux systems) are capable of replacing the entire firmware of individual ECUs with a new version. However, modular updates or changes to the software during operation are not taken into account.

The EU-funded Horizon 2020 project TAPPS [8] has developed an open platform for CPS software, which consists of an "app store" for security-critical and security-uncritical applications (or functions) as well as the software and hardware layers necessary for the assurance of security and real-time properties. The update management is based on virtualization techniques which were used to run a Linux and a FreeRTOS system on the same hardware. The platform requirements for running such a software stack naturally limit the applicability of such approaches in resource-constrained scenarios.

The Dynamic Software Updating(DSU) [4] mechanism describes the concept of replacing one or more functions during runtime. As one of the first contributions to this topic, the approach provides an extended toolchain for annotating the changes of the software in a high level language. The developer then selects a safe point in time to replace the function, at which point the software execution is paused, updated and then resumed. More recently, a similar approach, presented in [5], uses indirection to replace functions in the running software application. However, this leads to a constant overhead for each function call due to the use of indirection for each updated function. Additionally, the program execution has to be paused to migrate to the new function, similar to the approach from [4]. While the approach presented in this paper also induces a runtime overhead due to indirection, it does not require the target system to be paused during an update.

Furthermore, there are live patching solutions available for the Linux operating system. A popular solution is kGraft [7], where new kernel functionality is inserted into the memory and referenced by the updated function. The approach also features migration procedures, including a special "reality check" which decides if a redirection is appropriate based on the consistency of the overall system state. The contribution of this paper is closely related to the technical solution of this Linux-based update approach However, while such live-patching systems are based upon resource-intensive software frameworks such as Linux, our contribution focusses on exploring and analysing a live-patching mechanism for systems with direct access to the memory of a microprocessor system.

3   Overall Update Approach

This work considers an update approach for a system architecture which consists of three parts. The *Microprocessor system* is an embedded system consisting of a microprocessor, memory modules as well as I/O peripherals. This system is the target of the update and is executing software that should be changed during run-time. The embedded system is running software written in C and uses a shared memory for its instructions and data. The *Distribution system* is the source of update files and is not in the scope of the online update process itself. We therefore assume that the update files are already available on the *Update system* and have been securely transferred to the system and omit the communication details between those systems. Finally, the Update system is responsible for controlling and updating the Microprocessor system, which we will explain in the following section.

3.1   Update Procedure

The update procedure starts with the development of C-based software functions for the microprocessor system. As shown in Fig. 1, the source file is compiled into an object file, which is then processed by the linker. The linker script contains the necessary memory layout information to map all relevant object file sections to sections of the final memory layout. The result will be saved in an ELF file.

Next, a script converts the ELF file into a memory dump of the target microprocessor memory, which discards all ELF metadata and copies the loadable

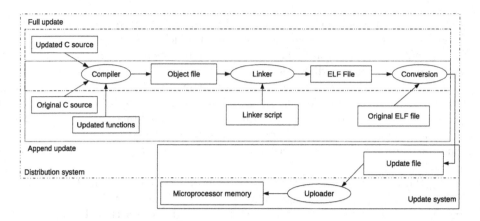

Fig. 1. Update workflow

ELF sections to their corresponding memory addresses. The file format consists of one word on each line as well as the address in which it is written. This file is used to populate the linear address space of the microprocessor. Additionally, as each word is one microprocessor instruction, we can easily change or replace instructions in the file. The update itself is implemented in two different variants:

Full Update. The full update completely replaces the software on the microprocessor. To achieve this, the update procedure can pause, halt, and even reset the microprocessor and consequently discard its current state.

Append Update. The append update allows replacing user-defined functions of the existing software by appending a new version in unused memory space, thus allowing the software to continue its operation and to retain its current state.

The following section describes the different flows of the full and append update approaches.

3.2 Full Update

The full update approach resembles the typical process of updating software on a processor. As described above in the basic workflow, the engineer writes new functionality in the existing C source code. After compiling and linking the program, the update file contains the complete memory of the full program. The update process consists of the following steps:

1. The distribution system initiates the update process by transferring the file to the update system and signaling the start of the update. The update system is idle while waiting for the signal and the microprocessor system is still executing the outdated software.
2. In the next step, the update system pauses the microprocessor, such that it can safely write to the whole microprocessor memory content while ensuring

that the microprocessor does not read any instructions or data from it. This is to avoid the execution of a combination of partly updated instructions which could lead to undefined execution behaviour of the microprocessor.
3. As soon as the microprocessor is paused, the update system writes the contents of the update file into the memory of the microprocessor.
4. Finally, the update system resets the microprocessor. While the update system returns to the idle state, the microprocessor system can now execute its updated software.

3.3   Append Update

The append update follows a different approach: instead of replacing the whole program binary, we only consider parts (i.e. C functions) that actually change. To avoid the problem of pausing the microprocessor to change multiple lines in the memory, we instead place the updated functions in a dedicated memory section and update a jump instruction at the start of the old function.

The left side of Fig. 2 depicts the typical microprocessor memory structure consisting of instruction segments, constants, and dynamic data. To update a function in the program, we duplicate the function in the source code, apply the source-level updates, and place the generated binary content of the new function in a dedicated memory section of the ELF file. We then copy this section to the dedicated memory region in the target memory layout, as depicted in the bottom part of Fig. 2.

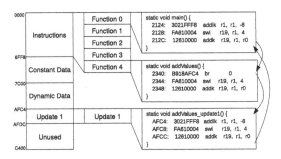

Fig. 2. Microprocessor memory overview

The next step is to integrate the updated function into the existing control flow of the program. We achieve this by redirecting any calls to the old function to the updated one. Since we are able to atomically write on a word granularity to the target memory, we are able to replace a single instruction in an atomic manner. This allows us to replace the first instruction of the old function with a branch instruction redirecting the processor to the new function instead. In Fig. 2 we can see the addition of the new function as well as the branch instruction. Function 4 gets changed and the first instruction becomes a branch to the memory section of update 1 in which we can see the updated function. Any subsequent call to the outdated function will be redirected to the updated version of the function. As we don't need to pause and reset the microprocessor system anymore, the interaction between the update and the microprocessor system is much smaller compared to the full update.

However, there are some restrictions on functions eligible for this update procedure, which needs to be considered during the development:

– The signature of the function (and the calling convention) must stay identical (i.e. all types, including the return and argument parameters have to be the same, including the ordering of the parameter types).
– The function symbol must have external visibility in the final compiled ELF file. Features like inline expansion of a function cannot be used, as they would hide the function and thus make it impossible to update them.
– The parallel execution of both old and new function has either to be prevented in the program or we have to make sure that both version can run without complication at the same time.
– If the updated function is called multiple times from another function or if it is used recursively, we have to make sure that the behaviour of the function stays the same. Otherwise we have to defer the update until the recursive function call has been completed.

4   Implementation

This section presents the prototypical implementation of the approach to demonstrate its applicability on an embedded microprocessor platform. We have chosen the ZedBoard Zynq-7000 ARM/FPGA SoC Development Board which consists of two main components, an ARM Cortex-A9 dual core (called processing system) and an Artix-7 FPGA (called programmable

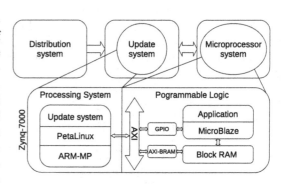

Fig. 3. Implementation overview

logic). Figure 3 provides an overview of the systems involved in the update process as well as their communication links.

The update system is running on the ARM processing system on top of a Linux operating system. The microprocessor system consists of a Xilinx MicroBlaze softcore instantiated in the FPGA along with a dedicated Block RAM as instruction and data memory. We use an AXI bus for the communication between the update and the microprocessor system. A GPIO is used to pause and reset the MicroBlaze processor. An AXI BRAM controller is used to access the dual-ported instruction and data memory of the MicroBlaze from the update system. The goal of the prototype implementation is to demonstrate the following scenario: a defective function (see Listing 1.1) is to be updated with a corrected function (see Listing 1.2).

For both update variants (full and append) we start with the same program loaded in the MicroBlaze memory: A basic program that calls the function from

Listing 1.1 is compiled and linked for the microprocessor, copied into the memory and then executed, such that in both cases the to-be updated software is being executed at the start of the system.

```
1  int addValues(int A, int B) {
2     return A + A; }
```

Listing 1.1. Defective Function

```
1  int addValues(int A, int B) {
2     return A + B; }
```

Listing 1.2. Corrected Function

4.1 Full Update

The full update has a mostly unchanged process compared to manually updating the binary on the processor. The function is updated in the source code, the program recompiled and relinked without any further changes. The resulting ELF file can then be converted to the format presented earlier. The update system now pauses the microprocessor via GPIO and writes the memory contents via the AXI interconnect. When this process has finished, it triggers the reset signal via GPIO and the microprocessor restarts with the updated function.

4.2 Append Update

In case of the append update approach, we change the update process such that the existing memory is not completely rewritten. Therefore, we create a new memory segment that will contain our updated function. Since memory segments are getting created during the linking process, we have to extend the linker script with a section for the new memory segment. Listing 1.3 shows how to instruct the linker to create a new segment .update_1 and to keep it in the final binary, even when it is not referenced by any other section. This is needed since the updated function symbol is not referenced in the original source code and would be removed otherwise.

With the new segment created, we can now add our updated function. To achieve this, we copy the old function addValues to a new version called addValues_update_1, as shown in Listing 1.4.

Additionally, we need to assign the function to the memory segment, which is annotated by the section attribute. When the program is compiled and linked after these changes, all old code sections remain unchanged; only the newly added segment is added behind the previous last segment to the ELF file. At this point, we can convert the ELF file to our update format and write the new lines of code with our updated function into the MicroBlaze memory. To finalize the update, the first instruction of the old function is replaced by the branch to the new function.

```
1  .update_1 : {
2     *(.update_1)
3     KEEP (*(.update_1))
4  }
```

Listing 1.3. Linker script extension

```
1  int addValues_update_1(int A, int B) \
2     __attribute__((used, section(".update_1")));
3  int addValues_update_1(int A, int B) {
4     return A + B; }
```

Listing 1.4. Updated function with section assignment

5   Evaluation

This evaluation compares the full against the append update using four different update scenarios (A–D):

0) **Initial program** running on the processor before an update occurs.
A) **Function replacement (same size)** A function will be replaced by the same/identical function.
B) **Function replacement (larger size)** The function from scenario A is getting replaced by a larger function with more instructions.
C) **Iterative function replacement (same size)** The same function (similar to scenario A) is updated multiple times.
D) **Replacement of multiple functions** Multiple functions will be replaced (each of them like in scenario A) at the same time.

The evaluation uses the Xilinx Vivado tool chain in version 2018.2 to build the PetaLinux for the update system, the bitstream for the FPGA, as well as software for the MicroBlaze processor. The hardware platform consists of a ZedBoard with all hardware components configured using their default clock values (CPU $666,\overline{6}$ MHz, DDR $533,\overline{3}$ MHz, Programmable Logic 100 MHz). Unless otherwise stated, the results of the following experiments were obtained from 100 runs.

The project sources for the implementation as well as the files to recreate this evaluation can be found at https://github.com/offis/mb-append-update. The repository also contains an example project with all intermediate steps and a short usage guide.

5.1   Memory Usage

The memory of an embedded system is always a limited resource. This experiment compares the amount of memory that will be written to the microprocessor memory by the update system, measured by counting the amount of lines that are present in the update files for both update variants. Since every line in the update files represent a word in the RAM, the result is also depicted in words.

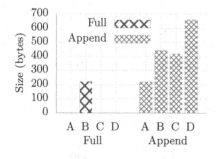

Fig. 4. Memory overhead

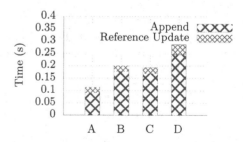

Fig. 5. Timing overhead

Figure 4 shows the relative overhead of the full and the append update compared to the baseline of experiment 0 which had a memory consumption of 13222 bytes. In scenario B, the function has been extended by 220 bytes. We can see the growing size of the memory in the full and in the append update. Scenario C shows that multiple replacements of a function do not affect the size of the full update, because in-place replacement has been used. With the append update, on the other hand, memory consumption is increased by further 198 bytes. In scenario D, the exchange of several functions of the full update behaves analogous to C, since these take the place of the old functions. The memory consumption of the append update corresponds to three times the replacement of a single function. The exchange of several functions in one update neither brings additional overhead nor saves memory. The experiments showed that, independent of the experiment, the number of instruction and the memory usage are linear to each other for the append update.

5.2 Duration of the Update Procedure

We have furthermore compared the duration of the update procedure of both full and append approaches using "perf" on the update system. For the full update, the measured time frame begins when the pause command is sent to the microprocessor and ends with the reset command for the restart of the microprocessor. In case of the append update, we have measured all necessary write procedures.

While the full update (scenario 0) takes 5.203 s, all variants of the append update are executed within 0.3 s. The reason for this is the different procedure of updating. While the full update rewrites the complete program into memory, the append update only adds a few lines. Figure 5 shows the timing overhead (i.e. the duration of all memory write operations) of the append update approach, in absolute numbers and with a refined view of their overheads.

5.3 Run-Time Overhead

There is a small run-time overhead in the append update, which results from the additional machine commands that must be executed after the update. As defined in the concept, each updated function brings one additional branch instruction which has to be executed. With the full update, this does not exist because the functions are completely replaced.

6 Conclusion

The evaluation of our proposed append update approach clearly shows its advantages and disadvantages. The memory usage of the full updates corresponds exactly to the size of the updated program and also scales with the size and number of functions. On the other hand, the append update grows with each update by the size of the new function.

For many microprocessor systems, the limited amount of required allocated but unused memory might be the most limiting factor of the append update approach.

Considering the duration of an update procedure, it is important to note that the microprocessor system is not available during the full update, which can cause an extended downtime of the system. On the other hand, the execution is not interrupted during the append update, which renders the time required to write the update irrelevant in terms of service availability interruptions. Additionally, the dual-ported block RAM allows for interference-free access to the memory while the microprocessor system is running. However, this is a special case due to the chosen platform and in general, arbitration for memory accesses would be necessary. For this reason, in general the reduced memory access overhead in the append update is of interest. Here, our evaluation showed that the duration of the append update was linear to the size of the updated functions.

For the distribution system and especially for over-the-air updates we can see an important difference in the amount of transmitted data. The full update always transfers the complete memory content, while the append update only has to transfer a few bytes of difference. However, using existing delta-transmission techniques could reduce this difference again in favor of a full update.

In contrast to the full update, the append update procedure also has a runtime overhead. Each replaced function leads to at least two additional machine instructions, but the overhead is insignificant compared to the usual function sizes.

References

1. Mender (2019). https://mender.io/
2. Babic, S.: Software update for embedded systems (2019). https://sbabic.github.io/swupdate/
3. Infineon: Software update over the air (SOTA) (2019). https://www.infineon.com/cms/en/applications/automotive/automotive-security/sotware-update-over-the-air/
4. Lee, I.: DYMOS: a dynamic modification system (1983)
5. Neamtiu, I., et al.: Practical dynamic software updating for C (2006)
6. OSTree maintainers: Operating system and container binary deployment and upgrades (2019). https://ostree.readthedocs.io/en/latest/
7. Pavlík, V.: kGraft: live patching of the Linux kernel. https://events.static.linuxfound.org/sites/events/files/slides/kGraft.pdf
8. Prehofer, C., et al.: Towards trusted apps platforms for open CPS (2016)
9. Wolf, M., et al.: Design, implementation, and evaluation of a vehicular hardware security module (2011)

Author Index

© IFIP International Federation for Information Processing 2023
Published by Springer Nature Switzerland AG 2023
M. A. Wehrmeister et al. (Eds.): IESS 2019, IFIP AICT 576, pp. 189–190, 2023.
https://doi.org/10.1007/978-3-031-26500-6

Printed in the United States
by Baker & Taylor Publisher Services